This book is dedicated to my family,
friends, colleagues, and Erika.
Thank you all for tolerating the time it takes to study,
prepare, design, write, edit and create
books on technology that are not rushed.
It is your patience that makes such publications outstanding pieces of work.

ABOUT THE AUTHOR

Robert J. Shimonski (Truesecure TICSA, Cisco CCDP, CCNP, Nortel NNCSS, Microsoft MCSE, MCP+I, Novell Master CNE, CIP, CIBS, IWA CWP, DCSE, Prosoft MCIW, SANS GSEC, GCIH, CompTIA Server+, Network+, Inet+, A+, e-Biz+, Security+, HTI+, Symantec SPS and NAI Sniffer SCP) is a lead network and security engineer for Danaher as well as a part time contract instructor and trainer. Robert's academics include a four-year degree from SUNY NY, military training in the United States Marine Corps, and hundreds of other training classes. Robert has worked in small-to-medium sized companies, as well as large enterprises (such as Avis Rent a Car).

Robert is known for his troubleshooting skills, being able to find and resolve problems very quickly, and bringing them to successful resolution. His specialties include overall network infrastructure design with Cisco, 3Com, and Nortel product lines, network security design and management with CiscoSecure, PIX firewalls, and Checkpoint NG, network management and troubleshooting with CiscoWorks, Sniffer-based technologies, and HPOV.

Robert has spent many years as a system engineer building solutions with Microsoft, Novell, Linux, and Apple solutions as well as having them all integrated into each other. He has spent time as a developer, and most recently, as a full-fledged web designer using technologies such as JavaScript, Flash, XML and scripting with Perl. He is the author of many articles and published books, including titles on Windows XP, Sniffer Pro, General Security, Web Design and many other areas of technology. You can contact Robert anytime at rshimonski@rsnetworks.net

ABOUT THE TECHNICAL EDITOR

Will Schmied (BSET, MCSE, CWNA, MCSA, Network+, A+) is a consultant, author, and the principal partner of Area 51 Partners. Will holds a bachelor's degree in Mechanical Engineering Technology from Old Dominion University. He currently resides in Newport News, Virginia with his wife, Allison, their children, Christopher, Austin, Andrea, and Hannah and their two dogs, Peanut and Jay. When he is not busy designing, configuring, training, or writing on wireless and wired networking technologies, you can usually find him in the back yard with his dogs or in the forest with his Cub Scout pack. You can visit Will at www.area51partners.com or www.netserverworld.com.

Windows® Server 2003
Clustering &
Load Balancing

Robert Shimonski

McGraw-Hill/Osborne

New York Chicago San Francisco
Lisbon London Madrid Mexico City Milan
New Delhi San Juan Seoul Singapore Sydney Toronto

The *McGraw-Hill* Companies

McGraw-Hill/Osborne
2100 Powell Street, Floor 10
Emeryville, California 94608
U.S.A.

To arrange bulk purchase discounts for sales promotions, premiums, or fund-raisers, please contact **McGraw-Hill/Osborne** at the above address. For information on translations or book distributors outside the U.S.A., please see the International Contact Information page immediately following the index of this book.

Windows® Server 2003 Clustering & Load Balancing

234567890 CUS CUS 01987654

ISBN 0-07-222622-6

Publisher
  Brandon A. Nordin
Vice President & Associate Publisher
  Scott Rogers
Acquisitions Editor
  Francis Kelly
Project Editor
  Monika Faltiss
Acquisitions Coordinator
  Jessica Wilson
Technical Editor
  Will Schmied
Developmental Editor
  Mark Cierzniak
Copy Editor
  Marcia Baker

Proofreader
  Mike McGee
Indexer
  Irv Hershman
Computer Designers
  George T. Charbak, Tara Davis
Illustrators
  Melinda Lytle, Michael Mueller,
  Lyssa Wald
Cover Series Design
  Jeff Weeks
Series Design
  Lyssa Wald, Peter F. Hancik

This book was composed with Corel VENTURA™ Publisher.

AT A GLANCE

v

CONTENTS

ACKNOWLEDGMENTS

I would like to thank everyone who was responsible for bringing this book to life. A warm thanks goes directly to my technical editor, Will Schmied. He not only served as a technical authority on some of my writing, but also as a slap in the head when it was needed. This book is only as good as it is because of our unending emails back and forth to 'make sure of things.' I would also like to extend my thanks to Franny Kelly, who served as a fantastic acquisitions editor and kept this book's vision intact. Also, a big thanks to all the other McGraw-Hill/Osborne folks who put in a lot of work, made sure everything was perfect, and helped get this book on the shelves. Lastly, I would like to thank you, the reader, for buying this book and wanting to work with High Availability solutions—I hope you found what you were looking for.

INTRODUCTION

High Availability is a term coined to explain a very simple concept: how to keep your systems available when you need them. To simplify the term, the process of designing, configuring, and maintaining it is by no means anywhere as simple as the term used. It is no small chore, and hence, it's massively complicated and requires a lot of planning. You have taken the right step by purchasing and reading this book. It will open the door for you to begin down the path towards High Availability, and more so, how to design and achieve it. It is incredibly important as a high level IT technician and/or an IT supervisor that you have the knowledge of High Availability deigning and planning in your bag of IT tricks. High Availability is no longer a coined term, but an integral part of your network and systems design.

High Availability is not just limited to load balancing and clustering. This book focuses not only on those elements as the most common form of High Availability design, but it also covers all the other areas of High Availability design that you need to be aware of. It's important to note that you need to read this book beginning with Chapter 1, because each chapter builds on the next. This book is meant to teach you from start to finish, all the details you need to know in order to be familiar with planning and designing a complete end-to-end High Availability solution.

Chapter 1, "Introduction to High Availability, Clustering, and Load-Balancing Technologies," exposes you to the world of High Availability concepts. You learn the lingo used to discuss High Availability solutions so that you can follow what is explained within the rest of the book. You learn the fundamentals of scaling, High Availability uptime calculations, definitions of some very important terms, why High Availability is so important, how to sell your management team on it, and how to use your team to build High Availability solutions. The chapter outlines the rest of the book and tells you what you need to know to survive the rest of the chapters efficiently.

Chapter 2, "Designing a Clustered Solution with Windows 2000 Advanced Server," is a very long chapter on how to build a Windows 2000 cluster and load balanced solution. The chapter is long because you learn how to completely plan out every little detail of the solution. You learn about planning SCSI, RAID, and many other items that need to be addressed before you install the Windows 2000 operating system, let alone the services that provide High Availability. This chapter is soup to nuts... you learn what you need to know to plan for a viable solution that works. You then install and configure a 2 node cluster using the clustering service and you also set up a Windows 2000 load-balanced solution using the NLB service—after which you troubleshoot it and see the most common problems that occur.

Chapter 3, "Designing a Clustered Solution with Windows Server 2003," is also a very long chapter on how to build a Windows cluster and load balanced solution, but this chapter focuses solely on the newest of the Microsoft Server-based operating systems: Windows Server 2003. Again, you learn how to completely plan out every little detail of the solution. I did not duplicate some of the content from Chapter 2, so it's important that you read Chapter 2 before you read Chapter 3. What's nice about this chapter is that it provides a way to do what's called a rolling upgrade of Windows 2000 to Windows 2003 in a 2 node cluster solution. This is important to know, because you will eventually have to upgrade your current solutions, and this is most likely how it will be done as to not disrupt your company when doing upgrades. This chapter is very detailed and you learn the finer points of Windows Server 2003 and how it differs (somewhat greatly) from the older versions of Windows when it comes to High Availability, clustering and load balancing. You then install and configure a 2 node cluster using the Clustering Service and you also set up a Windows 2003 load balanced solution using the NLB service—after which you troubleshoot it and see the most common of problems that occur.

Chapter 4, "Designing a Clustered and Load-Balanced Solution with Application Center 2000," gives you a fundamental view of add on products from Microsoft Application Center 2000. The Application Center 2000 product is not widely used, so our coverage of it here is minimal, but this chapter gives you enough to plan and install it, if needed. This chapter also discusses the important role that Application Center 2000 can play within your High Availability design if you choose to use it.

Chapter 5, "Designing a Clustered Solution with Windows SQL Server 2000 Enterprise Edition," explains one of the most important topics today: the proper planning and design of a 2 node SQL Cluster. It's very important that you know how to make your data storage highly available. As a matter of fact, if there is anything you want to make highly available, then it would be your data repository. This chapter covers the specifics needed to cluster SQL, and how to troubleshoot common issues, as well as how to configure some of the advanced settings to get your SQL Cluster to work.

Chapter 6, "Designing a Highly Available Solution with Windows Services," covers how to cluster specific services. In this chapter, you learn how to make specific services within Windows available if there is a failure to a system. For example, you may be interested in creating a Highly Available solution for your DHCP server. DHCP (Dynamic Host Configuration Protocol) is a service that allows you to dole out and manage all available IP addressing on your network. You may need to make this service (or others like it) redundant. This chapter covers a couple of these servers in great depth so that you can understand all the work that goes into planning, designing, and creating such a solution.

Chapter 7, "Building Advanced Highly Available Load-Balanced Configurations," covers advanced concepts with network load balancing. Where this chapter differs from Chapters 2 and 3 is that it covers a lot of the infrastructure planning and design that you need to do with Multicast and other configurations that are a little tricky without some guidance. You also learn a great deal more about using the Windows Server 2003 NLB Manager and some advanced troubleshooting.

Chapter 8, "High Availability, Baselining, Performance Monitoring, and Disaster Recovery Planning," covers monitoring and performance as well as baselining—all are very critical to the success of a Highly Available solution. This is a long chapter with facts on how to get the most out of your Highly Available solution. It is very important to know that once you set up your solution, it does what you expect it to do. This chapter also has a great amount of tips you can use to get more speed and efficiency out of your Highly Available solution, no matter how you configure it.

Appendix A, "Project Plan Sample," is a detailed listing of what you can use in your highly available project plan. These days, it's hard to pull off a project of this scope and magnitude without a project plan, and even sometimes without a project manager. This is your cheat sheet on how to build your own project plan to follow when rolling out a Highly Available solution.

Appendix B, "Advanced Troubleshooting: Event IDs," shows you some of the more common error messages found while working on a Highly Available solution—distilled here for your quick reference.

To summarize, it's critical you look at the possibility of a High Availability solution in your design no matter how big or small. Remember, this book talks not only about redundant servers failing over to another node, but also the need for redundancy in your WAN links, LAN connections, firewalls, and other devices on your network and systems.

—*Robert J. Shimonski*

CHAPTER 1

Introduction to High Availability, Clustering, and Load-Balancing Technologies

New York City, September 11, 2001 will ring in our minds and hearts for years to come, and history books will carry that date on through the decades to follow. Now etched in everyone's subconscious, a surreal feeling of unimaginable disaster will live on for eternity.

Shortly thereafter, a swarm of business continuity meetings seemed to crop up everywhere in organizations. Many meetings were about what would happen if such a disaster happened to their business . . . how would they continue to survive? Security and Disaster Recovery were suddenly more than mere buzzwords in the Information Technology (IT) industry. All of a sudden, we were all aware of how vulnerable we are, not only to attack but also to failure. Yes, the possibility your systems might never come back online was now a reality. Companies started to wonder if they had a disaster— big or small—whether their company business and livelihood, which might have run completely online via a web site, would be totally lost within minutes.

What to do? For the companies that ran their businesses online or those that depended on applications and systems to deliver the company goods, this now seemed critical and a top-level priority both to protect systems from disaster and to provide the customer base with services—no matter what.

This book lays the groundwork for planning, designing, and implementing Highly Available Solutions with Windows Technologies, present and future, and for making sure your systems have a better chance against failures of any kind. Disasters happen, but you *can* be protected. While you might never experience a disaster as great as the one on September 11, 2001, you could suffer a small problem like a power outage, which could cripple your business if it isn't fixed in time. Let's take our first steps into the larger world of continuous uptime and business continuity . . . Windows 2000 and Server 2003 clustering and load balancing.

INTRODUCTION TO HIGH AVAILABILITY

This book is made for anyone who needs to know how to get their systems up and running for as long as possible, and how to keep them there. Before you learn the details of how to configure Microsoft Technologies for continuous uptime, you need to understand how Highly Available solutions are created, why they're implemented, and what technologies you have in your arsenal with which to implement these solutions. You also learn about the design stages—the most important part to implementing Highly Available solutions.

In this section, you learn about the options you have for High Availability, why redundancy is so important, what scalability and reliability do for you, and some buzzwords in the industry, such as Five Nines, and what that provides for you. This chapter revolves around preparing you to understand what follows in the rest of this book. Please read this chapter first because it outlines the question of *why* you're implementing Highly Available solutions. If you don't, you'll find it difficult to work your way through the rest of the chapters, which focus on *how* to implement Highly Available solutions.

This chapter also focuses on an area I find critical to anyone who wants to implement a Highly Available solution: how to explain and justify a Highly Available solution to management, based on budgetary expenses. If you're in a management role, this chapter will explain why this technology is critical for the business climate of today and tomorrow.

High Availability

High Availability is the essence of mission-critical applications being provided quickly and reliably to clients looking for your services. If a client can't get to your services, then they're unavailable. Your company is making money to sustain the life of its business, which depends on only one thing: your client base can shop online. Nerve racking? You bet.

Not to sound overly simplistic, but systems up, servers serving, and the business running is what High Availability is all about. Systems *will* fail, so how will your company handle this failure? Anyone who has ever been in charge of a service that needed to be up all the time and watched it crash knows how the company's CEO or vice presidents look at their angriest. *High Availability,* the industry term for systems available 99.999 (called "Five Nines") percent of the time, is the way around this. *Five Nines* is the term for saying a service or system will be up almost 100 percent of the time. To achieve this level of availability, you need to deploy systems that can survive failure. The ways to perform this are through clustering and load balancing.

Throughout the book, you also learn about other forms of High Availability, such as Redundant Array of Inexpensive Disks (RAID) and redundancy, in all aspects of hardware and software components. You can see a simple example of a Highly Available infrastructure in Figure 1-1. Although this book focuses on clustering and load-balancing solutions, you're given the big picture, so you can prepare almost all your components for High Availability and redundancy.

Clustering and Load Balancing Defined

Clustering is a means of providing High Availability. *Clustering* is a group of machines acting as a single entity to provide resources and services to the network. In time of failure, a failover will occur to a system in that group that will maintain availability of those resources to the network. You can be alerted to the failure, repair the system failure, and bring the system back online to participate as a provider of services once more. You learn about many forms of clustering in this chapter. Clustering can allow for failover to other systems and it can also allow for load balancing between systems. *Load balancing* is using a device, which can be a server or an appliance, to balance the load of traffic across multiple servers waiting to receive that traffic. The device sends incoming traffic based on an algorithm to the most underused machine or spreads the traffic out evenly among all machines that are on at the time. A good example of using this technology would be if you had a web site that received 2,000 hits per day. If, in the months of November and December, your hit count tripled, you might be unable to

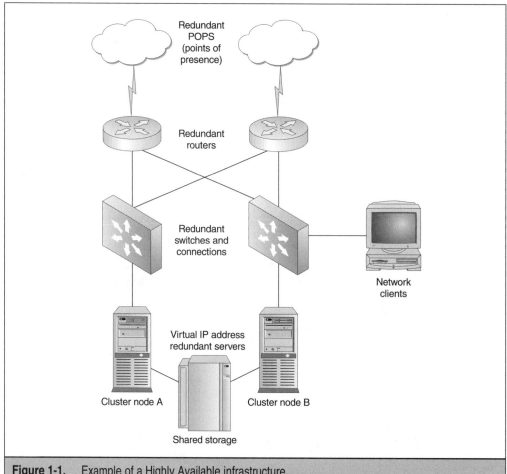

Figure 1-1.   Example of a Highly Available infrastructure

sustain that type of increased load. Your customers might experience time outs, slow response times, or worse, they might be unable to get to the site at all. With that picture fresh in your mind, consider two servers providing the same web site. Now you have an alternative to slow response time and, by adding a second or a third server, the response time would improve for the customer. High Availability is provided because, with this technology, you can always have your web site or services available to the visiting Internet community. You have also systematically removed the single point of failure from the equation. In Figure 1-2, you can see what a clustered solution can provide you. A single point of failure is removed because you now have a form of redundancy added in.

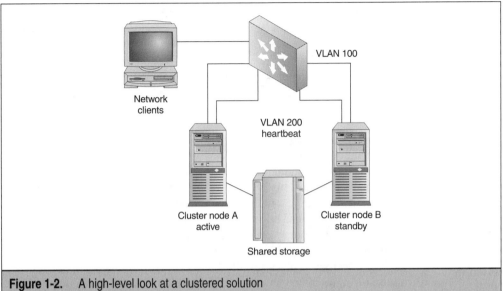

Figure 1-2.   A high-level look at a clustered solution

Pros and Cons to Clustering and Load Balancing

You could now be asking yourself, which is better to implement, clustering or load balancing? You can decide this for yourself after you finish this book, when you know all the details necessary to implement either solution. To give you a quick rundown of the high-level pros and cons to each technology, consider the following. With clustering, you depend on the actual clustered nodes to make a decision about the state of the network and what to do in a failure. If Node A in a cluster senses a problem with Node B (Node B is down), then Node A comes online. This is done with *heartbeat traffic*, which is a way for Node A to know that Node B is no longer available and it must come online to take over the traffic. With load balancing, a single device (a network client) sends traffic to any available node in the load-balanced group of nodes. Load balancing uses heartbeat traffic as well but, in this case, when a node comes offline, the "load" is recalculated among the remaining nodes in the group. Also, with clustering (not load balancing), you're normally tied down or restricted to a small number of participating nodes. For example, if you want to implement a clustered solution with Windows 2000 Advanced Server, you might use a two-node cluster. With load balancing, you can implement up to 32 nodes and, if you use a third-party utility, you can scale way beyond that number. You can even mix up the operating system (OS) platforms, if needed, to include Sun Solaris or any other system you might be running your services on. Again, this is something that's thoroughly explained as you work your way through the book. This section is simply used to give you an idea of your options. Finally, you have the option to set up tiered access to services and to mix both architectures (clustering and load balancing) together. You can set up the first tier of access to your web servers as load balanced and the last tier of access as your clustered SQL databases. This is explained in more detail in the upcoming section on N-tier architecture, " N-Tier Designs."

Hot Spare

A *hot spare* is a machine you can purchase and configure to be a mirror image of the machine you want to replace if a failure occurs. Figure 1-3 shows an example of a hot spare in use. A hot spare can be set aside for times of disaster, but it could sit there unused, waiting for a failure. When the disaster occurs, the hot spare is brought online to participate in the place of the systems that failed. This isn't a good idea because the system sitting idle isn't being used and, in many IT shops, it will be "borrowed" for other things. This means you never have that hot spare. For those administrators who could keep the hot spare as a spare, you're missing out on using that spare machine as a balancer of the load. Also, why configure the hot spare in time of failure? Your clients lose connectivity and you have to remove the old machine, and then replace it with the new one and have all your clients reconnect to it. Or, worse yet, the angry client shopping online could be gone forever to shop somewhere else online if it's a web server hosting an ecommerce site. Setting up a second server as a hot spare is redundant, but there is a better way. Set this second machine up in a cluster. Although the hot spare method might seem a little prehistoric, it's still widely used in IT shops that can't afford highly available systems, but still need some form of backup solution.

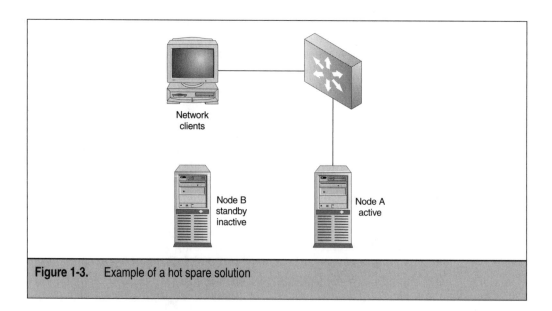

Network
clients

Node B
standby
inactive

Node A
active

Figure 1-3.   Example of a hot spare solution

A Need for Redundancy

You already learned about some forms of redundancy in the first few portions on this chapter in the discussion on clustering. Now let's look at why redundancy of systems is so important and what options you have besides a cluster. Being *redundant* (or superfluous) is the term used to explain exceeding what's necessary. If this is applied to an IT infrastructure, then it would be easy to say that if you need a power supply to power your server, then two power supplies would exceed what's necessary. Of course, in time of failure, you always wish you'd exceeded what you need, correct? The need for redundancy is obvious if you want to have your business continue operations in time of disaster.

The need for redundancy is apparent in a world of High Availability. Your options today are overwhelming. You can get redundant "anything" in the marketplace. You can purchase servers from Dell and Compaq with redundant power supplies: if one fails, the other takes over. You have redundant power supplies in Cisco Catalyst switches, for example. For a Catalyst 4006, you can put in up to three redundant power supplies. This is quite the design you want when configuring your core network. A redundant network can exceed hardware components and go into the logical configurations of routes in your routers and wide area network (WAN) protocol technologies, such as having your frame relay network drop off the face of the Earth and have your router dial around it using ISDN. All in all, redundant services are key to a Highly Available network design.

Manageability

With clustered solutions, you have the benefit of managing your systems as one system. When you configure clustering with network load balancing (NLB) and with Application Center 2000, you find that setting up and managing systems under one console, and monitoring performance under one console, makes your life much easier. Because we all know life as a Network and Systems administrator is far from easy, this can be an incredible help to your efforts.

Reliability

Reliability is being able to guarantee you'll have services available to requests from clients. Think about it: you buy a brand new car—don't you want it to be reliable? The theory is the same when dealing with mission-critical network services. If server components fail, you can plan outages that are usually at night and in off hours. What if you run 24-hour-a-day operations? You want to be able to absorb the disaster that occurs and reliably deliver the service you offer.

Scalability

Scalability is your option to grow above and beyond what you've implemented today. For instance, say you purchased two servers to configure into a cluster with a separate shared storage device. If you want to say the solution you have is scalable, then you would say you could add two more servers to that clustered group when the need for growth arrived. Scalability (or being able to scale) is a term you would use to explain that capability to grow either up or out of your current solution.

Scale Up

Scaling up is the term you use to build up a single machine. If you have one server—and that server provides printing services to all the clients on your network—you might want to increase its memory because, while performance monitoring the server, you see that virtual memory is constantly paged from your hard disk. The fact that you are "adding" to a single system to build it up and not adding more systems to share the load means you are scaling up, as seen in Figure 1-4.

Scale Out

Scaling out is clustering as seen in Figure 1-5. You have one server providing a web site to clients and, while performance monitoring, you notice page hits have increased by 50 percent in one month. You are exceeding limits on your current hardware, but you don't want to add more resources to this single machine. You decide to add another machine and create a cluster. You have just scaled out. You learn how to monitor performance in Chapter 8.

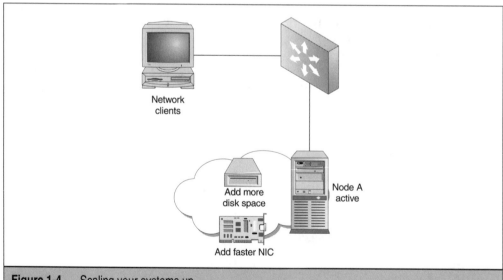

Figure 1-4.   Scaling your systems up

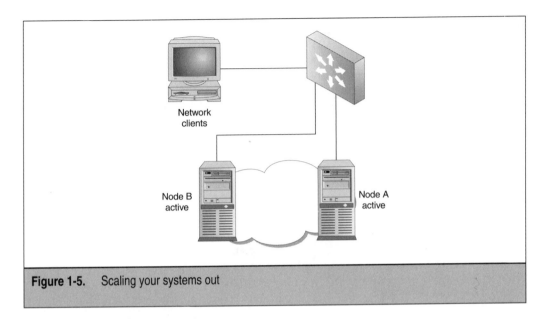

Figure 1-5.   Scaling your systems out

CLUSTERING WITH NT 4.0

Before you get into the high-level overview of clustering and load balancing with Windows 2000 and the Server 2003 platforms, you should know where this all started. I won't go over the history of clustering and how Microsoft got involved, but I'll give you an overview on why Windows 2000 clustering is a worthy solution to implement on your network.

Windows 2000 Clustering Services were first born on the Windows NT 4.0 Server Enterprise Edition. On hearing of its arrival and implementing the services, those involved quickly discovered this wasn't something they wanted to implement on their mission-critical applications. Microsoft Cluster Server, also code-named "Wolfpack," wasn't reliable. A plethora of problems occurred while running the service, including slow performance when using Fibre Channel and large amounts of hard disks that stopped serving clients altogether for no apparent reason, only to discover later it was another bug. This defeated the entire purpose for clustering in the first place and many quickly lost faith in the solution Microsoft had provided. Faith wasn't restored when most of the fixes you could implement were supplied from Microsoft in the form of a tool called: "Install the latest service pack."

Fast-forward to Windows 2000 and you have a whole different solution, which you discover throughout this book. All in all, the service has grown exponentially with the newer releases of Windows server-based OSs, and has become a reliable and applicable solution in your network infrastructure. If you plan to design an NT cluster, be aware that NT Server 4.0 doesn't support clustering, but it will work with load balancing. Windows NT 4.0 Enterprise Edition will work with load balancing and can be clustered with two nodes.

WINDOWS 2000 CLUSTERING AND LOAD BALANCING

When Windows 2000 was finally released to the public, I'd been running all beta and Release Candidate (RC) versions into the ground. Early on, I realized a winner was here. The system suddenly seemed less prone to the blue screen of death (BSOD) and reliability could be obtained. Now, years later, and after a few service-pack releases for quite a few bug fixes on clustering, this is still a force to be reckoned with. You should know that Windows 2000 Server doesn't contain the services to be clustered or load balanced. To mimic the Windows NT 4.0 Enterprise Edition, Windows 2000 Server has an "advanced" version, conveniently named Windows 2000 Advanced Server. This is the product you can cluster and load balance with. To compete in the high-end server arena, Microsoft also released a high-end version of Windows 2000 called Windows 2000 Datacenter Server, which allows not only clustering and load balancing, but also more flexibility to do it with by allowing four clustered nodes, instead of the limit of two with Advanced Server. Important design tips to remember are the following: when clustering and load balancing with Windows 2000, Windows 2000 Server won't support clustering and load balancing unless Application Center 2000 is installed; Windows 2000 Advanced Server will support a two node cluster and load balancing; and Windows 2000 Datacenter Server will support a four-node cluster and load balancing.

To understand Microsoft's position on this service, you should know Microsoft offers four types of clustering services. With Windows 2000, you have the Microsoft Cluster Server (MSCS), network load balancing (NLB), component load balancing (CLB), and a product called Application Center 2000. When you read about Application Center 2000 in detail, you'll realize it can help tie all the components together for you under one management umbrella. The Windows 2000 Clustering Service is thoroughly covered in Chapter 2 and an example of it can be seen in Figure 1-6. In the next chapter, you go step-by-step through the configuration and implementation of Windows 2000 Advanced Server Clustering and load balancing.

Windows 2000 Clustering Services

Windows 2000 Clustering Services enable you to implement some of the solutions mentioned thus far. You've learned about clustering and Windows 2000 has state-of-the-art clustering capability for your Enterprise solutions. Windows 2000 helps you by offering some great services, such as failover, Active/Active clustering, and rolling upgrades.

Failover and Failback Clustering

Failover is the act of another server in the cluster group taking over where the failed server left off. An example of a failover system can be seen in Figure 1-7. If you have a two-node cluster for file access and one fails, the service will failover to another server in the cluster. *Failback* is the capability of the failed server to come back online and take the load back from the node the original server failed over to. Again, this chapter simply lays

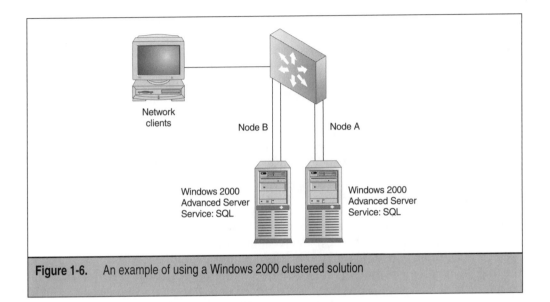

Figure 1-6.   An example of using a Windows 2000 clustered solution

the groundwork for the other chapters because, as you get into the actual configuration and testing of, say, SQL 2000, you could find that failover and failback might not always work. This is important to anyone who wants to run a SQL Server cluster.

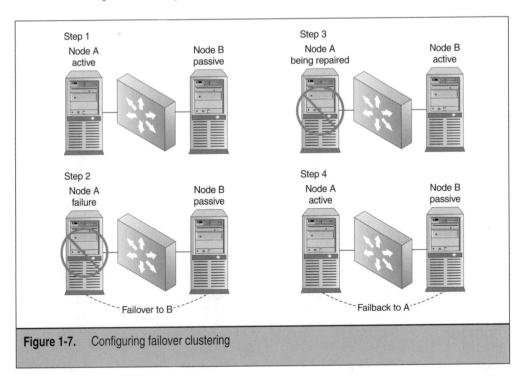

Figure 1-7.   Configuring failover clustering

Stateless vs. Stateful Clustering

Windows 2000 clustering functions as *stateful*, which means the application state and user state are managed during and through the failover. This is an important design question to ask yourself in the early stages of planning the High Availability solution. Do you want stateful failover? Most would answer "yes," so application state isn't lost. That can be equated as "what you were doing?" in time of failure. A *stateless* solution is one provided by network and component load balancing, where the state of the user and application aren't managed. An example of stateless versus stateful can be seen in Figure 1-8. As you become more involved with Application Center 2000, the explanation gets deeper.

Active/Passive

Active/Passive is defined as a cluster group where one server is handling the entire load and, in case of failure and disaster, a Passive node is standing by waiting for failover (as seen in Figure 1-9). This is commonly used, but most would argue that you're still wasting the resources of that server standing by. Wouldn't it be helpful if they were both somehow working to serve the clients needed data and still have the benefits of failover? That's what Windows 2000 clustering services can offer you: this is called Active/Active clustering. An example of this solution can be seen in Figure 1-10.

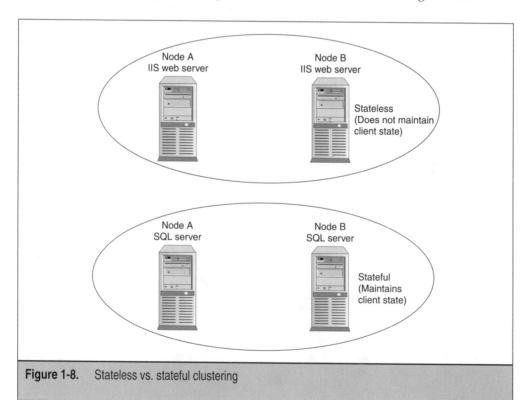

Figure 1-8.   Stateless vs. stateful clustering

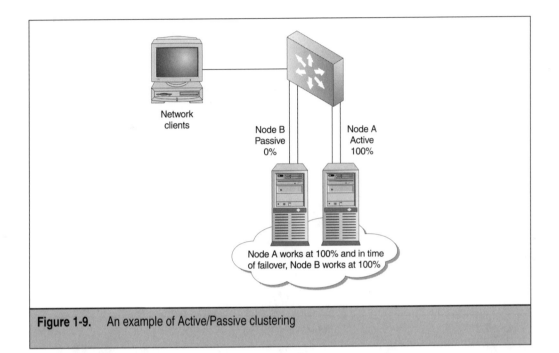

Figure 1-9.   An example of Active/Passive clustering

Active/Active

Active/Active clustering is when you want all servers in the cluster group to service clients and still be able to take up the load of a failed server in case of disaster, as seen in Figure 1-10. That said, a downside exists to using this technology. In Active/Passive clustering, you have a server producing 100 percent resources to clients. In case of disaster, the failed server fails over to the standby passive server. That node picks up the load and, other than a few seconds of change over time, there isn't any difference to the client. The client is still using 100 percent of the server's resources. In Active/Active clustering, this wouldn't be the case. You have nodes in the cluster sharing the load, thus, when one node fails and the other nodes must take up the load, this means you lost some of that percentage. In other words, you have two nodes providing services to the network clients. That's 100 percent of served resources. If one server fails, then the clients will only have one server in which to access and that would cut the percentage to 50 percent. This might not be noticeable in low-demand scenarios, but this is something to think about when planning your overall design. The best way to go about this is to determine the demand your servers will need and design your cluster solution around that demand. You also need to think about future demand, which brings us back to scalability. You learn about this in the section "Designing a Clustered Solution," where you can look at step-by-step design ideas you might need to consider.

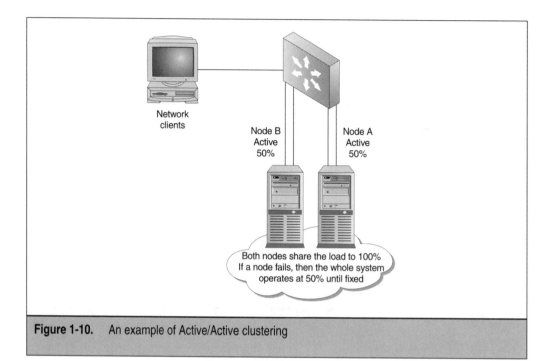

Figure 1-10. An example of Active/Active clustering

Rolling Upgrades

Rolling upgrades is a fantastic way to upgrade software on your production servers one at a time, without having a full-blown outage. Rolling upgrades is used for many reasons, including upgrading complete OSs, or applying service packs or hot fixes. The cluster node that needs work can be brought offline for maintenance, and then brought back online when the maintenance is complete, with no interruptions or only minor disruptions of service. You learn about performing a rolling upgrade in Chapter 2 of this book.

Network Load Balancing

Windows 2000 allows for load balancing of services as well. As just discussed, in an Active/Active cluster, you have load-balancing functionality. Another form of load balancing exists, though, which is if you have one IP address for an entire load-balanced cluster (with Windows 2000 Advanced Server, this scales to 32 nodes) and, using an algorithm, each node in the cluster helps with the entire data-traffic load. You can also use third-party solutions for load balancing in this manner, which you learn about shortly.

The way network load balancing (NLB) works is by having a driver sit between the TCP/IP stack and your NIC card. This driver is installed when you apply the service on every node in the cluster. All nodes participate by using one Internet protocol (IP) address, which is called a virtual IP address (VIP). Only one node will respond each time, but this will be a different node within the cluster. An affinity feature is used to weight the balance of the load when you configure NLB with Application Center 2000. (Application Center 2000, as you learn in Chapter 4, adds to the native NLB service that Windows 2000 Advanced Server provides.) You have multiple benefits for using Windows 2000 load-balanced solutions, which include, of course, balancing the load, transparent convergence, adding and removing servers as needed, and assigning certain servers in the load-balanced cluster certain amounts of the overall load and multicast-based messaging between nodes. You can see an example of a NLB solution in Figure 1-11.

Convergence

Windows 2000 has the intelligence to be able to know what nodes are in the cluster and, if one of them fails, it can reconverge the cluster based on this new number of nodes to continue balancing the load correctly. All Network Load Balancing (NLB)

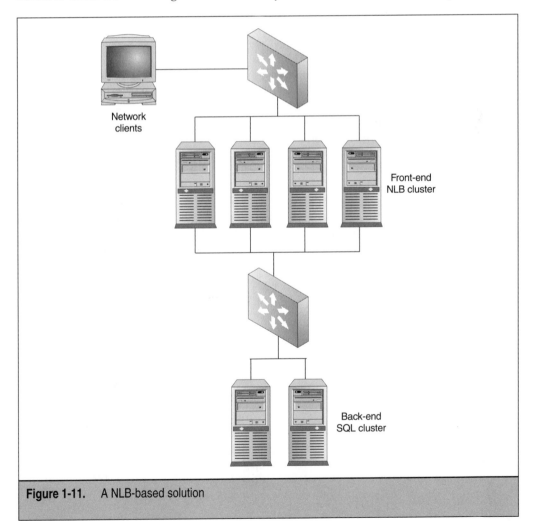

Figure 1-11. A NLB-based solution

hosts exchange *heartbeat messages* to inform the default host they're still active in the cluster. When a host doesn't send or respond to the heartbeat message, a process begins called convergence. During *convergence,* hosts that are still active are determined, as well as and whether they can accept loading. When a new host joins the cluster, it sends out heartbeat messages, are also trigger convergence to occur. Once all cluster hosts agree to the current status of the cluster, the loading is repartitioned and convergence ends.

The way NLB tracks which node is the *default node* (the node with the highest priority that keeps track of balancing the load to all other nodes in the group) and if that node is affected, can reconverge the group to elect a new default node. You see this in great detail while configuring load-balanced clusters and Application Center 2000-based clusters in Chapter 4.

Adding and Removing Servers

With Windows 2000 load balancing, you can easily add and remove nodes to the cluster. Windows 2000 Advanced Server allows for up to 32 nodes, so you can start off with 8 nodes and increase that number when necessary. When you configure Application Center 2000, you'll see this is an integral part of producing appropriate High-Availability solutions. Your load won't always be the same. Take, for instance, an ecommerce site that sells gifts on the Internet. In December, around Christmas time, the amount of hits, requests, and sales for the sight generally increases exponentially. That said, you'd want to design your load-balanced solution to be able to function normally with eight servers (you see how to baseline and monitor performance in Chapter 8), and then add servers to the group when times of availability need to be increased. You'll also want to be able to remove these servers when you finish. The beauty of this solution is you can lease server hardware when and where you need it, instead of keeping equipment you need to account for on hand all year. What's important to understand here is you're allotted that functionality, so you can plan for it because this chapter is where your initial design work takes place. If you need four servers to begin with, you'll have to baseline the servers on hand, and then, during periods of high activity and use, baseline again. You'll find your load is either over what you expected and you'll need to add a server or you'll find it's under your expectations and you can survive the additional hits with the hardware you have. Either way, you can only determine this by performance monitoring the systems and knowing how many hits you get a month. All of this is covered in the last chapter of the book.

Port Rules and Priority Assignments

The most difficult configurations on load-balanced solutions are Port Rules, affinity, and weighted assignments. These take a little time to plan and a lot of reading to understand fully if you aren't familiar with them. The mission of this book is to demystify these configurations for you, so you can plan, design, and implement them. The load of every node in the load-balanced cluster can be customized with *Port Rules,* which are used to specify load weight and priority. In Chapter 2, you learn about port assignments and affinity when you configure NLB on Windows 2000 Advanced Server.

SERVER 2003 CLUSTERING AND LOAD BALANCING

With the upcoming release of Server 2003 on the horizon, now's the time to start thinking about using this platform for your Clustered solutions as well. Windows 2000 will be around for quite some time. Companies haven't even moved away from NT 4 yet and they have little to no intentions of doing so. Microsoft will also take a stance at some time in the next decade and will look at what to do with Windows 2000 and its end of life (EOL) sequence. What's next, you ask? A product called Server 2003 will eventually replace Windows 2000. This book looks at clustering and load-balancing Server 2003. One of the most confusing pieces of Microsoft's new naming convention is that it has also retired its Backoffice solution and upgraded the name to Server 2003 Enterprise servers, ("Backoffice" is the name that applied to running Exchange 5.5 or Proxy 2.0 on top of Windows NT 4.0). Windows 2000 also has services that can be added to it, such as Exchange 2000 and Internet Security and Acceleration (ISA) Server 2000, which are the subsequent upgrades from the previously mentioned products.

Windows Server 2003 Enterprise Servers

The name Server 2003 can be confusing. I want to demystify this term, so you understand how it will be referenced throughout the remainder of this book. You have the OS, which is slated to succeed Windows 2000 Server and the Server 2003 Enterprise server line, such as SQL 2000. And then you have the products just mentioned, like Exchange 2000 and ISA 2000. My goal is to cover the configuration and installation of clustered services that combine with most of these services. SQL 2000 is covered in great detail because it's a big player in N-tier architecture. You'll most likely be involved with N-tier architecture while configuring High Availability solutions.

Windows Server 2003

At press time, the full version of Windows Server 2003 wasn't yet released and is currently in RC2. It's almost out of testing and ready for full production. After you read this book, you'll already know how to configure and cluster the full version of Windows Server 2003. The program's release should be in sync with this book's release. What I want to accomplish is to lay out the overall strategy and enhancements, so you can consider this product in your upgrade or migration path for the future. Or, even more important, you could find the product's enhancements are so superior, you might want to wait for its release to implement it immediately. Let's look at where Server 2003 is going with clustering and load balancing.

Server 2003 Clustering Enhancements

First, your clustered node count went up. In Windows 2000 Advanced Server, you were locked down to a two-node cluster, but Server 2003 Enterprise version will allow for four-node clusters. (Datacenter Server moves up to eight nodes). Also new to Server 2003 is load balancing for all its Server 2003 versions. Windows 2000 server was incapable of NLB, but Windows Server 2003 is capable. Another huge addition is adding the Window Cluster Service in Server 2003 to Active Directory. A virtual object is created, which allows applications to use Kerberos authentication, as well as delegation. Unless you have the hardware, it doesn't matter. If you do have the hardware, though, 64-bit support is now available. New configuration and management tools have been added, which you read about in great detail in Chapter 3. They do make life easier. Network enhancements have also been made to make network traffic run smoother so as to include a multicast heartbeat default option where unicast traffic is only used if multicasting fails entirely. You have options to make communication more secure as well. New storage enhancements have also been worked into the product to allow more flexibility with a shared quorum device. And, you have new cluster-based troubleshooting tools, which you look at closely as an enhancement.

Server 2003 Load-Balanced Enhancements

A brand new management utility is being offered in Server 2003 load-balancing services. You now have a central management utility from which to manage NLB clusters. You see this in detail in Chapter 3 and make comparisons to Application Center 2000, as necessary. You can now configure virtual clusters. This is a huge step up because you previously had limitations on how you perform IP addressing on load balanced clusters, but now you can configure clustering almost like switch-based virtual local area networks (VLANs). You learn about this in Chapter 3. You also have Internet Group Membership Protocol (IGMP) support, which is to have multicast groupings configured for NLB clusters. Another greatly needed enhancement is the inception of Bidirectional Affinity in what you need to implement to have server publishing while using ISA Server 2000. Bidirectional Affinity is what is used to create multiple instances of NLB on the same host to make sure that responses from servers that are published via ISA Server can be routed through the correct ISA server in the cluster. Two separate algorithms are used on both the internal and external interfaces of the servers to aid in determining which node services the request.

As you can see, huge enhancements exist to the new Server 2003 technology, which you learn about in great detail in Chapter 3 when we discuss load balancing and clustering Windows Server 2003. You need to review the basics here so you can plan for it, if necessary. All the major differences will be highlighted, as we configure the clustered and load-balanced solutions. Chapter 3 covers the granular details of configuration and implementation of Server 2003.

APPLICATION CENTER 2000

With the creation and shipment of Application Center 2000, Microsoft placed itself on a map few others could reach. Application Center 2000 is the future of cluster management. This Server 2003 enterprise server platform adds massive functionality to your clustered and load-balanced solutions. You already know Windows 2000 Advanced Server can provide for you with load balancing and clustering, so now you'll learn about the benefits Application Center 2000 can add. Microsoft wanted to expand on the NLB and clustering functionality of Windows 2000 Advanced Server and it created the ultimate package to get that done. Microsoft Application Center 2000 is used to manage and administer from one central console web and COM+ components. This was a problem in the past without Application Center 2000. Many customers complained about how archaic it was to manage their clusters and load-balanced solutions, so Microsoft obliged them with the Application Center 2000 Management Console. Through this console, you can manage all your cluster nodes and all your clusters in one Microsoft Management Console (MMC) snap-in. Health monitoring also created a snafu, which was unmanageable. As you see in Chapter 8, you can monitor the entire cluster from one console, instead of having to do performance monitoring on every cluster node separately with Microsoft Health Monitor. You'll also see that configuring a cluster without Application Center 2000 can be difficult.

In the next few chapters, you learn to configure clustered and load-balanced solutions, and then, in later chapters, you do the same thing using Application Center 2000. You'll see clearly that the management of difficult settings becomes much easier to configure and manage. Application Center 2000 also provides the power to manage your web sites and COM components, all within the same console. This is important because, many times, most of what you'll be load balancing are your web site and ecommerce solutions. You also have some other great add-ons, such as the capability to use alerting, and so forth. Using Windows 2000 and Application Center 2000 to manage your cluster can be seen in Figure 1-12.

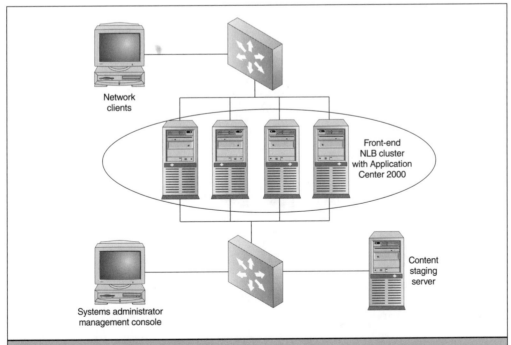

Figure 1-12.   Using Windows 2000 and Application Center 2000 to manage your cluster

Component Load Balancing

In times of High Availability, you might not only need to cluster and load balance entire server platforms, but also critical applications that use Component Object Model (COM) services of COM and COM+ for short. Most high-availability demands come from the need to produce services quickly and reliably, like application components for an online store. You might need to load balance specific servers and pages, as well as the COM+ components shared by all servers within the group. With component load balancing (CLB), the possibilities are endless. CLB is new to Windows 2000, once you install Application Center 2000, and it offers something that wasn't available in the past with older versions of NT 4.0: the capability to scale up to 16 clustered nodes of servers dedicated to processing the code for COM and COM+ objects. CLB clustering and routing also needs Application Center 2000, which you use to implement this solution. Chapters 4, 6, and 7 cover the granular details of configuration and implementation of Application Center with Microsoft Servers. An example of CLB can be seen in Figure 1-13.

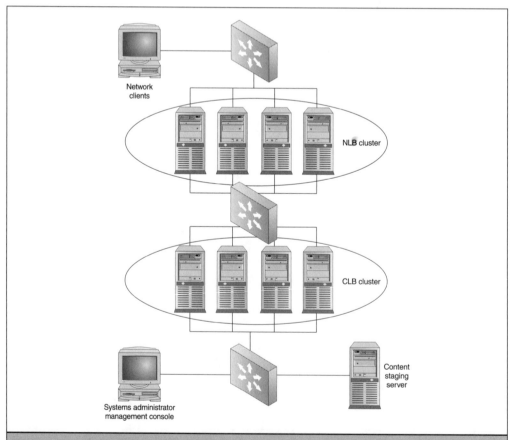

Figure 1-13.   An example of component load balancing

HIGHLY AVAILABLE DATABASES WITH SQL SERVER 2000

SQL Server is by far the most up-and-coming database product today. With its lower-than-average cost against the bigger players like Oracle, SQL Server eats up more and more market share as it continues to be promoted and moved into more infrastructures. That said, more companies are relying on its uptime. For those who don't know what *SQL Server* is, it's the Microsoft database server product. SQL Server 2000 (a Server 2003 Enterprise product) is mentioned here and is covered in depth throughout the book because it's an integral part of web-based commerce sites and it's finding its way into nearly every product available that does some form of logging or network management. I think it's clear why this product needs to be clustered and highly available. An example of SQL Clustering can be seen in Figure 1-14. Chapter 5 covers the clustering in granular detail. You also learn some little-known facts about what clustering this product costs, how to convince management this product is relatively cheap to cluster, and why clustering it makes sense.

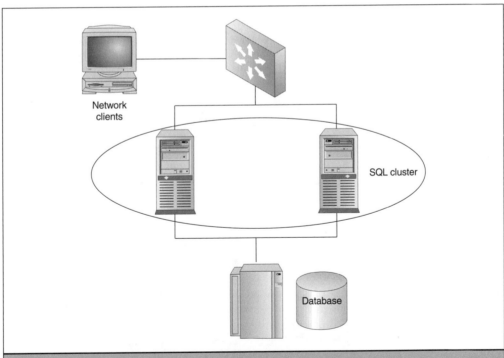

Figure 1-14.   Configuring clustered solutions with SQL 2000

DESIGNING A HIGHLY AVAILABLE SOLUTION

Now that you know all the basics of High Availability, clustering, and load balancing, you need to learn how to develop its design. This is, by far, the most important phase in any project. Many networks have been built with good intentions but, because of the lack of design done in the early stages of rolling out the solution, it always wound up costing more, taking longer, or not panning out as expected.

In this book, I hope to get you to a point where you can completely bypass that scenario. I want you to be the one who designs the proper solution and correctly budgets for it in the early stages of development and project planning. First, you need to develop *what* you're trying to accomplish. This section gives you an overall approach to any solution you need to accomplish. In other words, I won't go into deep detail here about Application Center per se, but you'll get an overall thorough process to follow up until you need to design the Application Center task within the project. When you get to the appropriate chapters where each technology is different, I'll include a design phase section to help you incorporate that piece of technology into your overall design and the project plan you want to create. For this section, you need to get that overall 40,000-foot view of the entire project. This is critical because, without the proper vision, you might overlook some glaring omissions in the beginning stages of the plan that could come back to haunt you later.

To create a great solution, you first need to create a vision on what you want to accomplish. If this is merely a two-node cluster, then you should take into account what hardware solution you want to purchase. Getting involved with a good vendor is crucial to the success of your overall design. You could find each vendor has different costs that won't meet your budget or each vendor might have clustering hardware packages with shared storage solutions, which meet your needs more clearly than other hardware vendors. For instance, you could find you'd like to have servers with three power supplies instead of two within each server. You might decide you want your management network connection to be connected via fiber or Gigabit Ethernet and have your shared storage at the same speeds. You have much to think about at this stage of overall design. Something else to think about is what service do you want to provide? You must understand that the product you're delivering needs to function properly and you need to know what the client level of expectations is. You could have a client who has a specific Service Level Agreement (SLA), which he expects you to honor. When I shop for new services, I always want to know what's in the contract based on my own expectations. You might also want to get an overall feel of the expected deadlines. By what date does this solution need to be rolled out live into production? This is important to plan for because, based on what pieces of hardware you need to purchase, you could have lead time on ordering it. Remember, if the hardware is sizable and pricey, you might need to account for a little more time to get it.

Another consideration is budget. This is covered in its own section because budget warrants its own area of discussion. You also need to consider the surrounding infrastructure. I once encountered a design where the entire clustered solution was laid out in Visio format and looked outstanding, but the planners didn't account for the fact that they didn't order the separate switch for the Management VLAN. Although this was a painless oversight, my hope is this book can eliminate most of these types of errors from ever occurring.

Creating a Project Plan

By creating a project plan like the one seen in Figure 1-15, you have a way to keep track of your budget needs, your resources—whether the resources are actual workers or technicians of server-based hardware—and many other aspects of rolling out a Highly Available solution. Make no mistake, creating a Highly Availability solution is no small task. There is much to account for and many things need to be addressed during every step of the design during the setup and roll out of this type of solution. Having at least a documented project plan can keep you organized and on track. You don't necessarily need a dedicated project manager (unless you feel the tasks are so numerous, and spread over many locations and business units that it warrants the use of one), but you should at least have a shared document for everyone in your team to monitor and sign off on.

Pilots and Prototypes

You need to set up a test bed to practice on. If you plan on rolling anything at all out into your production network, you need to test it in an isolated environment first. To do this you can set up a pilot. A *pilot* is simply a scaled-down version of the real solution,

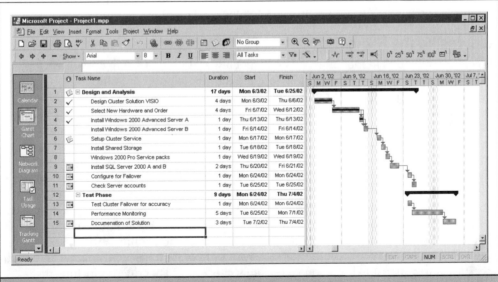

Figure 1-15.   Example of a sample project plan with Project 2000

where you can quite easily get an overall feel of what you'll be rolling out into your live production network. A *prototype* is almost an exact duplicate set to the proper scale of the actual solution you'll be rolling out. This would be costly to implement, based on the costs of the hardware but, if asked, at least you can accurately say you could set up a pilot instead to simulate the environment you'll be designing. Working with a hardware vendor directly is helpful and, during the negotiation phase of the hardware, ask the vendor what other companies have implemented their solutions. I can usually get a list of companies using their products and make contacts within those companies, so I can see their solutions in action. And I hit newsgroups and forums to deposit general questions to see what answers I turn up on specific vendors and their solutions. You could also find the vendors themselves might be willing to work out having you visiting one of their clients to see the solutions in action. This has worked for me and I'm sure it could also be helpful to you.

Designing a Clustered Solution

Now that you've seen the 40,000-foot view, let's come down to 10,000 feet. Don't worry. In upcoming chapters (and starting with the next chapter), you get into specific configurations. To understand all the new terminology, though, it's imperative for you to look at basic topology maps and ideas, so we can share this terminology as we cover the actual solution configurations. As you look at clustering Windows 2000 Advanced Server in the next chapter, we'll be at ground level, looking at all the dialog boxes and check boxes we'll need to manipulate. First, you need to consider the design of a general cluster, no matter how many nodes it will service. Let's look at a two-node cluster for a simple overview. Now let's look at some analysis facts.

Addressing the Risks

When I mention this in meetings, I usually get a weird look. If we're implementing a cluster, is that what we're using to eliminate the single point of failure that was the original problem? Why would you now have to consider new risks? Although you might think this type of a question is ridiculous, it isn't. The answer to this question is something that takes experience to answer. I've set up clustering only to find out that the service running on each cluster was now redundant and much slower than it was without the clustering. This is a risk. Your user community will, of course, make you aware of the slow-down in services. They know because they deal with it all day.

Another risk is troubleshooting. Does your staff know how to troubleshoot and solve cluster-based problems? I've seen problems where a clustered Exchange Server 2000 solution took 12 people to determine what the problem was because too many areas of expertise were needed for just one problem. You needed someone who knew network infrastructure to look through the routers and switches, you needed an e-mail specialist, and you needed someone who knew clustering. That doesn't include the systems administrators for the Windows 2000 Advanced Servers that were implemented. Training of personnel on new systems is critical to the system's success . . .and yours.

Have power concerns been addressed? I got to witness the most horrifying, yet hilarious, phenomenon ever to occur in my experience as an IT professional. One of the junior administrators on staff brought up a server to mark the beginning of the age of Windows 2000 in our infrastructure, only to find out the power to that circuit was already at its peak. The entire network went down—no joke. (Was that a sign or what?) This was something I learned the hard way. Consider power and uninterruptible power supplies as well. Power design is covered in more detail in Chapter 2.

Designing Applications and Proper Bandwidth

What will you be running on this cluster? This is going to bring you back to planning your hardware solution appropriately. In each of the following chapters, you'll be given a set of basic requirements, which you'll need to get your job done with the solution you're implementing. Of course, when you add services on top of the cluster itself, you'll also need to consider adding resources to the hardware.

You should also consider the bandwidth connections based on the application. Bandwidth and application flows can be seen in Figure 1-16. Some services will use more bandwidth than others and this must be planned by watching application flows. In later chapters, we'll discuss how to test your clustered solutions with a network and protocol analyzer to make sure you're operating at peak performance, instead of trying to function on an oversaturated and overused network segment.

You also need to consider whether your applications are *cluster aware*, which means they support the cluster API (application programming interface). Applications that are cluster aware will be registered with the Cluster Service. Applications that are noncluster aware can still be failed over, but will miss out on some of the benefits of cluster-aware applications. That said, you might want to consider this if the whole reason you're clustering is for a mission-critical application that might not be cluster aware. Most of Microsoft's product line is cluster aware, but you might want to check with a vendor of a third-party solution to see if their applications function with the cluster API.

Determining Failover Policies

Failover will occur through disaster or testing and, when it does, what happens is based on a policy. Until now, we've covered the fundamentals of what failover entails, but now we can expound on the features a bit. You can set up polices for failover and failback timing, as well as configuring a policy for preferred node. Failover, failback, and preferred nodes are all based on setting up MSCS (Microsoft Cluster Service) or simply the Cluster Service.

Failover Timing   *Failover timing* is used for simple failover to another standby node in the group upon failure. Another option is to have the Cluster Service make attempts to restart the failed node before going to failover node to a Passive node. In situations where you might want to have the primary node brought back online immediately, this is the policy you can implement. Failover timing design is based on what is an acceptable

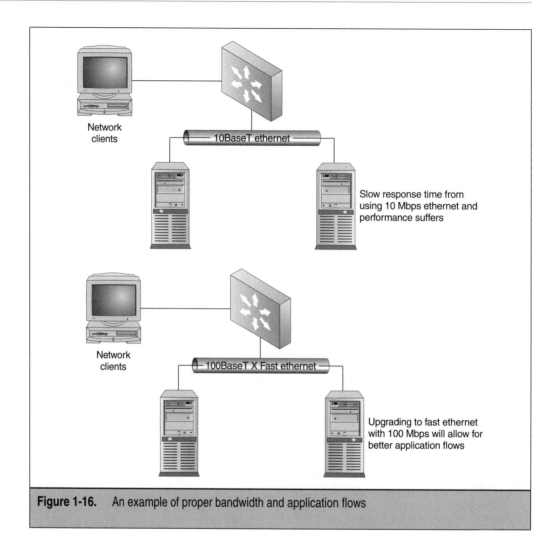

Figure 1-16.   An example of proper bandwidth and application flows

amount of downtime any node can experience. If you're looking at failover timing based on critical systems, where nodes can't be down at all, which is based on 99.999 percent, then you need to test your systems to make sure your failover timing is quick enough, so your clients aren't caused any disruption.

Failback Timing   *Failing back* is the process of going back to the original primary node that originally failed. Failback can be immediate or you can set a policy to allow timing to be put in place to have the failback occur in off-hours, so the network isn't disturbed again with a changeover in the clustered nodes.

Preferred Node   A *preferred node* can be set via policy, so if that node is available, then that will be the Active node. You'd want to design this so your primary node could be set up with high hardware requirements. This is the node you'd want to serve the clients at all times.

Selecting a Domain Model

I've been asked many times about clustering domain controllers and how this affects the design. You can cluster your domain controllers (or member servers), but an important design rule to consider is this: all nodes must be part of the same domain. A simple design consideration is that you never install services like SQL on top of a domain controller; otherwise, your hardware requirements will go sky high. When designing a Windows 2000 clustered solution, you'll want to separate services as much as possible. Make sure when you cluster your domain controllers that you also take traffic overhead into consideration. Now, you'll not only have to worry about replication and synchronization traffic, but also about management heartbeat traffic. Be cautious about how you design your domain controllers and, when they're clustered in future chapters, I'll point this out to you again.

Limitations of Clusters

But I thought clustering would be the total solution to my problems? Wrong! Clustering works wonders, but it has limits. When designing the cluster, it's imperative for you to look at what you can and can't do. Again, it all comes down to design. What if you were considering using Encrypting File System (EFS) on your clustered data? Could you set that up or would you need to forego that solution for the clustered one? This question usually doesn't come up when you're thinking about clustering a service because all you can think about are the benefits of clustering. You should highlight what you might have to eliminate to support the clustered service. In the case of EFS, you can't use it on cluster storage. That said, you'll also need to use disks on cluster storage configured as basic disks. You can't use dynamic disks and you must always use NT file system (NTFS), so you won't be able to use FAT or any of its variations. You must also only use TCP/IP. Although in this day and age, this might not be shocking to you, it could be a surprise to businesses that want to use Windows 2000 clustering while only running IPX/SPX in their environments. This is something you should consider when you design your clustered solution.

Capacity Planning

Capacity planning involves memory, CPU utilization, and hard disk structure. After you choose what kind of clustered model you want, you need to know how to equip it. You already know you need to consider the hardware vendors, but when you're capacity planning, this is something that needs to be fully understood and designed specifically for your system.

Determining Server-Capacity Requirements

After you choose a cluster model, determine how to group your resources, and determine the failover policies required by each resource, then you're ready to determine the hardware capacity required for each server in the cluster. The following sections explain the criteria for choosing computers for use as cluster nodes. Look closely at storage requirements. Each node in your cluster group must have enough storage to contain systems files, the applications and services installed, swap space for paging, and enough free space for scalability. You'll want to set up one system and analyze your storage requirements for that system, so you can roll it out identically to the other systems in your cluster group.

A *quorum device,* which is a shared storage device that both cluster nodes will use together, needs to be factored in as well. You need to look at size requirements and the needs of your business. Your CPU must be able to process without consistent strain. Although we know a CPU peaking occasionally to 100 percent is normal, riding consistent at a high level isn't normal. During your pilot and assessment stages, you need to know what applications and services will require higher CPU requirements: SQL Server 2000, for instance, is a resource hog.

The CPU and memory requirements needed should be closely analyzed for your clustered solution. You also need to consider the CPU requirements on nodes with which failover might occur. A good design methodology to apply here is to design the perfect node, and then duplicate it for the Passive node. Memory (or RAM) needs to be addressed as well. When you do capacity planning, always oversize your memory. The more data that can be stored and pulled from memory, the faster your system will operate—it's that simple. In any case, always look at the minimum requirements while doing your design work and make sure you test to see what you need to apply.

Planning for Fault-Tolerant Disks

Your cluster design needs to implement the use of fault-tolerant disks. Although we won't delve deeply into the use of fault-tolerant disks, where and how you should implement them when the need occurs will be highlighted. As of this section, you need to know where fault-tolerant disks come up in the overall design. When you plan for fault-tolerant disks, you should consider RAID. RAID support makes sure the data contained on your clustered disk sets is highly available. Hardware RAID, which can be implemented in a shared device among the cluster members, can almost guarantee you won't lose data or make sure it's recoverable if a disaster occurs. You should factor into your initial design that you can't use software fault-tolerant-based disk sets for cluster storage. Also, always consult the Microsoft Hardware Compatibility List (HCL) for any hardware purchasing you plan to do, especially with extravagant and expensive hardware solutions such as RAID and clustering solutions. If you're going to implement a RAID solution into your High Availability design (wise choice), then you need to consider which version of RAID you want to implement.

Raid Version	Fault Tolerant?
Raid 0	No
Raid 1	Yes
Raid 5	Yes
Raid 0+1	Yes

When you configure RAID, you'll want to design at least one of the most popular and functional versions of RAID into your infrastructure. RAID 0 is used only as a speed enhancement, enabling multiple drives to be written to and read from simultaneously. RAID 0 is disk striping without parity. Although it accounts for faster disk reads and writes, no fault tolerance is involved whatsoever in RAID 0. If a disk failure occurs, you can't rebuild the rest of the data by inserting a new disk into the set. Raid 1 is the beginning of fault tolerance within RAID, but it's slower, depending on which version of RAID 1 you implement. RAID 1 with mirroring is achieved by using two disks within a system on the same motherboard controller. When data is written to one disk, it's then written to the second disk achieving fault tolerance.

When one disk fails, the other has a working version of the data ready to go. With *mirroring,* you have a single point of failure, which is removed from the equation when you implement RAID 1 disk duplexing. This is the same as mirroring, except you're now working from two disk controllers on the motherboard instead of one. RAID 5 is the fastest and most common RAID version used today that also offers fault tolerance. Disk striping with parity (RAID 0 does not have this) offers fast reads and writes, while maintaining a separate disk to store parity information. This will be essential to re-create the disk if a failure occurs. Raid 0+1 or (RAID 10) is the combination of RAID levels 0 and 1. For design purposes, you need to implement something highly fault-tolerant if you want to maintain a highly available posture to your clients accessing resources. Cost is the only factor from this point. RAID 5 and RAID 10 are the best options, but they cost the most. Examples of RAID 0, 1, and 5 can be seen in Figure 1-17.

Optimizing a Cluster

Optimizing your cluster is something you learn throughout each chapter of this book. In each new section, you learn all the ways you can enhance performance, while looking at particular services like structured query language (SQL) and Internet Information Server (IIS). Some general design-optimization techniques you can, again, look at are to make sure you have plenty of hard disk storage, fast connections between your nodes and the shared storage, high-end CPUs and using Symmetrical Multiprocessing (SMP) when your services call for it, and adjusting virtual memory within the servers to appropriately handle paging and swapping.

One item many designers overlook is size and placement of the paging file. This can seriously affect your performance. When you configure your first cluster, you'll

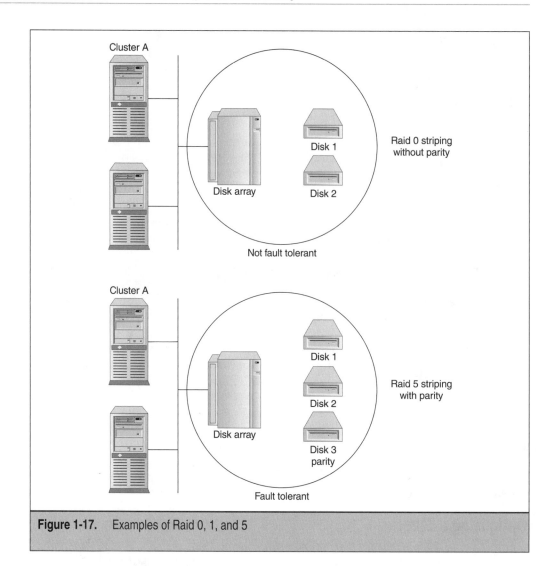

Figure 1-17. Examples of Raid 0, 1, and 5

look at this in great detail. But make sure you plan for it, while you allot for free disk space on the nodes themselves. You must take into consideration that the paging file can't be located on a shared bus storage solution. The best way to design this for high performance is to set up a separate physical drive in each node and use only that drive for paging. Placing the Pagefile.sys on a shared bus or an extended partition can severely impact your performance. Now that you understand where to put it, let's look at how to set up. Set a page file at two times the amount of physical RAM you have installed.

Also, be aware that you never want to set the virtual memory to be larger than the amount of free space you have on a disk. Last, always watch the performance of virtual memory with the system monitor to see exactly how much virtual memory you're using. In Chapter 8, you look at performance monitoring on your cluster.

VIPS, VMACS, and Other Addressing Concerns

When you lay out the design of a cluster, you can account for IP addressing to rear its head because, without logical addressing, how would your services work? In this section, you look at the design methods you should consider with both logical and physical addressing of your clusters. You can see an example of a virtual IP in use on a cluster in Figure 1-18. In each chapter of this book, you'll look at it over and over with each cluster and service you configure but, for design purposes, you need to be aware of what you'll need to consider overall.

You must be aware that TCP/IP is the only protocol you can use with the Windows 2000 clustering and load-balancing solution. That said, it's important for you to concentrate on planning your TCP/IP addressing architecture early in the design. When we get into the actual configuration during the next chapters, you'll see why this is so critical, but you need to make sure you have such addressing accessible. I once had a situation where, in the design and planning stages of an Internet-accessible design that used publicly assigned IP addresses from the Internet service provider (ISP), I realized someone might not have taken that into consideration with the block the company had

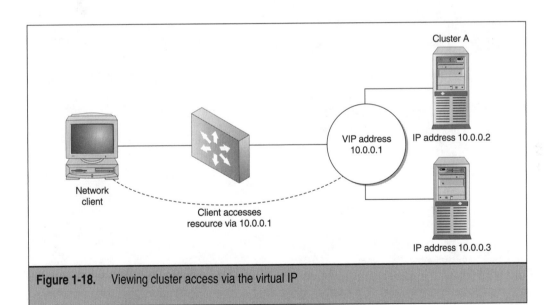

Figure 1-18.   Viewing cluster access via the virtual IP

been given. They were locked down to the few addresses they already had and they had absolutely no room to grow. To build forward from that point, we had to get the ISP involved to get a new block with much more capacity. You need to get that high-level view of design finalized before implementing the technology. An example of a load-balanced solution while considering IP can be seen in Figure 1-19.

The Heartbeat

You might wonder how the nodes communicate with each other. Nodes in a cluster communicate through a management network (as seen in Figure 1-20) exclusive to

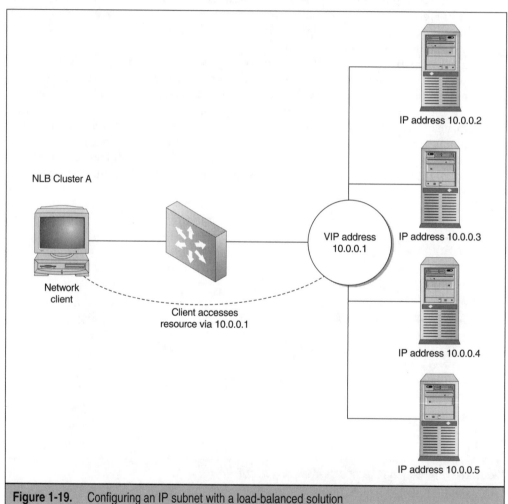

Figure 1-19.   Configuring an IP subnet with a load-balanced solution

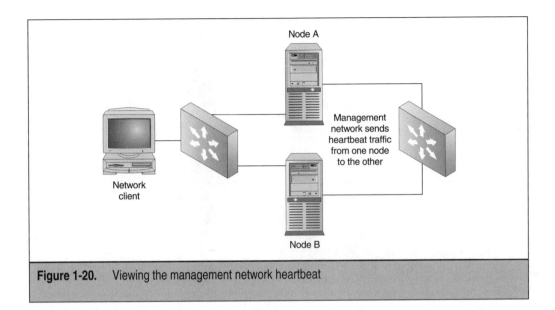

Figure 1-20.   Viewing the management network heartbeat

them. You can plug all network connections into a hub and have everything in one shared collision domain, but to design your network properly, you might want to consider having a high-speed, dedicated connection from one node to another that only contains management-based traffic. This traffic is affectionately called the heartbeat. The *heartbeat* is simply packets sent from the Passive node to the Active node. When the Passive node doesn't see the Active node anymore, it comes up online.

Designing a Load-Balanced Third-Party Solution

Many times, you might want options to be present when deciding what load-balanced solution you want to apply to your infrastructure. Although many solutions are available and covering all these technologies would warrant its own publication, this book discusses some of your options and why some are better than others.

Cisco Local Director is a product I've used. Cisco puts out a solid load balancer to direct traffic to an array of servers. The use of a Cisco load balancer can be seen in Figure 1-21.

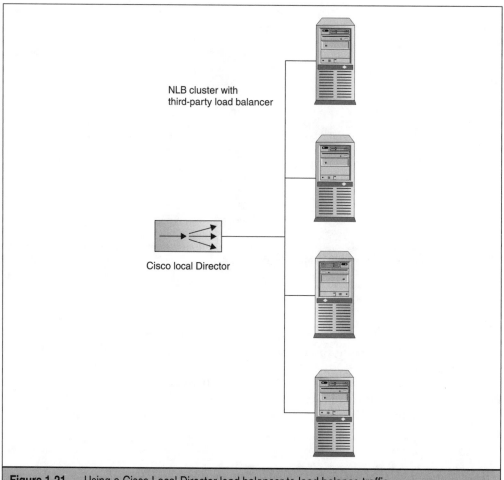

NLB cluster with
third-party load balancer

Cisco local Director

Figure 1-21. Using a Cisco Local Director load balancer to load balance traffic

N-TIER DESIGNS

N-tier is more than a buzzword: its entire design logic in highly availability design is a formidable force. You can't look to design a highly available solution and not come across the mention of N-tier technology. N stands for any number. When you wrote $2 + n = 3$, this was a simple formula in algebra to solve the number as being 1 or, for the sake of a formal solution, $n = 1$. N was something you had to solve for. In the context in which it's presented here, N is any number that makes sense. If you were going to set up two layers of access for your Highly Available solution, you could safely say you're creating a two-tier design.

Three-Tier Designs

Now that you understand what N-tier design is, let's look at the most popular and widely used design used today when designing highly available solutions. The *three-tier design* is a three-tier architecture used to lay out three distinctly separate layers of services used on most ecommerce configurations and designs used today. This design is also known as a *three-tier system architecture.*

Counting backwards from three, you'll look at the most highly secured layer, which is where your database sits. Of course, your database is what contains your data and also your client information, so keep this layer separate from the servers running your web sites. Then, if they're penetrated by hackers, you'd have a separate layer of protection for both your front-end systems and your back-end databases. You can separate each layer via a firewall, which is another design task you'd need to look into.

The third tier is the SQL Server back-end database. This is where your data is stored. This tier (or layer) is known as the *data services layer.* When considering design, you'll want to cluster your SQL databases and make sure they're protected via a firewall. In Chapter 5, you learn not only how to cluster SQL, but also how to open ports on the firewall to let transitions through to the other tiers and the back-end network. (Remember, your SQL server implementation needs to be designed as a cluster with MSCS where your IIS and component clusters in the first two tiers will be using NLB.)

The next layer in the three-tier layer is called the *business logic layer,* which is where much of the development and component coding takes place for access between the web servers themselves and the back-end databases. The second tier sits in the middle and consists of ASP code, ADO, COM+, and anything else used to build the data into XML-based formats or other formats and specifications. The second tier also has some shopping cart software components if configured. You can see an example of a three-tier design in Figure 1-22.

The last layer in the three-tier design is Layer 1, the presentation layer. This is generally what the web site visitor or ecommerce shopper sees when purchasing over the Internet. Although components run here as well, this will make more sense to you once you're configuring Application Center 2000, which allows for CLB-based clustering and load balancing.

You might wonder where N-tier design and architecture fit into clustering and load balancing. Well, again, they fit into the whole picture of High Availability. In this book, you'll look at clustering services such as WINS and DHCP, but these aren't always considered mission-critical services. The web servers running your ecommerce software are probably mission-critical and sustain the livelihood of your business, so they would be more susceptible to being clustered and load balanced. Because this is the case, you'll frequently come in contact with N-tier design and architecture. Therefore, you should remember them and know how to design around and within them.

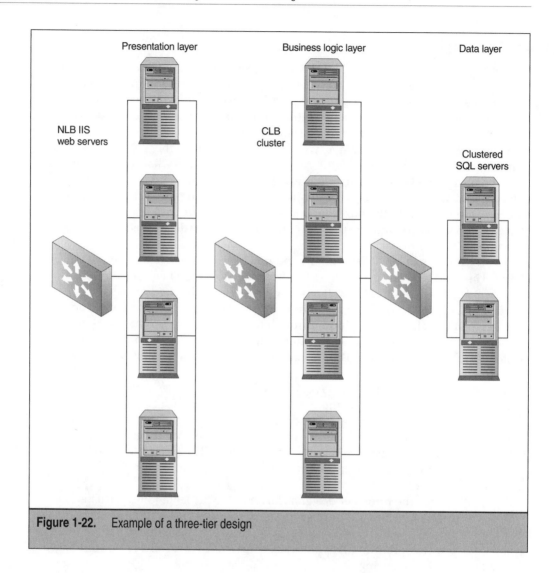

Figure 1-22.   Example of a three-tier design

SECURITY AND REMOTE ACCESS DESIGN

Cluster-based security is also a big deal in today's architectures. Security in general is a big deal to anyone's network infrastructure, but it's more important in any clustered and load-balanced solution available via the Internet. You need to be concerned. In this section, I'm simply pointing out some things you need to be aware of for your initial design, but never fear. As we move forward to configure more and more solutions, I add tips and notes every step of the way where you'll need to configure security-based solutions. As mentioned with three-tier designs (as seen in Figure 1-23), you'll have to implement a firewall (or two to make them redundant as well) to protect your data from intrusion.

You should take all this into consideration early in the designing phase. Many times, this is overlooked until later and purchasing sets of redundant firewalls can overinflate your preplanned budget. You also should be concerned about remote access into your network to manage, troubleshoot, and do maintenance on your cluster from a remote location, home, or business office. Assessing a cluster from a remote location can be seen in Figure 1-24.

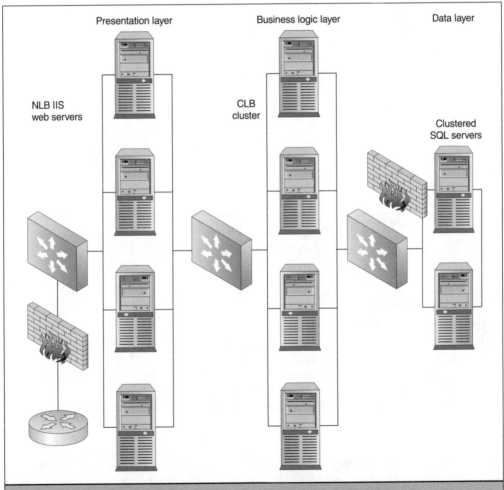

Figure 1-23. Assessing security concerns on your three-tier clustered solution

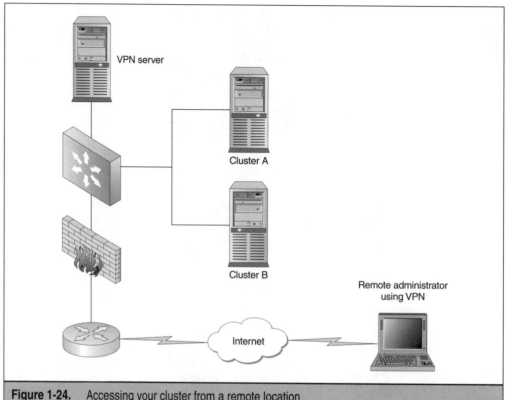

Figure 1-24.   Accessing your cluster from a remote location

HANDLING THE COSTS

High Availability involves cost—there's no way around this. Whenever you want to implement highly scalable and available solutions, you have to pay for it. This is something that isn't always allocated for in the IT budget. To buy an exact duplicate system for disaster reasons, when many more things are needed, is usually frowned upon. In this section, you see how to understand the costs involved and why you need to understand the ramifications of not having this type of solution in place.

Budget

Budget—a word that can strike terror into everyone's heart. If anyone needs to plan and design networks, then a budget will become a big reality to you. Everything that's scalable and redundant comes with a huge price tag. Remember, you're essentially buying everything you need at least twice. If a solution costs $100,000 (which is pretty cheap), then you could be looking at an added $60,000 for redundant features. When we discuss Return on Investment (ROI) and Total Cost of Ownership (TCO), why you might want to make such an investment will make sense. A nice design ethic I apply when doing purchases and high-level design planning is to plan big and buy modular. If you purchase a server with a chassis that can handle two power supplies and only purchase one power supply up-front, you can always come back later when you have more money to purchase the additional component.

ROI and TCO Fundamentals

Explaining a major disaster to your vice president isn't something you want to do, especially when you can't get the services the company depends on back online. This needs to be flagged in the early stages of your accepting any job where your responsibility is to provide services to clients.

What I generally do when coming onboard to any business is to find out what the acceptable amount of downtime is for any service provided today. In other words, if the company depended on an Enterprise Resource Planning (ERP) package, I'd ask how much downtime they can afford to have, if and when a disaster occurs. Most are usually caught off guard by this question and, believe me, it's an important question to ask. I usually get answers like "We can't have any downtime whatsoever!"

My next step is to show the company just how vulnerable they are. This is quite simple because you only have to explain that hard drives will fail because they have a mean time before failure (MTBF), power supplies will fail at times, and so on. After that, the point you want to get across is usually understood. This is when you explain where redundancy comes into the design. With redundancy, that disk failure won't be a showstopper because you have RAID enabled. The power supply failure will mean nothing because you have redundant power supplies. Again, the list goes on, but so does the extra cost. The extra cost is easily justified by doing a ROI analysis.

A real ROI analysis needs financial information, which you might not be privy to but, for the sake of this book, let's pretend you do get the company's profit count for the year. If you can do some math and determine that the company, with the use of the IT infrastructure, makes, say, 1 million dollars per month, then you can easily explain what a one-week outage would cost the company. One week of downtime for a company that earns 1 million dollars a month is going to cost that company $250,000. Think back to my $60,000 redundancy cost. Doesn't seem so bad now, does it? This is how you have to explain it and make others understand it.

Unfortunately, in my experience, a disaster is what it takes to get people to understand the ramifications of what can happen. To backtrack to the introduction of this chapter, we also briefly looked at September 11, 2001, and the disaster of losing the World Trade Center Towers. During this time, getting equipment for replacements was extremely difficult. I tried to order a Cisco Catalyst core switch and found that lead times for buying were all pushed out.

You can also explain to management that you might not even get the equipment you need when the disaster hits and your one week could multiply to two. Half a million dollars lost because an initial investment of $60,000 was not undertaken.

Another horror that must be understood is how this can affect your clientele and business partners. I experienced a loss of a server because of a failed power supply for a company that needed to share information with another company through an extranet-based VPN. The business that did practice solid Disaster Recovery and redundancy techniques wasn't happy at all with the company that didn't practice them. In this situation, not only did you lose money, time and productivity, but you damaged a business relationship. Customers can also lose faith in you completely if you have an outage of that magnitude. Imagine right now if amazon.com went down for two weeks. Don't tell me you wouldn't run to other vendors and never come back.

That said, the Return on Investment is outstanding if you ever need it but, then again, if you decide not to do it, then you're gambling: all in all, this is a game of chance. You can also justify that the gear you buy won't be sitting idle waiting for the active equipment to die. It can be used for load balancing, assist in upgrading software, and enable you to segment your network into an N-tiered architecture. Sounds like an easy sell to me. Your total cost of ownership of TCO can also be justified because, in the unlikely event of disaster, you've justified owning every last piece of that equipment.

CREATING YOUR DESIGN PLAN AND IMPLEMENTATION TEAM

Now you've sold management on it and you have your budget to buy equipment. Who will plan, design, test, configure, implement, develop, and troubleshoot it? I hope you thought of this because, up until now, we've only looked at things to think about. Now, you have to gainfully employ staff for planning and rolling out this solution. An important point is this: you need to know the size and importance of the project you're about to undertake. Research and development needs to be done, and you need to test and plan the initial design. This takes time and you don't want to rush.

Creating the Project Plan

Let's use an example of a simple two-node cluster for an explanation. If you want to implement a two-node cluster, the first question I'd ask is, "Is this box already in production and do we have to cluster it?" If that's the case, then you need to analyze what's going on with the production box today. If this isn't the case, then it's simple to plan for new hardware and software installs. All this needs is to be taken into consideration for the project plan.

I mention this because I believe every high-level implementation is worthy of a plan. I can't see anything happening without it. Every time you involve resources and time with any implementation, you need some form of plan. Sound simple? It is. If you're in a large enterprise, I'd assume you have some type of project manager on staff and that's who you need involved, especially when you roll out an N-tier solution. If the project is small enough, a supervisor can probably plan and manage a simple file-share cluster solution. Again, this all depends on the size and scope of the solution. You should also keep the plan on paper or in a ledger that can be passed down. My preference is to use Project 2000 (a Microsoft Office application), but if you don't own a license for it, a ledger or a book will work.

The Team (Human Resources)

You also need to consider human-based resources into your design. In this chapter alone, we covered many diverse topics, some of them relating to IP addressing and network engineering, some relating to system engineering, and others based on the development of COM components. We covered Internet web site development, and ecommerce software. We looked at supervision and management's level of involvement, and we even looked at large implementation being managed by a project manager. You can't survive a project alone. I know the nature and blood of a true IT guru is to want to know it all and do it all, but face the facts: it could well be impossible at times to keep up with rolling out a solution of this size. Make sure you analyze what components will be involved with your implementation and get the right people in place. If you need to hold an initial meeting with major department heads, you might be able to pinpoint what resources you need early, so everyone is on the same page as to who will be available when.

Management's Approval and Getting Started

Now that you have the plan, the budget, and the go-ahead, what do you do now? Well, now you read this book from cover to cover. You learn the intricacies of software and hardware configurations to make the solution work! Seriously, I hope this chapter has been an eye opener to all the things you need to consider before you get to the configuration side of clustering. Once you have the go-ahead from management and you have your plan, you need to consider every design in a unique way. As you get involved in the next chapter, you'll look at every design in detail as you learn how to configure it. It's imperative that you read all the Notes and Tips, so you can learn from other's mistakes. Also imperative is that you look at every clustered solution as being unique because every server and its contents are different from company to company and from server room to server room.

This chapter's purpose was to give you the foundation on which to plan and design a proper High Availability solution within a network. Although you could go through hundreds of pages of text researching what would be right for each unique network situation, you have enough here to build a foundation.

In the next chapter, you learn about the setup and configuration of Windows 2000 Advanced Server in a clustered and load-balanced scenario.

CHAPTER 2

Designing a Clustered Solution with Windows 2000 Advanced Server

In this chapter, we walk through the start-to-finish process of designing, installing, and configuring all aspects of a Windows 2000 clustered solution in a failover design. The cluster will contain two nodes, both running Windows 2000 Advanced Server. The nodes will be set in an Active/Passive configuration. We'll make shared storage the purpose for the cluster and have a client access this data. While accessing the data, we'll simulate a failure and the clustering of the data will be successful. This could prove quite interesting because so much work is involved just to get to that point.

In the second half of this chapter, we look at the design and implementation of rolling out a Windows 2000 Advanced Server highly available network load balancing (NLB) solution. We cover the two solutions so closely that, at the end of this chapter, you'll know which one you'll want, need, or be in a position to implement based on hardware, software, resources, and support. First, we'll look at the most difficult to implement: Microsoft Cluster Server (MSCS). While you read this chapter, remember all networks will be different in design, so the most important part of this chapter is planning the Highly Available solution within your environment. The more time you take to plan both the clustered and load-balanced server solutions, the better your chance of success.

DESIGNING A CLUSTERED SOLUTION WITH WINDOWS 2000 ADVANCED SERVER

This section of the chapter covers two important areas of your high-availability design: hardware and software. I broke this up because, as you'll see by the end of the section, it's important to plan out, purchase, and configure your hardware properly before starting with the Windows 2000 Advanced Server cluster configuration, which is software-based. If, for any reason, you have problems configuring your hardware systems and shared SCSI bus, you won't be able to install the clustering service on your nodes. Make sure to pay close attention and work out all the possible bugs you can have with your hardware.

Where to Begin

High-availability system implementations should begin with a project plan. You need to lay out what you're going to do before you do it. The combined length of this chapter and the previous one should tell you something. You need to know many facts ahead of time to implement a simple cluster successfully. This doesn't include adding SQL server or Internet Information Server (IIS) to the mix. This is a pure vanilla cluster solution. That said, you need to know what resources you'll put where and what kind of money you need to buy not only one set of hardware, but all the redundant pieces to make it highly available. You should begin the whole evolution with a project plan and you might even want to get a Project Manager involved if you feel the solution and the cost are big enough to warrant it.

NOTE   Sample project plans are within the appendixes of this publication. I included them so you have a place to start with your planning and you can tweak them to fit your own needs. As in any project, you always want to do a preimplementation design.

The Design Phase

Clustering must be designed, plain and simple. There's no "winging it" here. You'll see by the end of this chapter, there's much to think about if you want to put a Highly Available solution in place. The *Design phase* of any project is one of the most important pieces of the project because it outlines the budget dollars needed to buy what you need and the resources you need to allocate to the project tasks. Resources aren't just servers and cables; resources are also people. You need to configure a switch with a virtual local area network (VLAN). Do you know how to do that? You might know how, but you might not have access to those systems and could need to get another department in your organization involved. Whatever your situation and no matter how unique it is, my main objective is to get you to think about all the work you need to lay out and accomplish before you even get on the server console to configure the cluster services.

PLAN YOUR HARDWARE ROLL OUT

In this section, you walk though all the hardware installations and configurations you need to accomplish prior to, and during, the installation of the Windows 2000 Advanced Server operating system (OS). Be aware of the common pitfalls technicians fall into while planning a clustered solution. Most of these pitfalls are in ordering and configuring the appropriate hardware. Although you can get away with a test lab with 2 PCs and a couple of network interface cards (NICs) to test your clustering services, when you go live with the real deal, your head will spin when you see what hardware you need to purchase and implement. You can apply most of what you learn in this chapter to nearly any hardware vendor. I like the Dell and Compaq Server-based hardware lines, but you need to decide what fits your budget and what your OS platform works with best. Some server hardware vendors have management utilities that function with certain OSs and, as long as you do your research before ordering, you should be fine. Be sure to take a trip to Microsoft's web site and review the Hardware Compatibility List, discussed later in the next section, to see what Windows 2000 Advanced Server runs with for beginners. Then pick a few vendors, such as Dell or Compaq, and ask to see demos or have meetings to discuss what you want to do. You'd be surprised what kind of education you can get from presales support.

Microsoft's Hardware Compatibility List

Microsoft's Hardware Compatibility List (HCL), found at **http://www.microsoft.com/ hcl**, is your way to verify that your hardware and its firmware will function properly with the Microsoft Windows 2000 Advanced Server OS. The HCL is where it all begins for planning and installing your hardware for the planned cluster. This should be followed religiously. Some vendors won't support you if you deviate from what they have certified. Buy service contracts if you feel you might need added support because the cost of the calls can add up if you don't plan for them in the beginning. A support contract you can use 24/7 could be something valuable to you in an emergency. Remember, this is a book about high availability, so this also counts into the equation.

The Servers and Presales Support

You need to purchase two servers and the recommendation is that they're identical. Many vendors sell clustered solutions, so you know you're getting a certified product in a set made to be clustered. The servers will come with exactly what you need in the way of hardware and you might even get added management software for managing the servers. Don't be embarrassed about getting presales support and do designs with the vendors' technicians. This is a genuine learning opportunity for you. I don't recommend that you build your own servers if your solution is one on which the company depends. You can build one, of course, but, again, the recommendation is that you purchase a premade set, get the vendors presales support and design work, and then make further plans from there. There's nothing like building your own servers to be clustered (you wind up spending close to the same amount of money) only to have it crash on you later. Then, you need to get out the magnifying glass to find the problems. It's much easier to have a vendors' knowledge base and a support system available if you need them. If you build your own servers, make sure you have identical hardware, get all the drivers you need, and check them against the HCL. You might also want to get well-known hardware, so you can use the online knowledge bases, if needed.

You must understand that all software and hardware have problems. Although one could have less than others, they all inevitably have some problem or incompatibility. A clustered solution is the last place you want to find that. Remember what I said about the foundation you want to build. Imagine installing your company's e-mail solution on a cluster (with Exchange 2000) only to have massive problems later and, possibly, crash a system that was made not to crash. It won't look good for you, I promise. This section isn't meant to frighten you. It's meant to give you tips on where I've seen failure or have had problems myself.

Power Supplies

Use redundant power supplies. For the price of a power supply, you might as well double them. Redundant power supplies are inexpensive and give you total piece of mind. Many systems offer you the availability to put in three power supplies as well.

Power and Uninterruptible Power Supply (UPS)

I've seen a design team go through the painstaking mechanics of designing a Highly Available solution only to leave out one of the most important features. It's this simple: no power, no server. You can have two power supplies mounted in a server—all on the same breaker and lose power. All power is lost, regardless of what redundancy you implemented. Nothing is more embarrassing than having to explain why redundant servers, power supplies, and all this other great stuff is useless to you in the first major power outage.

What about power surges? I had the opportunity to be onsite at a location with known power problems. The business continuously suffered from brownouts and all kinds of fluctuations in power. It wasn't apparent yet, but all the servers mounted in the server room were also affected and they weren't protected. Power supplies and fans were blowing out and failing like crazy. Why? Simple—a power supply is supposed to get one regulated voltage to it and, if exceeded, could damage the power supply or, worse yet, the server's components. All they needed was a simple *Uninterruptible Power Supply (UPS)*. A UPS is a battery in a box that takes one source of power and converts it into another. If you get a power surge in one end of the UPS, it always dishes out the regulated voltage needed to power the servers or any network hardware for that matter (except laser printers).

UPSs also come with software that allows the server to shut itself down when disaster strikes. If power ceases, then your UPS unit can only keep the server running for so long. The UPS will shut the server down correctly. Some UPS software will also send you a page to your phone or alphanumeric pager if necessary. As a recommendation, you can use any UPS systems that meet your power standards and life- (or up-) time before shutdown, but I like American Power Conversion (APC)–based UPSs the best from my experience working with them throughout the years. They seem to provide some of the best performance, battery life, and options available.

Server Mounting and Racking

Most of the time, you can choose between rack-mountable hardware and stand up–based towers. This is up to you and what your server room or environment looks like, but it's also something you need to consider when predesigning your hardware solution. Make sure you know what space you have to work with. If you use a stand-alone tower, make sure you have a rack or table that offers stability, security, and a raised environment. Placing all this equipment on the floor is ridiculous. All this high availability and one good flood can take it all away. A raised floor environment is the way to go in any server room today. If you do go for the rack-mounted hardware, make sure you plan out your rack, how much space you'll need (in U units where 1U is about the equivalent of 1.75 inches). There's nothing like explaining to management why you need to invest a thousand dollars in a new rack because you ran out of space. If you get two servers with a shared storage device, you could be looking at about 10U. Be sure to plan this carefully and accurately.

Make sure your cabling is not only secure, but also looks neat. This is important when you have to sift through blobs of cabling trying to trace down a patch cable that might have been damaged. Your design should also be augmented with good documentation of cable layout, cable management devices, and a clean environment for your cabling. Although this isn't a chapter on cabling, every piece of your design can be affected by something else. For instance, if you make your cable runs too long, past limits, it could have a negative effect on your response time or your signal transmission. Be aware of the negative impact of any area of poor design when building your Highly Available solution.

Environmental Considerations

ESD safety is something that all technicians need to practice by having proper ESD safety precautions in place, like properly grounding yourself while working on your systems. You're playing with fire if you work with hardware that isn't grounded properly. Even if you simply plug in the chassis of the server and hold on to the case (with the server plugged in to a properly grounded outlet), you and your hardware are on safe ground. Most professional rack systems come with a grounding strip, so if you set it up correctly, then you only need to hold on to the rack where the server is mounted. Most rack mount servers come with sliding rails, so you can open the server while it's still mounted to do maintenance and touch the rack to ground yourself. No, you needn't embarrass yourself by wearing a wrist strip for electrostatic discharge (ESD), but I think you'd be more embarrassed if you're reprimanded for damaging an $8,000 server. ESD is also created from a lack of humidity in the room in which you're placing your servers. You should have a dedicated server room with a raised floor, fire extinguishers, or a Halon system available, as well as temperature control to make sure the room is cool and not too dry. This is preferable and can help eliminate the possibility of ESD.

Locked Cases and Physical Security

I was told a long time ago that a thief wouldn't be a thief if you locked your stuff up and didn't give someone the opportunity to take it. Yes, sometimes issues, such as security breaches, robberies, and other bad things happen, but when you make it difficult for security to be breached, you'll see a lot less theft. I recommend you put your servers in locked cases or racks, or lock the server room door and only allow trusted and authorized access. I once had the opportunity to go to a remote site and found an unlocked console with the administrator logged into the server. This is dangerous and should be avoided at all costs. In a following section, you learn how to set up an account for your clustered servers.

Central Processing Unit (CPU)

When planning the hardware for your system, you need to consider what kind of Central Processing Unit (CPU) is needed for the servers. The CPU brand is all a matter of preference (as long as it's on the HCL). We need to discuss what speed rating you might need or how many CPUs you need for your systems. When you plan your server CPU, you need to take many things into account and at varying stages. First, you need to get the minimum hardware requirements for Windows 2000 Advanced Server, which is simply a 133 MHz or higher Pentium-compatible CPU. For today's standards, though, I'd go from 500 MHz to 1.3 GHz. Also, be aware that Windows 2000 Advanced Server supports symmetrical multiprocessing, so you need to take that into consideration when ordering the server. Windows 2000 Advanced Server supports up to eight CPUs on one machine. That's just for the operation of the Windows 2000 Advanced Server processes and services that are running.

We haven't yet discussed what we'll find when we install, for example, SQL Server 2000 on top of the cluster. In Chapter 5, you learn about the clustering of SQL in great detail, but this is something you should start thinking about now. Never shortchange yourself. Always think about what you're putting on the server and plan accordingly for the proper hardware needed.

Memory Requirements (Physical and Virtual)

Max out your memory when possible. If you take a normal production Windows 2000 server with antivirus services and a few running applications on it, you'll find your memory is quickly used up. Always preplan what you'll be running on your server and get enough memory to support the services you plan to run. Although Microsoft says the minimum for Windows 2000 Advanced Server is 128MB of random access memory (RAM), you'll find 256MB is more efficient.

Always remember, more memory can't hurt. Production systems today run anywhere from 512MB to 1GB of memory on Windows-based systems. Many system engineers don't take into consideration the fact that antivirus software is now a mandatory piece of software you need to implement on your systems and it runs *memory-resident*, which means it's permanently located in your computer's memory. Other items that run in memory are services such as Domain Name System (DNS), SQL, or IIS. If you view what Exchange Server 2000 runs in memory, you might be surprised. Investigate how much memory you'll need and, if possible, max it out. Slow response time isn't something you want from your Highly Available solution.

Virtual memory and swap file size also need to be taken into consideration. If you plan to run a system without allocating ample virtual memory size, your server might crash. I've seen disks run low on space, and swap files grow and crash the server. Having a separate physical disk assigned only for Swap file use is wise. One tip to follow is never to assign your swap file to an extended partition: this only slows the server down and creates problems. Make sure you configure this before you go live with the cluster solution because you'll have to reboot the system when you set the swap file. The Task Manager is also a great utility to get a quick baseline of memory use and how the systems function while under load not only to include memory, but also CPU statistics. In the last chapter of this book, this is covered in granular detail.

NIC's Cabling and Switch Connections

NIC connections are one of the most important pieces of hardware you need for your cluster. While all the hardware in your cluster solution is important and equally critical, the NIC you choose will determine how quickly your data can travel to and from your clustered servers, as well as your shared storage device. You need to prepare this based on the types of configurations you plan on designing. In other words, for a simple two-node cluster, you need a minimum of four network cards. Why would you need this many? Well, you need to separate your cluster management network from the public network from which the clients access the server. If you have two servers, they both need to access the network for client access. This is self-explanatory, but many ask, then what's the cluster management network? This is also called the *heartbeat segment*, where the servers communicate back and forth to make sure the other is there for failover and failback situations. When we configure the software, we'll discuss this in more detail, but justify why you need the hardware you're requesting. When designing your hardware, it's also important to make and attempt to keep the NIC cards identical. This isn't mandatory, but it's helpful for troubleshooting and updating system drivers.

Also important is to design the Heartbeat network separate from the network connections that the network clients will use to access the servers. This is where knowing how to configure a switch is helpful. When you look at configuring the software in a later section, you learn to set up separate VLANs for your Heartbeat network. To keep life easy, you can also use a crossover cable between the NIC cards. This is simple, indeed, but you lose the power to monitor traffic on the interface with the switch if you want to check for CRC errors or any other problems, such as runts and jabbers coming from the NIC. This is one reason I would advise using a separate switch or VLAN to separate the networks.

Network card speed is also a critical factor to design beforehand. The day and age of 10BaseT networking with a shared access hub are, hopefully, over in your network environment, although many places still have this outdated technology.

Many administrators (and CIOs) live by the old adage, "If it ain't broke, don't fix it!" They see no reason to move away from functioning solutions that are already in place. Unfortunately, while this might work with your grandfather's '57 Chevy pickup, it doesn't hold true in the IT world, where issues such as end-of-life (EOL) support, network growth, and software evolution make upgrading to newer, more capable hardware an inevitable fact of life. Most often, network and systems administrators don't take into account the possibility of a network slowdown (or what seems like a system slowdown) that can be fixed with a simple changing of network infrastructure from hubs to switches. A *hub*, which might only run at 10 Mbps at half-duplex, won't allow optimized transfer of data on a network segment between systems. If you replace a hub with a switch that runs at 100 Mbps at full-duplex (or even 1,000 Mbps), you'll see massive network performance gains in your design. I recommend that if you design a clustered or load-balanced solution, you optimize the LAN segment as much as possible with the following design guidelines:

- Use Fast Ethernet at 100 Mbps full-duplex at a bare minimum. Running at Ethernet speed (10 Mbps) isn't recommended unless you can't afford to purchase a switch. These days, though, switches are cheap.

- Run Gigabit Ethernet (1,000 Mbps) anywhere you can, especially if your servers are located in a server farm located on the network backbone. The *network backbone,* which is the largest data transport area on your network, should be as fast as possible and optimized as quickly as possible. If you connect your clustered and load-balanced systems directly into it, then you'll see massive speed gains.

- Test your connections after you implement them. Make sure you check all the links and see they're running at the speeds you want. Many times, I've seen network connections running on *autoconfigure,* which detects that connected systems are running at (speed and duplex) to negotiate a selected speed and duplex rate. This often winds up negotiating the wrong speeds and, although you could have your systems running faster, speed and duplex settings are set to run at slower speeds, like 10 Mbps.

Check your duplex settings. You can either run at half-duplex or at full-duplex. With Ethernet, you have a Transmit (tx) and a Receive (rx) set of channels on your network devices, like NICs and hubs or switches. When you use standard Ethernet running at 10 Mbps with, say, a hub, you need to use carrier sense multiple access with collision detection (CSMA/CD). In layman's terms, this simply means when a system on a network segment wants to transmit data on the network medium, it has to make sure no other device is using the network medium at that exact time. It "senses" the medium with one of its channels, and then sends or transmits data when it doesn't sense anything. *Multiple access* simply means many hosts share the same medium and have the same access point to the network, which is shared. *Collision detection* means the host on the shared segment is able to know a collision occurred. It knows it needs to back off and go into a random-number countdown to try transmitting again. Because of how this algorithm works, saturated segments of your network might cause the network to oversaturate (usually anything over 40 percent using Ethernet) and cause a network slowdown. Changing to switches at 100 Mbps at full-duplex enables you to remove this issue from your network, thus, making things at least ten times faster than the speed they ran originally. Full-duplex means both the tx and rx channels transmit and receive at the same time (which pushes you to 200 Mbps) and, because the switch maps devices to ports and keeps this map, you needn't rely on the CSMA/CD algorithm, which improves network speed and efficiency. Make sure you're running at 100 Mbps full-duplex, if you can afford the equipment to run it. You can also monitor traffic on the better equipment (which we discuss later) and provide not only highly available services, but also fast ones. With *Fast Ethernet* and *Gigabit Ethernet*, you can configure the switch to operate at full-duplex (eliminating collisions from the CSMA/CD equation) and increase the speed even more. You can also create Fast and Gigabit Ethernet crossover cables for the Heartbeat network, if needed.

One last design tip to mention is this: if you can, check with your server hardware vendor to see if the server board supports hot plug cards. *Hot plug cards* (or any hot plug technology, for that matter) are hardware devices that can be removed and reinstalled in a powered up and operational server. The beauty of this design for Highly Available solutions is you never have to reboot your server, thus disabling it on the network. You can have a problem with a PCI NIC, and then remove and replace it without downing the server. For a truly highly available design, you might want to consider this as an option to be able to pull your card in and out of a system running nearly 100 percent of the time.

Small Computer System Interface (SCSI)

Your storage situation also needs to be designed, purchased, and configured properly. Small Computer System Interface (SCSI) is the most widely used system today for storage and drives. The SCSI system is used to exceed the current EIDE limitations of two channels and four drives, where SCSI can use either seven or fifteen devices, depending on the system used, and exceed speeds because of the bigger system bus.

Although this isn't a chapter on how to set up any SCSI system in any PC or server, I'll point out the points of major concern while setting up a highly available Windows 2000 Server Cluster. As with all other hardware, you'll want to verify that your SCSI solution is on the HCL. Redundant? Perhaps, but redundancy is a way of life you'll have to grow accustomed to if you want to design and support a viable Highly Available solution. Why wouldn't you check something you plan to invest big money in? Go online and look it up. If the SCSI system you want to use is good to go with Windows 2000 Advanced Server, then you need to configure the SCSI system per the vendor's guidelines and recommendations. Always ask for the documentation books for all the hardware you buy. Many times, you don't get it (you get scaled-down documentation) and, you'll find in times of disaster, this information is important. Also, so many different systems exist with vendor-specific firmware, it would be fruitless to discuss them all here.

You could write an entire book on SCSI systems alone. This is why I recommend you get all the presales support and documentation you can and install everything per those guidelines.

When you design your SCSI system, think about how many devices you want to host from one SCSI chain. In other words, are you going to configure six drives in each server? How many devices can you fit on the bus? For instance, you can use SCSI Wide Ultra-2, which runs at about 80 Mbps and can handle up to 16 open slots on the bus. SCSI Ultra-3 can operate the same except at speeds of 160 Mbps. It depends on what you purchase (what you need) and what the vendor sells. It's all a matter of preference and what the systems sold come with. Some systems come as a "standard" (cookie cutter) configuration, so be aware of this when you place your order. When ordering SCSI systems, you also need to consider both internal and external SCSI systems. If you use an internal system, then you're probably running your hard drives on it. If you set up an external chain, you're probably going to connect to a shared storage device or quorum solution. Other items of interest when designing a SCSI solution are to pick the interface type.

You can use a single-ended system (SE), a high voltage differential (HVD), or a low-voltage differential (LVD). SE systems are generally cheaper, but they're less robust (such as covering shorter distances) than LVD or HVD systems.

If you use HVD, then you can use twisted-pair cable, which can be used in conjunction with an extremely long cable run (it can be employed in distances longer than SE and LVD). HVD is rarely used, but be aware of its existence if you're asked during the initial design. Also, HVD and SE are incompatible. LVD systems are probably the most common form of SCSI you'll see in production. LVD signaling is excellent because of low noise and low power consumption. LVD is useful because you can switch the mode if you want to configure SE devices on the bus.

Be aware of the host bus adapter (HBA) if you're installing in the server. And, make sure it doesn't conflict with the system's basic input/output system (BIOS) if you're installing the SCSI equipment. If you're installing the SCSI equipment, make sure the system's BIOS knows to look at the SCSI card for booting purposes. The SCSI system, as with all the other hardware listed here, needs to be configured correctly before you start installing clustering services. By purchasing a predesigned server solution from a vendor, you can usually avoid many of the problems and questions associated with SCSI- and BIOS-compatibility issues.

Advanced SCSI Configuration

Now that you have the cards installed in the system, you need to start configuring the SCSI devices. The documentation provided by the hardware vendor for each system might vary with the configurations you need to make, so I'll highlight points to look up if they can't be generalized or made generic to any installation. You need to make sure you're properly terminating the SCSI bus—both internal and external—otherwise the system might not function. By using a cluster (which is the case here), you can share the SCSI bus between your nodes when shared storage needs to be accessed, but you still need to make sure you have proper termination. You must also configure every device on the bus with a unique ID. Remember, if you're using a shared SCSI bus for any reason, you need to make sure you have unique IDs for both servers sharing the bus. In other words, if the HBA default for ID number seven, for example, is on both systems, then you'll have a problem. You need to configure one of the servers as seven and, perhaps, configure the other server as five or six (preferably six). Also be aware of what you assigned and document everything to the last ID number. If you have an issue where the SCSI bus resets, you're in hot water. If this feature exists on the vendor's documentation, you should disable the resetting of the bus when applicable.

Configuring the Shared SCSI Bus

You need to understand how the shared SCSI bus works to get the Cluster Service to install properly and prevent your NTFS partition on the shared storage media from corrupting. When you normally configure SCSI (not in a two-node clustered solution), you would place the HBA into your server (or PC) and make sure each end is terminated properly. The termination can be both internal and external, and will eliminate line noise. The shared SCSI bus must consist of a compatible and, hopefully, identical PCI HBA in each server. You can install them one at a time and test them in each system. Remember, both servers will connect to the same SCSI bus. This isn't easy to picture because you're probably used to thinking that all chained devices need to be devices and not servers but, in this instance, it will be another server. Again, this raises a question of assignable SCSI IDs.

The first server you install the SCSI card in will probably default to the highest priority ID and take ID 7. If this is the case, then you want to configure the other server to take the ID of ID 6. You want the HBAs in each server to have the highest priority. The MSCS will manage and control access to each device. You can also have more than one SCSI bus to add more storage. Look at your vendor's documentation closely if you need to install this feature. You should also be aware that the OS drives (where Windows 2000 Advanced Server might be installed and not the Quorum device) can also be a part of the shared SCSI bus. Using ID 6 and ID 7 for the host adapters on the shared bus is important when it comes to having the highest priority, so start there with your ID assignments and work your way down.

SCSI Cables: Lengths, Termination, and Troubleshooting

Don't shortchange the implementation phase to save money when you're building a high-availability system. How many times have you seen a company buy a $35,000 switch, and then buy cheap cabling and cheesy NICs?

What's the point? This kind of thinking also goes with your SCSI implementation. SCSI problems can be traced to bad or cheap cables. To tell if you have good cable, either ask the vendor to verify the quality of the cable or eyeball it yourself. Thicker (harder to bend) cable is of better quality than flimsier cabling.

You also have different types of cables. One of the more common cables for SCSI implementation is the Y cable (better known as a Y adapter), which is recommended when using a shared SCSI bus. Y cables are better because the cable adapter allows for bus termination at each end of the chain and it's fully independent of the HBAs. Y cables also allow for continuous termination when maintenance needs to be performed, so they're the perfect piece of hardware when you want to build a high-availability system. When using the Y adapter, a node can disconnect from the shared bus and not create a loss of termination. Another trick to termination is to make sure that when you terminate the bus on the ends, if you have HBAs in the middle of the bus, a technician needn't terminate the SCSI chain.

Cable Length and Termination

Cable lengths also need to be addressed in the SCSI design. If you want to go into the kilometer range, you should consider Fibre Channel (discussed in the next section), but if you want to go about 20 to 25 meters (although the longer you go, the slower it could become), then SCSI is good enough. You should stay in the six-meter range or under for good design measures. If you extend too far, you'll also have signal problems and, again, you don't want this in a high-availability solution. Review total allowable limits based on which type of SCSI you use (SCSI-2, SCSI-3, and so forth). All implementations have different ranges, speeds, and allowable IDs. When using the MSCS, be aware that active termination of the bus is recommended and preferred on each end of your bus.

Passive termination isn't recommended because it hasn't proven to provide constant termination as active termination does. What does this all amount to? High availability. If you skip one detail, your system goes down, and you've spent all this money (and time) for nothing. While designing the shared SCSI bus, you should never put termination on anywhere within the center (or middle) of the bus: put it only at the ends. Never count on termination that's automatically applied by the HBA. Make sure you've terminated it and verify it by reading the HBA documentation.

Test Your Connections

When you finish planning the cable and running your connections, you should test it to verify that it works before moving ahead. Check with your vendor documentation to use the verification tools that come with each HBA. Going through each vendor tool would be fruitless because most are configured differently, but they will verify that you have unique IDs and solid connections on your cable runs.

One thing you should do to test your cable and termination is to check one node at a time. You still need to check one node at a time because, once you begin the installation of the OS (if it isn't already installed), you stand the chance of corrupting the quorum. When you install the Cluster Services, the disk cable and termination will be verified when the service shows online within the Cluster Service. If you do have problems, the best bet is to power down a node and run the verification tools on the HBA with the aid of the vendor's support or documentation.

Now, let's look at a faster and lengthier type of shared storage medium called Fibre Channel. We only briefly look at this alternative to SCSI because our implementation focuses on using the SCSI-shared bus and shared storage that connects via the SCSI bus.

Fibre Channel

Although SCSI is the most common and widely known technology, another technology has arisen that you should be aware of when configuring your clustered solution. *Fibre Channel* is a high-speed (gigabit) communication technology that allows the transfer of data on a network type media (like optical fiber), giving you more distance limitations in the "kilometer range" (or about six miles), instead of shorter distances offered by most SCSI technologies. This option allows for 100 to 1,000 Mbps transfer that wasn't capable until now.

In the future, when 10 Gpbs Ethernet is finally commonplace, speeds will reach infinite possibilities. Other than spanning longer distances and working at a higher bandwidth, Fibre Channel is also capable of connecting to a separate switch (Brocade makes excellent ones) for intelligent switching, and provides even more accurate and faster speeds for transfer. You might want to consider this when building a Storage Area Network (SAN) where data is saved in multiple places. This is the ultimate in high availability, redundancy, scalability, and efficiency, but it's more expensive.

Three main types of Fibre Channel interfaces and coaxial exist, and twisted pair isn't part of them. You can use point-to-point, arbitrated loop (Fibre Channel Arbitrated Loop FC-AL), and cross point or fabric-based switched. If you plan to build a back-end SAN, consult with a vendor for a demonstration and get yourself up to speed on this complex technology.

Quorum Devices and Shared Storage

A quorum is a shared storage solution that you connect to your two-node cluster. Let's look at some important design points you need to consider for your implementation. The quorum disk should always be a separate physical or logical device if using Redundant Array of Inexpensive Disks (RAID). If the quorum isn't designed and configured properly, you're looking at having massive failover problems in production. If you want your cluster to have a "split-brain" mentality and have a failover situation to another passive node sharing a single storage space, you need to configure your quorum properly. When breaking down the design of a quorum disk or disk set, make sure you never share the quorum as a partition of a resource disk, especially if you have multiple resources used on the two-node cluster. Also, never make the server boot disk (where the system and boot files reside) on the shared quorum.

Although this might seem obvious, I've seen this design step missed. This can be confusing because you could put everything on the same bus (all disks and quorum, which you do in this chapter) and accidentally use the wrong disk when working with a shared SCSI bus. You learn to eliminate that possibility later in this chapter.

Always use RAID for the shared storage. Not implementing a RAID solution on a cluster that you're trying to make highly available is a mistake. Refer to Chapter 1 for RAID types if you need to select one. Disks fail! All disks have a mean time between failures (MTBF) and they will fail. Add into the equation the commonly improper mounting of disks (upside-down or sideways) that could put more stress on the read/write heads and you're cutting that MTBF even shorter. Would you run your data on something you knew would fail? Using RAID can also give you the 99.999 percent uptime on the disks. Remember, this book is about high-availability systems and it would be a mistake not to mention the importance of RAID in your solution.

With shared disk use, you have more design requirements to consider. When you're using a shared disk and you're booting the system, you can verify that all devices (disks) attached to the SCSI bus have, in fact, initialized, aren't generating errors, and can be seen from both of the nodes in the two-node cluster. Errors can be seen in the following illustration. You can verify that all devices have unique ID numbers (mentioned earlier in the chapter). If you do get errors, stop immediately, jot down the error, and look it up on the vendor's knowledge base online or in the documentation you asked for when you purchased the system. I can't stress enough the importance of wiping out all errors before you start the software portion of the cluster implementation.

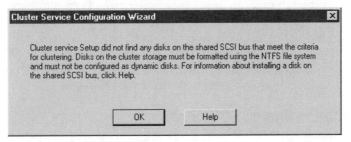

Use RAID 5, which uses parity, and don't mistake the use of RAID 0, which only increases read and write speed though striping. In simple terms, *parity* is a technique of using a binary bit to check the validity of data when moved from one point in storage to another. *Striping* is the placing of data contiguously across multiple physical disks acting as one logical unit for the purpose of speed gains and fault tolerance. RAID 0 isn't fault tolerant and RAID 5 is for a highly available design.

Which would you use? Fault tolerance, of course! Fault tolerance is the insurance you take in your system to ensure its uptime. I've seen the configuration of RAID 0, in lieu of RAID 5, done so many times, it's almost unbelievable because it costs so little to add a little more storage space with fault-tolerance capabilities to your system. You have to make sure you configure the shared storage as RAID 5. The best way to configure this RAID solution is with the vendor's installation or setup disk, which most new servers have included with their server platforms. I don't suggest setting up a cluster solution on an old server. Remember, the key reason you're doing this is high availability. One critical server failure and all that redundancy is worthless, especially with your shared storage where all your business's key data is located.

Sometimes you can set your backup software solution on the same shared bus. You can also set it up on another server that accesses the bus to collect the data and send it to tape but, regardless, make certain you implement a backup solution with your shared storage. If you can't regenerate a set, then you're in trouble. Have some form of tape backup available to avoid accidental deletions and viruses. Always check the HCL for hardware that's acceptable for use with Windows 2000 Advanced Server and make sure you double-check with all your vendors if you dare mix and match different hardware platforms with your servers against your shared quorum. I am all for keeping things uniform and, although it was beaten into me from the military, it works.

If I have a problem with any cluster solution that I can't figure out quickly, one call to a single vendor set usually has me up and running quickly, instead of spending hours scanning through every possible situation the problem can be resulting from. Although I expect you to make your own judgment on what hardware vendor you prefer and feel offers comparable pricing, I'll use Dell as an example. One purchase on a complete cluster solution with a shared storage quorum with a support option enables you to make a call on the whole system and get support with the entire solution, not just a piece of it. If you mix and match, you'll get into a kluge of "vendor blame," confusion, and frustration. Although you can mix, I recommend you keep it uniform.

Last and, most important, you need to know how to avoid corrupting your shared storage solution during the install. Before you start your software install, you have to boot up your nodes one at a time to configure the disks and install the OSs or you risk the chance of corrupting the disks to which the nodes are both connected. I only highlight this here, but I'll explain it as we begin to prepare the OS install.

Problems with the Shared SCSI Bus

I want to wrap up this section with some other design issues you might come across while implementing your shared SCSI bus. This is a short summary of the most common (and some uncommon) issues you could experience while configuring this hardware solution.

If you need to troubleshoot the shared SCSI bus, make sure you ground yourself to protect from ESD when working on the internals of the servers and other related hardware. When working with devices on the bus, you should connect only the physical disk or other similar RAID devices to the bus. If you want to connect CD burners or other types of devices to the bus, you should install a second SCSI bus. When designing this highly available system, it's preferable to keep things uniform and separate. Don't inundate the bus with extra devices. Again, check the cabling and make sure it's within specification, and verify that all the components are terminated within guidelines.

When you work with SCSI controllers, be aware of multiple problems that could occur if prior planning and design isn't properly thought out. You must verify that all SCSI devices are compatible with the controllers you have installed. If you're using basic/standard SCSI devices, you can't mix and match differential devices. Be aware of what you purchase. This is an even better reason to buy a complete cluster package from a vendor.

When you buy a SCSI controller, be aware that some controllers have "smart" capabilities and will automatically handout IDs based on the feature. If you're creating a shared bus, though, this could lead to unexpected problems. I've seen the IDs assigned within each server, and then the technician had to go back and manually assign it anyway because a bad order in priority was handed, out or it caused other problems which disabled the use of the system.

If you do, in fact, try to buy your own SCSI equipment to create a shared bus, be careful you don't mix the smart devices with devices without this feature set. Last, when configuring the controllers, make sure you configured all parameters identically when it comes to data transfer rates. A good design trait is to keep all parameters identical, except for obvious settings like IDs, which can't be identical and must be unique.

Adding Devices to the Shared SCSI Bus

If you want to add devices to your SCSI bus, you need to follow a sequence of events. If you need to add a device to the shared bus, you must power down everything. If you have your cluster up and running, and you try to add a device, you might experience problems with the cluster service software, the OS, the hardware, or all three.

The odds of successfully adding devices to a live system aren't in the technician's favor because of the difficulty level, so plan this portion out properly before committing the system to a live state. Remember, this is a shared bus between all systems. You can't power down a single node to service anything on the shared bus. You need to power down everything. To add a device, use the controller software (from the vendor). Check the troubleshooting tool software on the controller to verify termination and proper ID selection.

Next, turn up one of the nodes and, when booted, open the Disk Administrator to work with, format, assign letters to, and add disks, if needed. Once you're done, use the Cluster Administrator to add a disk resource for the cluster. Now that you've verified the disk is live and online, you can power up the other node and have it rejoin the entire cluster. You shouldn't have any problems, but check the Event Viewer anyway, just in case.

RAID Considerations

A *RAID array* or a *disk array* is generally a set of physical disks that operate as one logical volume. The *array* is a set of disks that are all commonly accessible (usually high-speed) and managed via some form of control software or firmware that runs on the actual disk controller.

When configuring a quorum or shared storage solution, RAID is your best bet at highly redundant solutions. What if you spend big bucks on totally redundant servers and other appropriate hardware only to have a single disk failure? You would be out of business. In the world of high availability, you must implement RAID. RAID was covered in Chapter 1, but remember, you need to be aware of configuring it for your cluster solution.

While doing the initial hardware configuration for your cluster, be aware that some systems you purchase might do an initial "scrubbing" of the drives before you use them. I mention this here not only to alert you to when and why it needs to be done for RAID preparation, but also because time could play a factor when developing your project plan.

Disk scrubbing can take a long time, especially if it's the first time you're configuring the system. *Disk scrubbing* is the process of the RAID controller checking data for bad blocks within your RAID array and also making sure your parity matches. Disk scrubbing is like a massive Scandisk for RAID systems. Scrubbing can either be done on the initial power up of the system or during system operation, depending on the vendor hardware. This is why you need all the documentation and support you can find when working with a hardware vendor. It's imperative to your success. You also want to factor in some time when you initialize a RAID-5 volume because creating parity for the first time takes a little while.

For the last item, make sure you get hot swappable drives with your RAID array. It's easy to pop in a new disk and regenerate the data from parity without having to power down the entire system, which you might have to do in some cases. Make this one of the questions you ask your hardware vendor when you plan your high-availability design. The sequence of events you need to follow to rebuild a RAID set is time-consuming if you can't hot swap the drives.

Cluster Server Drive Considerations

Configuring your drives is probably the most important preinstallation design and configuration step you can take. You have much to consider. For instance, can you use a dynamic disk with Windows Cluster Services on a shared disk? I'll answer that in a moment but, more important, most technicians don't think about that before they begin installing, only to find themselves faced with problems and errors.

Final Hardware Design Considerations

Make sure you balance your technologies with speed because if you make something too fast on one end and too slow on the other, you create a scenario for a possible bottleneck. To put this another way, it's like putting a firehouse up to a one-inch by one-inch hole and letting the water go full blast. If you can't buffer the overflow, then you'll have a massive bottleneck. This is something to think about as we get into faster and faster speeds. This goes for SCSI, fiber, and UTP copper, or any other technology discussed up until now. I've seen instances where this wasn't followed and the server performance wasn't optimal, which raised many question in postproduction review.

One last tip I highly recommend is all hardware should be identical (if possible) for a production system: vendor-supported and documented. When hardware is identical, it can make configuration easier and eliminate potential compatibility problems or offer a quicker, more consolidated solution to the problem you could encounter. Make sure you keep a written log of all settings and configurations that you can share with others in the organization, perhaps via an intranet. Your log can contain SCSI ID assignments, topology maps, vendor contact information, web site URLs, drivers—anything you think you might need to make your life easier in a time of panic.

PLAN YOUR SOFTWARE ROLLOUT

Now that you've seen the most important aspects of setting up your hardware, let's look at the details of creating a two-node clustered solution with Windows 2000 Advanced Server. This section begins with a general overview of things you should take into consideration for your clustered node design. I'm a full believer in a methodical and proper design. Anyone can install software with minimal skill and effort, but the true mark of an expert comes with design and troubleshooting. Here are some considerations you should be aware of.

Preinstallation Configurations

As mentioned earlier, when you read the quorum section of the chapter, before you start your software install, you have to boot up your nodes one at a time to configure the disks and install the OSs. Otherwise, you risk the chance of corrupting the disks to which the nodes are both connected. During the install of the Cluster Services and advanced configurations you're asked to boot one node at a time. This is the reason for that request. Also, make sure you have all your licensed software, hot fixes, service packs, drivers, firmware upgrades, and vendor-management software available before you begin the install.

Get the right people involved as well. I'll promote a project plan at this time, but if this is unfamiliar to you, then get a project manager or a department supervisor involved. Make sure the management team knows what help you need before you need it. Generally, IT support staff is so busy that asking for someone's help on-the-fly might not be possible. Schedule the time of resources from other departments in advance. This keeps everyone happy and looks more professional for you. You might also want to set up a test lab and practice with the software install before you go through with the production install.

Installation and Configuration

Now that you know all the preliminary work leading up to the actual installation, you need to look at the specifics for installing the software and getting your cluster operational. When you buy the hardware, it almost always comes with some form of installation disk with drivers on it. You can either order the software from the manufacturer or pull the software you need off the Internet. Please confirm that the drivers you get are certified for Windows 2000 and digitally signed because that could also cause you a problem during the install. In the next sections, I highlight specifics you should follow to make the best of your install.

Windows 2000 Advanced Server Installation and Advanced Settings

It's important for you to configure only one server at a time and only power up one server at a time. Failure to do so could result in corruption of the shared storage solution.

Let's begin by designing and implementing the solution for your first node. Take some masking tape or some other way to mark your server with temporary names (like Node 1 and Node 2), so you don't confuse them. This happens often and it especially happens when you're configured through a KVM (keyboard, video, mouse) switch where you're switching from node to node via the KVM. These are only temporary assignments: Node 1 and 2 are fine for now. To begin, start your install on the first server in your cluster. You need to know on what drive you're installing the OS and, if you prepared properly, you'll have a separate drive for the OS and a separate drive for the data you'll be using of the services you'll install. You needn't do it this way; it's just a good design recommendation.

You can also have a separate drive only for your swap file if you have the drives available. Make sure you have enough space to install the OS and for swap file growth if they're on the same drive. You need to keep 3GB to 4GB of space available for this purpose. Microsoft has the basic minimum requirements set at about 2GBs for the install and about 1GB free space but, as always, make sure you plan for future growth. If you're installing SQL on the same drive, you'll need to account for the space it requires. Although we'll cover all fundamental requirements in the chapters ahead on SQL, you can always visit Microsoft's web site for products not mentioned in this book or visit vendors' web sites for their requirements.

During the install, choose to be part of a workgroup for the time being. You'll join a domain later. If asked either to be a part of a workgroup or a domain, select the workgroup option. When asked about protocols and addressing for adapters, you can configure your NIC adapters with drivers, but don't configure them with IP addressing at this time. You can do that later during the configuration phase.

Last, make sure you name your server something that represents your cluster, such as Cluster-Node-A or something similar, so you know which system is which when you do advanced configurations. You need to reserve a separate NetBIOS name (not used on the network anywhere) for the entire cluster, so make these names meaningful to you. Node A and Node B, or Node 1 and Node 2 should be good enough for that purpose.

Before you take the next step, place the i386 Directory from the Windows 2000 Advanced Server installation CD-ROM on each cluster node. If you have the space, add it and change the search path in the Registry to access it when you install future services for the server. You need this information not only when you install the Cluster Service, but also for installing IIS or nearly any other Backoffice/Server 2003 platform on your clustered servers. The next steps after you have a basic installation of Windows 2000 Advanced Server on both systems are to make sure you have all applicable service packs and hot fixes available for your system. Many security holes and system bugs are fixed with these updates, so install them. Configure your server to access the Internet and pull all updates from Windows Update on the Microsoft web site. You can visit the Windows Update site (as seen in the following illustration) by viewing the following URL: **http://v4.windowsupdate.microsoft.com/en/default.asp**.

Microsoft pledges it won't send any information on your drive to Microsoft itself, and it archives your system to find what you do or don't have. This is done rather quickly. You're then asked what you want to install from here and, as you can see in Figure 2-1, Service Pack 2 for Windows 2000 is a selectable option. This is a quick way to get the most updated software available from Microsoft and it takes all the guesswork out of it. You can customize Windows Update to download and install only what you want installed by selecting specific components, hot fixes, or entire service packs.

The site will scan your machine for what you need to install and give you the options on what to install on your system. At press time, you want to install Service Pack 3 and all post-Service Pack 3 hot fixes on your system.

Once you complete your Service Pack install, make sure your entire hardware install is also current with the latest revisions or service packs on software and firmware on your SCSI cards or BIOS. If an update is needed, now is the time to do it. Remember, it's better to do all this now, rather than when your system is in production and you have to down it.

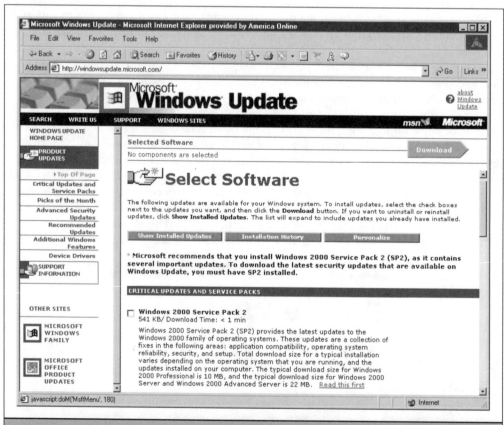

Figure 2-1.   Selecting Service Pack 2 to be installed on your server

Although Chapter 1 explained that having a cluster makes it easier to down and repair a production system, that doesn't mean you want to be put in that position. A Systems Administrator might not be at his happiest if he gets called in the middle of the night to fix a system that crashed. Do all your testing and checking now before you have users connected to the production system. Unforeseeable issues always pop up here and there, but keeping them to a bare minimum is always something you should strive for.

Now, once all packs and fixes are in, boot up clean and make sure you aren't getting any errors. When I say errors, I mean anything visible from the start of the boot process to the end. You might have a problem with Windows Advanced Server itself, where you get a Service Control Manager error pop-up. If you do get any errors while booted into Windows, you should immediately check the Event Viewer. (I recommend checking it anyway, whether or not you get errors, for good measure.) You can get to the Event Viewer by opening the Computer Management console in the Administrative Tools folder within your Start menu programs. In Figure 2-2, you can see the Computer Management console with the Event Viewer. In the Details pane of the console, a potential problem exists with the Dynamic Host Configuration Protocol (DHCP) service, so flag that and check it before moving on to the next steps of the configuration. To select an error event, simply double-click it.

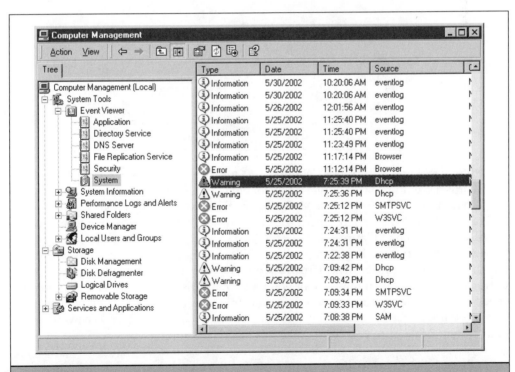

Figure 2-2.   Using the Event Viewer to troubleshoot your server

Once I open the event (in the following illustration), I can see what the problem is and it isn't a real problem at all. Because I haven't yet configured my IP addresses on my NIC cards, Windows 2000 Advanced Server was kind enough to notice this and assign an IP address from the Automatic Private IP Addressing (APIPA) range, so it can try to communicate with other nodes on the local subnet. This error will be meaningless once we configure TCP/IP correctly later in the chapter, but it's important for you to look at potential problems you might be having. You can also see browser errors on the Event Viewer System log, which we'll address in the "NetBIOS and WINS" section of this chapter.

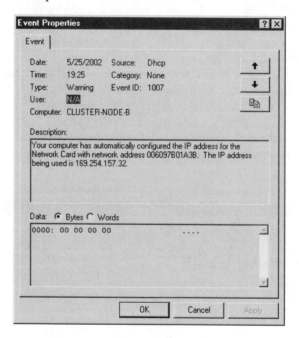

Other places you can check in Windows 2000 Advanced Server for a quick visual of your status are in the system applet's control panel located in the Device Manager. You can also find this in the Computer Management MMC console. By opening the console, you can verify if you have a problem with your system's hardware by reviewing the visual icons, as seen in Figure 2-3.

If you see a large red X (shown in Figure 2-3) on a piece of hardware, this means it was disabled by the system. The hardware could have created a problem serious enough to warrant its operational removal, or you might have disabled it. Either way, you can check here to make certain. If you see a yellow exclamation point or a yellow question mark, you might need to reinstall drivers or you could have unknown hardware in your system. Make sure you clean up all this before continuing.

If you use antivirus software, install that now. Check to make sure it's installed properly and that you downloaded and installed the most current virus definitions.

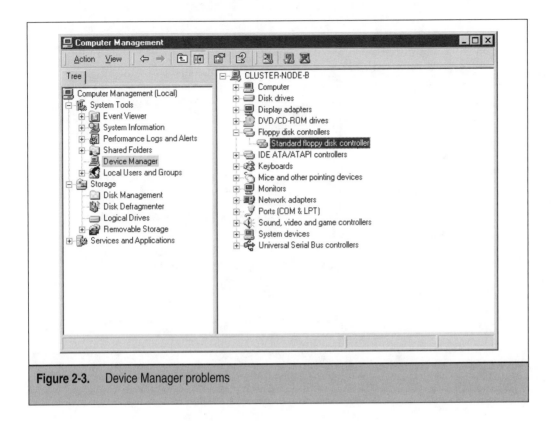

Figure 2-3.   Device Manager problems

PRECLUSTER SYSTEM CUSTOMIZATION AND CONFIGURATION

This section deals with configuring the cluster service installation, as well as noting preinstall configurations and other configuration planning considerations.

Disk Drive Configuration

After both servers have Windows 2000 Advanced Server installed and configured, you need to make sure your hard disks and shared storage (quorum) are all visible and configured correctly. Let's look at the configuration of the drives on each server. First, power up Node A (remember, only power up one node at a time, so you don't corrupt the shared storage) and open the Disk Management utility.

You can view the Disk Management utility (as seen in Figure 2-4) by going to Start | Programs | Administrative Tools folder, and then selecting the Computer Management MMC. If you don't have the Start menu programs extended from the taskbar properties,

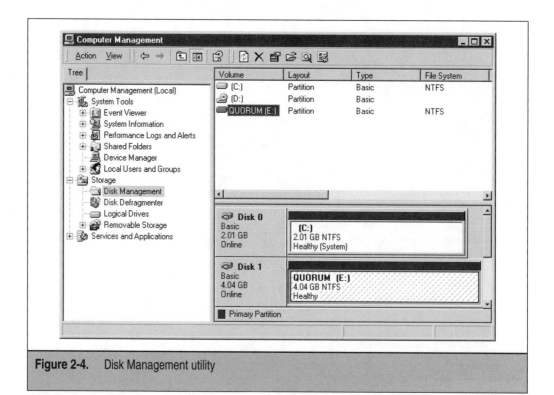

Figure 2-4.   Disk Management utility

you can quickly access it by going to the My Computer desktop icon, right-clicking it, and then selecting Manage. If you need yet another place to pull this console from, you can go to the Control Panel and access Administrative Tools. When you open the console, you'll see a Storage icon. Expand it to expose the Disk Management Folder. When you select the folder, it takes a moment for Windows 2000 Advanced Server to pull all the current information and display it. Then you can configure the shared disk array you already set up in the first portion of this chapter.

Create disks with user-friendly names, so you know what you're looking at. Because this is a shared bus, you can see what you have in the server and what you're connected to externally.

Make sure you format all drives with the NT file system (NTFS), which is based on permissions that are more efficient than the file allocation table (FAT). To format your drives, you can select the drive itself by clicking it, right-clicking it, and then selecting

Format from the menu options. Remember, formatting the disk wipes out all data on it. Once you select format, the Create Partition Wizard will prompt you to begin. This is the easiest way to create a formatted partition. Let's walk through it and configure our quorum device. First, the welcome screen, as seen in the following illustration, prompts you to create a partition on a basic disk, which is important.

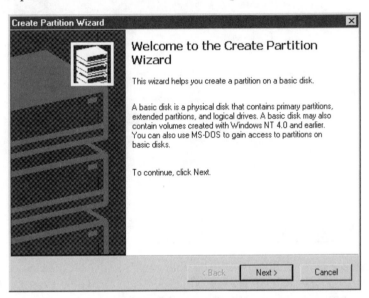

Once you begin formatting, read the welcome screen to get your definition of the basic disk. In Windows 2000, you have the option to make a disk basic or dynamic. A b*asic disk* is a physical disk that contains primary partitions, extended partitions, or logical drives. Basic disks can also contain spanned, mirrored, striped, and RAID-5 volumes created using Windows NT 4.0 or earlier. MS-DOS can access basic disks, whereas a *dynamic disk* is a physical disk managed by Disk Management. Dynamic disks can contain only dynamic volumes (that is, volumes created with Disk Management). Dynamic disks can't contain partitions or logical drives and MS-DOS can't access them.

Now that you have your disks laid out, you need to remember they all need to be basic disks. Next, you want to select the type of partition you need. In the next illustration, you can see you have an option to select either primary or extended (then logical) partitions. Set up a *primary partition*, which is defined as a volume you create using free space on a basic disk. As you can see in the following dialog box, it also lets you know you can set up to four primary partitions on a basic disk or you can create three primary partitions and one extended one. Our example is a basic setup, so we'll select only the primary partition.

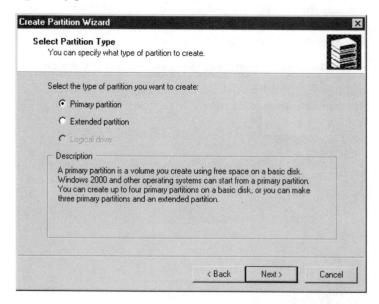

As you can see in the following illustration, you can now set the size you want to make your partition. Here, we'll use the entire disk and all available space. The 4GB I allocated for my four folders, which only contain 500MB of data, is more than enough and gives me additional room for future growth until I need to redo the entire system. If you preplan your cluster, you'll know exactly what you need in the future.

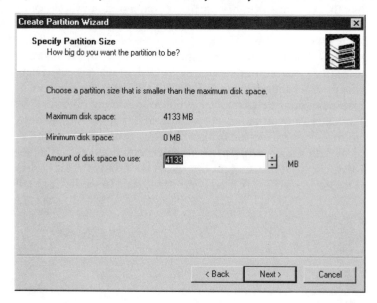

Next, you can assign a drive letter to your disk. Assigning drive letters in a cluster solution is different than assigning drive letters for a standard standalone system. Because both nodes will be accessing this shared storage device, you need a common drive letter that both nodes can access. You might want to set your drive letter fairly high and not have your cluster nodes run login scripts. If you configure your nodes to access—for example, drive F—and you add some disks to your nodes, both nodes might not be pointing to the same drive and common storage space anymore. Assigning your shared storage high-drive letters, with a Z ranking and working your way down as you configure storage, is safer. This is because many systems administrators commonly use lower drive letters in login scripts to assign shared logical drives on systems running the login script. Most commonly, you can avoid this by starting with Z and working your way down. Checking with your systems' administration staff to verify what letters in drive mappings they might be using today would also be safe. In addition, be careful when you assign your nodes to a domain in which you could be running login scripts that could also conflict or alter your drive mappings. You can avoid this error by configuring the user properties correctly, which is explained later in the chapter. The next illustration shows the option of changing the drive letter.

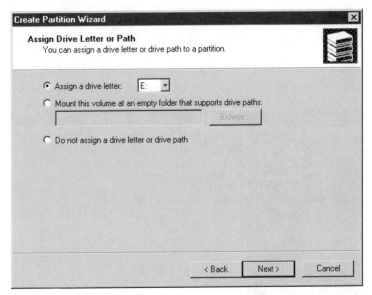

Now you need to format your drive. Formatting your drive with NTFS is imperative. Keep the allocation size as default and add a user-friendly name for the volume so you can quickly identify it. I named it "Quorum" to denote this is the shared storage repository.

In the following illustration, you can see where you can set the volume label and file system type.

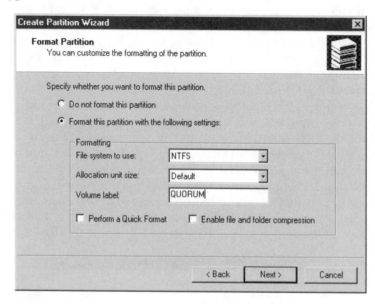

You have now completed a format and configuration of your drive. You'll be greeted with a completion window, as seen in the next illustration.

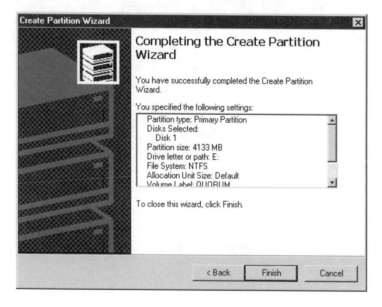

You should copy-and-paste the setting information to add to your documentation. This makes information easier to recall during troubleshooting scenarios.

Page File Configuration

You need to make sure the servers have a properly sized system-paging file. Although many arguments exist about what size you should set, you should consider the following characteristics for your clustered nodes:

- Never put the page file on a shared drive like the quorum.
- Never put the page file on an extended partition. The best idea is to purchase a separate drive and install the page file (Pagefile.sys) on its own drive.
- Never set the page file on a drive with small amounts of free space.
- Never set the page file size bigger than available space on the drive it resides on.

If you find your system running improperly, you might want to view the Task Manager, as seen in Figure 2-5, and check how your virtual memory is used against what you physically have in your machine. To open the Task Manager, right-click your taskbar, and select it.

Pay attention to the physical memory section and make sure you're running enough physical memory to meet the demands of the system. If you look at the Memory Usage bar and see that it runs higher than what you have available, then you are probably *disk thrashing* (constant paging to disk) and excessively using virtual memory. (A review of performance monitoring memory use is in Chapter 8.) If you find your system runs poorly, you might want to look at that chapter to start resolving problems on your production network equipment before you go live with the cluster service. To set the page size properly, look at the amount of physical RAM you have and add 11MB to that number. That's it. Remember to place the paging file in the correct location (on its own physical disk instead of the logical drive) or you can damage system performance.

Configuring Network Properties

You need to preplan your network properties seriously before you install the Cluster Service. In this section, we configure TCP/IP communications and media speeds, so your nodes communicate properly. We test this as well. It's important for you to have communication with all hosts that play a key role in your implementation on the network before continuing with the cluster install.

If you don't have access to IP addressing assignments, you need to contact the department that assigns them. In larger IT shops, you'll find that TCP/IP management is closely monitored and you might have to get a Lead Engineer or Manager involved to get a block of addresses you can use.

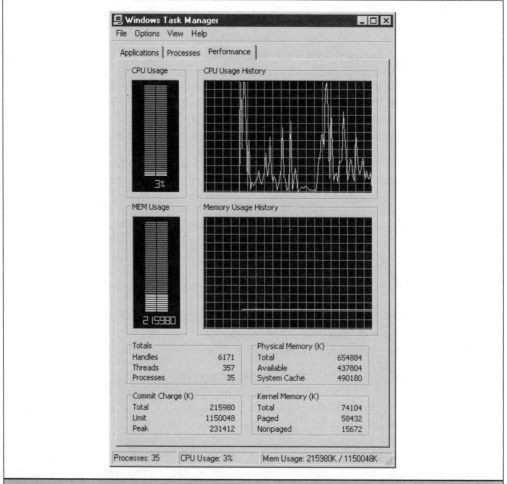

Figure 2-5. Windows Task Manager Memory and CPU details

The IPs you use need to be static (not doled out from DHCP, which hands out IP addresses via a configured scope) and they don't necessarily need to be on the same subnet. You can configure the cards on different networks because you'll be dividing the cluster into two halves. One half is the LAN connection, where your clients will come to access the clustered resources. The other is the Heartbeat Connection network or the Management network, which is the node-to-node connection where the clustered servers communicate with each other to make sure they're operational. The best design method to use in this scenario is to have two different subnets dividing the publicly accessible network and the private Heartbeat network. This keeps both networks separate. I explain all the IP address assignment and network connections in the following sections.

Heartbeat Connection and Client Access

The first thing that needs to be done when configuring network properties is to make sure you have two connections available to configure. Open your network and dial-up connections by right-clicking My Network Places and selecting Properties. Or, you can open it from the Control Panel. When you open the dialog box, you see the Make a New Connection Wizard applet and, if your install went properly, you see two connection icons, as listed in the next illustration. If you don't see two connections, you need to open the Device Manager discussed earlier and make sure you have the drivers installed correctly for the network card. After you have properly configured the drivers, the network connection should appear.

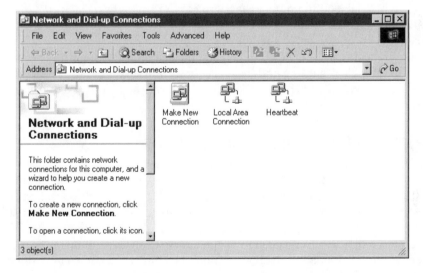

Windows 2000 has a great way to view your network connections. When using Windows NT 4.0 Enterprise Edition, you had to open the general TCP/IP properties and drop down to each NIC card listed in the properties to view its settings. Windows 2000

has improved this method by letting you give a friendly name to your connection. When you view the network connections for the first time, you'll see they're named (by default) Local Area Connection and Local Area Connection 2. To rename the connection, simply right-click the name, and select it. In this example, you can call the connection by its assignment, which is Heartbeat. You don't want to name just any old interface. You want to name the interfaces as you have them cabled in the system. The Heartbeat network connection would be either the crossover cable you ran from one node to the other, or the dedicated hub, switch, or VLAN you configured for the management network.

If you already cabled the server and don't know which is which, this is simple to determine. With Windows 2000, you can unplug the network cable and it will pop up in the system tray (systray) on the bottom right-hand side of your desktop. If you unplugged the Heartbeat network cable, you'll see the icon appear with a big red X through it. Hover your mouse pointer over the connection icon and it will give you a small description and details pane that either says Local Area Connection or Local Area Connection 2. Make a note of which one it is, and then go back to your Network Connections dialog box. Right-click the appropriate connection and rename it to Heartbeat. Make sure you plug the cable back in. The icon should disappear, unless you configured it to always appear, which we'll do later in the section. Now, make sure the other network connection is also labeled to your satisfaction. For example, this is labeled Local Area Connection, which is its assignment. This is the connection where your network clients will make requests of the server's resources.

The second node can be configured exactly the same way as the first one as far as the network connection naming and basic configurations. You're only working on one node at a time, so you won't corrupt the shared storage set. Configure this one when the time comes to bring up the second node.

IP Addressing and NIC Card Configurations

I discuss the entire TCP/IP connection settings here, but only do one node at a time. Keeping a notepad next to you and jotting down notes on how to configure the other node helps. Then, you can simply do it after you read this and configure the first node.

Now that you have your node network connection properties labeled correctly, you can begin to configure your TCP/IP properties. The dialog box shown in the following illustration has a title bar that reads Heartbeat properties. The bottom of the dialog box shows a check box that enables the Show icon in taskbar when connected option.

Die-hard Windows veterans know this is a slight mistake in wording as the icon really appears in the systray but, no matter, you understand the difference. You should check this box to help you look at something quickly. Simply hover your mouse over the connection (it will read heartbeat in the popup) and you can double-click it to get to the properties quickly. You can also see incoming and outgoing data flow by hovering your mouse over the icon or by double-clicking it.

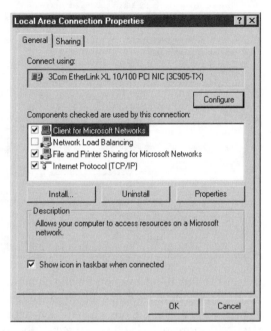

I selected two identical 3COM NICs for both servers and, because they are identical, they're named in an ordinal fashion. Be sure to document which connection goes where and apply labels on the server. Feel free to get a nice *P-Touch*—a device that enables you to make labels—with markable tape to label everything you feel you need to see on the server. Also, always take notes to log in as documentation later, to use for troubleshooting. You can configure the NIC from here, as well as in the Device Manager discussed earlier.

Your next configuration centers on the TCP/IP protocol. As mentioned in prerollout design, you can't use anything but TCP/IP. Not IPX/SPX or AppleTalk—only TCP/IP.

Highlight your TCP/IP protocol and select the Properties button. You will open a dialog box, as seen in the next illustration.

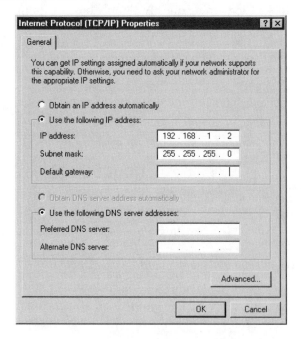

You now need to configure static IP addressing for the clustered nodes. You should have any server, printer, or network device set statically and configure all your network clients' PCs and laptops to grab an address from a DHCP server. You will need to configure four interfaces with IP addresses. I list them here initially, so you can implement for the second node that you'll need to configure. These are the settings I configured on my servers, so yours might be different or you can choose my settings. Just make sure you understand the concepts explained. I also configured my Node A, so I'm in the process of configuring Node B now. I set the TCP/IP addressing as follows:

- Cluster-Node-B has a Heartbeat Connection IP address of 192.168.1.2, with a 24-bit subnet mask.

- Cluster-node-B also has a Local Area Connection IP Address of 10.0.0.3, with a 24-bit subnet mask.

- Cluster-node-A has a Heartbeat Connection IP address of 192.168.1.1, with a 24-bit subnet mask.

- Cluster-Node-A has a Local Area Connection IP Address of 10.0.0.2, with a 24-bit subnet mask.

Both Cluster-Node-A and B have a default gateway of 10.0.0.1 /24 and I'll be logging into a domain controller with an IP address of 10.0.0.4, with a 24-bit subnet mask. I'll break these settings down for you as you configure it step-by-step. Figure 2-6 shows you what this will look like on a topology map.

Once you get deeper into the install, you'll see another address is needed. Don't worry about this now, though. Just remember I mentioned earlier that you'll need to

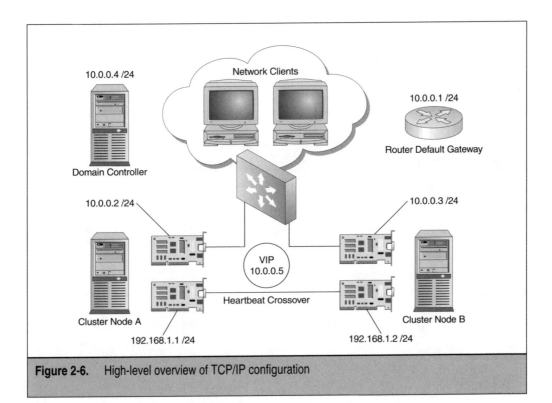

Figure 2-6.   High-level overview of TCP/IP configuration

allocate five IP addresses and a specific NetBIOS name for the cluster you're configuring.

We've just configured the IP address for one node (192.168.1.2 /24). This is for the Heartbeat network. Now you need to configure the node's other network connection, called Local Area Connection. You can select that one the same way you selected the Heartbeat network, by right-clicking the icon in the Network Connections dialog box and selecting Properties. When you open the dialog box, you need to configure it the same way as you configured the Heartbeat connection, except you enter the IP address of 10.0.0.2 with a 24-bit subnet mask. On this network connection, however, you must configure more than just an IP address and a subnet mask. The server needs a default gateway on the local segment to which it's connected. Remember, this server needs to respond to and serve resources to the network clients. You might have to configure a default gateway (local router) if you have clients accessing your cluster from other networks or from across a wide area network (WAN).

You eventually need an IP address for every resource you set up in your cluster. If you set up a SQL Server 2000, you need a new IP address for it (something like 10.0.0.6 /24), but you'll still be using the two-node cluster with IP addresses of 10.0.0.2 and 10.0.0.3. If you know you'll be setting up quite a few clustered solutions, you might want to ask your Network Engineer (or slot them yourself) for a block of IPs. You could use 10.0.0.2–10.0.0.10 for the nodes and quite a few resources. If you expect more growth, then block out some more.

Advanced Configuration and Troubleshooting for Network Connections

Getting this right before the installation of the Cluster Services is important. Make sure you open the Device Manager, as seen in Figure 2-7, and view the NICs for any possible errors. Next, select each of them, one at a time, and double-click them to access their properties.

When viewing the NIC properties, as shown in the following illustration, you can pinpoint bus locations and see if the card is enabled. A handy troubleshooter option can help you if you need it. You can use the troubleshooter, but the explanations of the problems are rather vague and basic, so it might not help much.

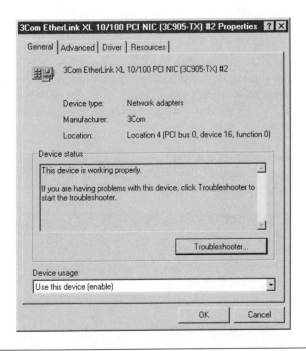

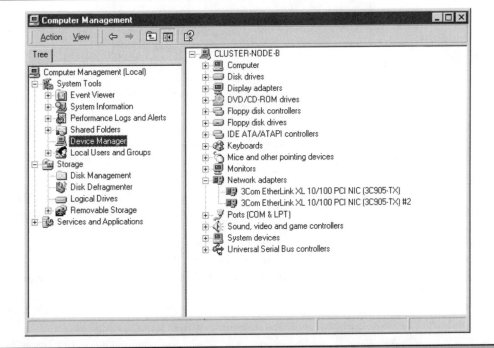

Figure 2-7.   Viewing multiple NICs in the Device Manager

Next, click the Advanced tab (as seen in the following illustration), so you can learn how to configure (or hardcode) the speeds for your NIC card manually if they didn't autonegotiate properly or if you want to tweak a few milliseconds out of your system by eliminating the time it takes to autonegotiate from the NIC to the Switch port. By viewing media type, you can select to put the card at different speeds, but if you hardcode this, make sure you know how to configure the switch on the other side of the connection, in case it has a problem. I've seen cases where a skilled technician hardcoded the NIC at 100 Mbps and couldn't figure out why he lost the connection when plugged into a Cisco 1900 Catalyst switch. Well, the 1900 series switch ran at 10BaseT and, because a high-level overview and topology map wasn't used, he assumed the speed was 100 Mbps because it was a Cisco switch.

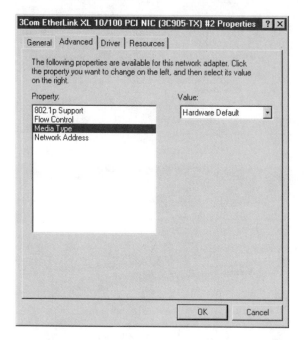

Now, after you configure all your IPs, speeds, and connections the way you want them, you need to run a test to make sure it all works. Because we've done this step-by-step—checking along the way—it's easy to see problems and immediately eliminate or fix them without having to backtrack too far in the installation.

Use the command prompt for your troubleshooting. This can be pulled up quickly by going to the Start button and opening the Run dialog box. Type **CMD,** and then

press ENTER. You open a Command Prompt window, as shown in Figure 2-8. Check
to see what your configuration is set at by typing **IPCONFIG /ALL,** and then press
ENTER. This will show you all your configuration statistics. You should jot down (or
copy-and-paste) this information for your log and documentation. You should have
Cluster-Node-A or B (or whatever you called your clustered servers). You should also
have your Local Area Connection configurations exactly as you entered them. And, you
should have your Heartbeat configurations just as you entered them in the network
properties. If you have any discrepancies, backtrack until you find your error. Next,
type **PING** and try to make contact with your server from a network client (or another
server). Because the Heartbeat connection is listed here, you might be unable to connect
yet—until the other server is up and running. What I generally do is set up a VLAN for
the Heartbeat and ping all NICs from within a Layer 3 switch. This is the easiest way to
verify the connectivity of your clustered node set.

Finally, you need to power down the first node you configured and power up the
second node to configure its IP addressing as well. You can do this now or wait until
you completely finish all configurations. Most of the major ones have been discussed,
but we can explore a few more topics to improve your clustered and Highly Available
solution.

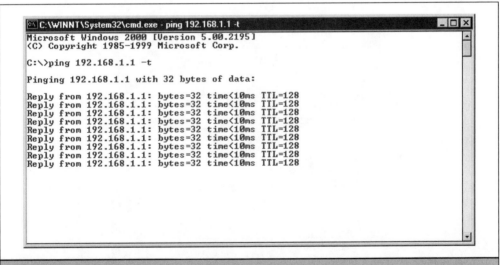

Figure 2-8.   Using the PING command to test connectivity

NETBIOS and WINS

NetBIOS is a protocol without legs. I won't give a history on the NetBIOS protocol, but it's an integral part of pre-Windows 2000 network communications. Unless you have 100 percent Windows 2000 rolled out across your infrastructure, you're stuck with WINS to find and use resources on the network. Many places where I work still run Windows 95, so NetBIOS will be a part of our IT-based lives. We need to set up NetBIOS properly on a Windows 2000 clustered solution. In the following illustration, we revisit the network properties for our Heartbeat connection. Open the network properties, and then go to the advanced settings within the TCP/IP protocol stack. Click the WINS tab and you can disable the NetBIOS resolution use for your Heartbeat connection. It's a point-to-point connection and it's unneeded. You don't want to disable this for your LAN that your network clients access because it could create a problem with NBT resolution (NetBIOS over TCP/IP). You can, however, add another configuration tweak into the cluster node for better performance when you disable it on the back-end connection.

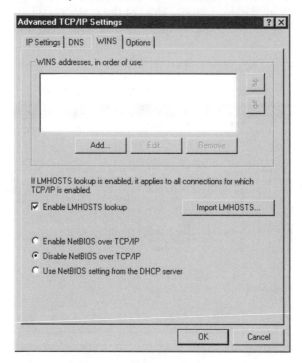

NetBIOS is broadcast-based and when you implement a Windows Internet Naming Service (WINS) server, you can have all NetBIOS names and services log directly to a database on a server, which cuts down broadcasting tremendously. You can configure your network to use such a feature to control performance and bandwidth utilization on your cluster segment.

Also, you might find your system's Event Viewer could be filling up with unnecessary browser announcements from your server participating in browser wars. The network browser service manages a list of servers and services running on your network, so all clients can find them. This is used to build a list of systems and services found within My Network Place (formerly Network Neighborhood) for you to access. Unfortunately, this creates unwanted traffic and fills your logs with nonsense about elections (who will be what type of browser) and other issues about servers being unable to participate in or losing an election. For a dedicated server set to provide a clustered resource, you can safely assume your domain controllers can float this list around and your cluster should ignore the possibility of using it or participating in it.

The only way to kill the *Browser Service* (the service that runs on the Windows server that allows for browser list elections) without stopping the Server Service or disabling File and Print Sharing is to attempt a registry hack. This is safe and easy, but as always, you should know that changes are hard to reverse and make sure you have a backup of your registry before attempting the following hack.

You can disable the NetBIOS browser wars by making our cluster node not participate in a browser election. Simply open your Registry Editor by clicking the Start button, select Run from the Start menu, and type **regedit** in the Run dialog box. Press ENTER and you will open the Registry Editor, as seen in the next illustration.

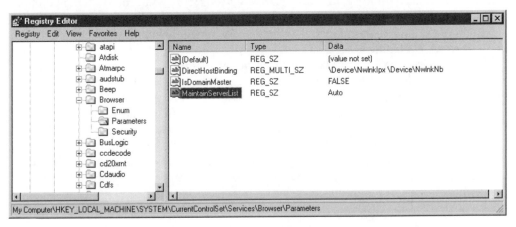

Browse to the following path: HKEY_LOCAL_MACHINE\SYSTEM\ CurrentControlSet\Services\Browser\Parameters and double-click the MaintainServerList string. You open a dialog box, as seen in the following illustration.

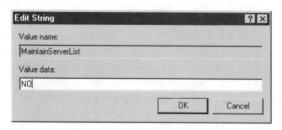

Change the setting from Auto to No. This will stop you from participating in the browser wars that fill up your Event Viewer logs.

Last, you still need a reserved name for the entire cluster. A fact of networking with NetBIOS is you can't duplicate NetBIOS names, so this name must be unique on the network. This is why you need to plan on the cluster name having its own unique NetBIOS name because, if you accidentally duplicate it, you might have networking problems when the system goes live. We use this name later when we run the install for the cluster services. You need to name each of your cluster members, and then name the entire cluster. You'll see this clearly when we go through the installation and configuration of MSCS.

User Accounts and Security

A domain user account for your Cluster Service needs to be configured on the domain controller where your servers will authenticate. Both cluster nodes need to be part of a domain or the service won't install, which means they'll have a computer account on the domain controller.

When you join the domain, you use a service account that we'll create later in the chapter. I simulated a failed install to show it can't be done until you join a domain, which you see soon. To create an account, go to a domain controller on your network and create a new account. You can do this by opening the Active Directory Users and Computers MMC console. Go to your Administrative Tools folder in the Control Panel. Create a new account by right-clicking the Users folder in the console, and then create a new User object in the directory. You'll open a new dialog box, as seen in the next illustration. You can name this account anything you want, but follow the naming convention dictated by your organization.

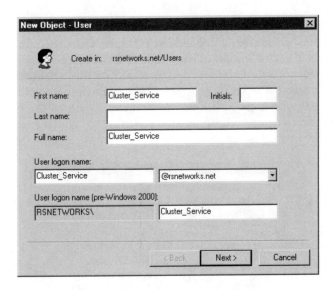

If your organization doesn't implement a naming convention (this is a bad thing), then make up an account that you'll know by looking at the name, for example, Cluster_Service. When you finish, click Next, and then select a password that can't be guessed or easily hacked. I generally select a password from a phrase (which is one of the best ways to create a secure password). You can use something like, "My dog loves to play catch with a black Frisbee," and use the first letter from each word, which creates the password, MDLTPCWABF. Now that you've selected a good password, select the two check boxes, as seen in the following illustration, for Password never expires and User cannot change password. Uncheck the option to have the user change the password at the next logon.

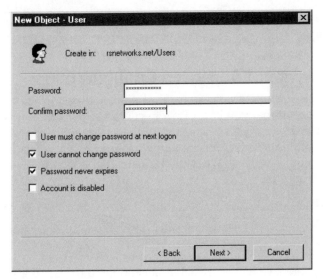

Click Next and finish the User objects' basic settings. Once you finish and the new Cluster_Service object is created, you need to configure it further with one quick tweak I mentioned before. You don't want to run login scripts that could conflict with drive mappings used on the cluster for shared storage because this might cause a problem. Be aware of this or create a separate script and assign it explicitly to the user, so it won't alter the drive mappings on the clustered nodes. If you have a problem with this, either take the script out or designate the specific user with a customized login script, as seen in the next illustration.

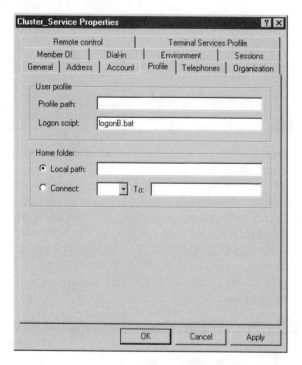

Cluster Service Account Advanced Configuration

In this section, I discuss other ways to configure the account, Cluster_Service. The reason it's so important that you know how to configure this account is this: if you ever change anything with this account, if someone else accidentally changes something, if you assign a different account, or any reason whatsoever, you'll need to know how to reconfigure the account in which we named Cluster_Service from before. Note these important points about the Cluster Service account:

- The account must be a domain account (created on a domain controller)
- The account must have local administrative rights to every node in your cluster

If you need to add the account to local machines, all you need to do is open the Computer Management Console for each node and go to the Local Users and Groups icon. Select the Groups folder, and then add the Cluster Service account to the Local Administrators group.

NOTE   This only works if you're clustering nodes that are not, in fact, domain controllers themselves. Otherwise, the Local Users and Groups account won't let you change anything.

The Cluster Service running on your Windows 2000 Advanced Server needs an account (Cluster_Service) that can function with the following rights.

- Act as part of the OS
- Back up files and directories
- Increase scheduling priority
- Increase quotas
- Log on as a service
- Restore files and directories
- Lock pages in memory
- Load and unload device drivers

If you need to grant these rights manually, you can do so from another management console (MMC), called the Local Security Policy, as seen in Figure 2-9. To open the console,

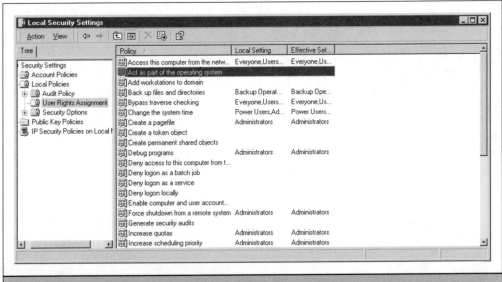

Figure 2-9.   Configuring Local Security Policy settings

go to the Control Panel, and then to the Administrative Tools folder. Once within this folder, you can see the Local Security Policy. To change the settings, go to the Local Security Policy | Security Settings | Local Policies | User Rights Assignment. In the Preview pane of the console, you'll find the policies you need to adjust.

By default, all rights listed here are given to the Local Administrators group:

- Act as part of the OS
- Back up files and directories
- Increase scheduling priority
- Increase quotas
- Log on as a service
- Restore files and directories
- Lock pages in memory
- Load and unload device drivers

And all are granted, except for the following three:

- Act as part of the OS
- Log on as a service
- Lock pages in memory

The last three aren't granted by default and are highly needed for the Cluster Service account, so if you need to re-create the account, you'll need to set these rights explicitly. Remember, it isn't okay simply to place the user account in the Domain Administrators Group. You need to make explicit assignments into the Local Administrators Groups.

Domain Connection

You're almost ready to run the Cluster Services. One last step you need to accomplish is to join a domain. You must be part of a domain to run the Cluster Services on the node you're attempting to create a cluster with. If you attempt to join or create a cluster by installing the service, you're stopped because you aren't part of a domain and you're given an error message, as seen in the following illustration.

To join a domain, you need to open the System applet from the Control Panel. Once opened, click the Network Identification tab. You can tell from here whether a server is part of a domain. In the next illustration, you can see the cluster node we're trying to configure Cluster Services on isn't part of a domain, but is part of a workgroup. Because the cluster node is part of a workgroup, you need to join the node to a domain. Again, you've preplanned all this already and have all the information you need available.

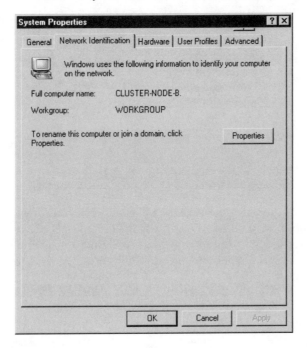

When you join the domain, you need the domain name and an account that enables you to add machines to the domain. The Domain Administrator (Administrator) account will do unless you made a special account to do this. If in a production environment, check with the person who does your User and Group Accounts, and make sure you have the right credentials.

Click the Properties button and you'll open the dialog box shown in the following illustration. You can make identification changes here and join the domain. Select the Member of Domain radio button and type in your domain name. (It is not case-sensitive.)

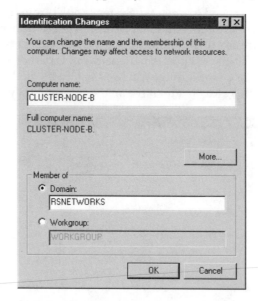

Click OK and wait for the domain controller to query you for your credentials. In the next illustration, you're asked to supply the credentials of a user with the permissions to add the server to this domain. It will take a moment and, as long as you have all the correct information, you should be fine.

Your last step (and one that spells success) is the acceptance into the domain from the domain controller. You'll see the Welcome dialog box, as seen in the following illustration. If you see a red X-bearing dialog box, backtrack until you find what you missed. Things missed can be anything from bad credentials to a disconnected cable connection, so be cautious of what problems you could possibly run into.

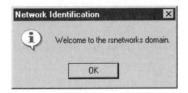

If everything else is fine up to this point, then you can move ahead. Again, although this is painstakingly methodical, you can't miss a step or else the cluster won't successfully provide you with the outcome of high availability. You might not even be able to install the service if you miss anything up to now. To finalize this section, power down the node you're working on, bring up the other node, and then follow the same steps. You should be able to reread this section and join the other node to the same domain without problems.

Clustering Service Preinstallation Checklist

I created a quick checklist, so you can verify that all the preplanning you did is completed and all the tasks are done. These are for the most important high-level tasks that must be done before you install the Cluster Service on the nodes. Before you install the Microsoft Cluster Service, you should have done the following beforehand:

- Design your cluster for your infrastructure, have appropriate support, resources, and budget.
- Have a log of all the details of your implementation to be transferred to documentation later.
- Configure all your hardware properly, using only items listed on the HCL.
- Install the hardware properly for your clustered solution. Take your time to step through every section of this chapter to make all the hardware settings appropriate to your solution.
- Verify the shared SCSI bus: termination, cables, IDs.
- Prepare all your drivers, licenses, software, firmware, and anything else you need before your installation begins.
- Install Windows 2000 Advanced Server, one node at a time. Go through all the details listed in this chapter to make all needed settings' adjustments and changes.
- Install all needed service packs and hot fixes.

- Configure the shared storage, NTFS files system formatting, and drive letter assignment from one Windows 2000 node.

- Make sure your NICs are configured properly and the IP addressing is configured correctly. Test your NIC's with ping.

- Make sure an available domain controller is always on the segment where your cluster nodes will reside. Your nodes need to be part of a domain.

- Check your Event Viewer logs to ensure they're clean of any big problems. You'll always have informational events and possibly warnings, but you should be concerned about critical errors that can be caught and fixed now.

- Have a NetBIOS name set aside for the cluster. This name should be something meaningful and easy to understand.

This should be a quick run down and overview of major points covered. Although you can do more tweaking, this is enough to get the Cluster Service installed and functional, so let's begin.

Clustering Services Installation

You've finally reached the point where you can install the Cluster Service. Although it seems we went through a ridiculous amount of work and effort to get here, you should now feel confident that you'll be building a nice house on a solid foundation.

1. First, open the Control Panel to view the applets. You'll find the Add/Remove Programs applet within. As seen in Figure 2-10, you have an option in the bottom left-hand side of the dialog box to install Windows-based services that come with the OS. Select this to invoke the Installation Wizard that will enable you to install the Cluster Service on your node.

2. After you open this dialog box, as shown in Figure 2-11, you can check the Cluster Service and press OK. The installation begins immediately.

NOTE Remember, you must have everything in place up to now or the Cluster Service won't install. Microsoft Windows 2000 Advanced Server will *not* install the service unless you have all components in place. If it isn't set up right, you'll be denied. This is the reason I've been so methodical up to now. I've tested this many times and it won't function properly if you don't do it correctly.

---

3. If you didn't add the i386 directory to your local drive, you'll be asked for the Windows 2000 Installation Media CD-ROM. If you're asked, install the service and you'll be prompted with the Cluster Installation Wizard.

4. This wizard will guide you as you install the Cluster Service and configure a virtual cluster. Your two-node cluster is almost finished.

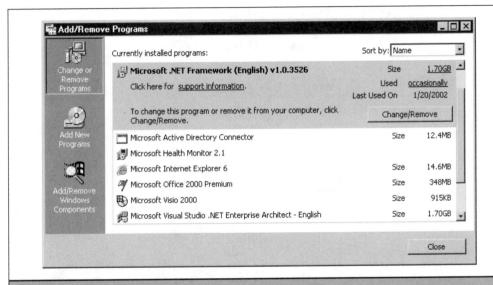

Figure 2-10. Using the Add/Remove Programs Control Panel applet

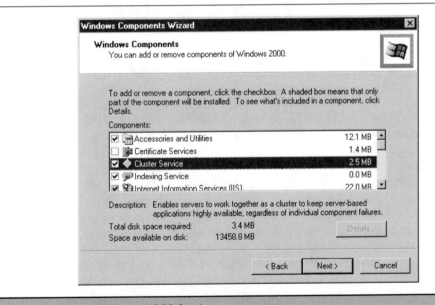

Figure 2-11. Installing the MSCS Service

5. Once you open the wizard, click Next and you'll be asked about the HCL again from Microsoft's online web site. In the following illustration, Microsoft asks you to verify that you did go to the web site and check your hardware against the list.

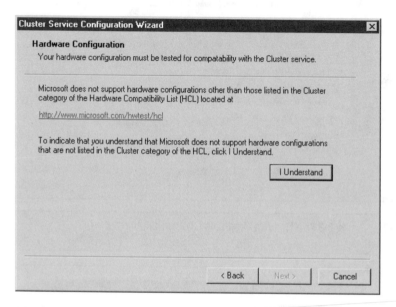

Microsoft isn't trying to be redundant here: it wants to make sure you checked and, by clicking the I Understand button, you're verifying that you did. If you look at Figure 2-12, you'll notice I've gone to the HCL site and it's helpful. I've used the HCL to build all the production clusters I've designed. We all make mistakes, but you want to minimize those mistakes. By visiting the HCL, you can help minimize many mistakes. Incompatible hardware and drivers will cause a blue screen of death (BSOD) on your production system, so make sure you verify everything in your preinstallation design.

After you confirm that you read the HCL and agree to having used it, you're basically done with the hard parts of the installation. As you can see, the most difficult portion of creating a two-node cluster was the preparation work. Installing the service is a piece of cake. Your next task is to create the cluster. In the following illustration, you must join or create a cluster, or make a new one. Select the first node in the cluster. In the section that follows, you'll add the other node to the cluster to create a two-node cluster.

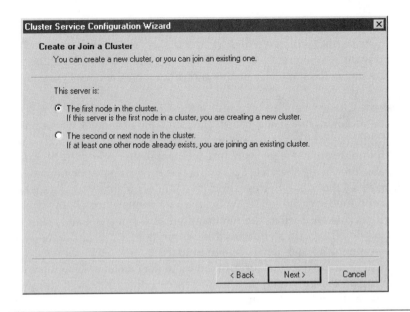

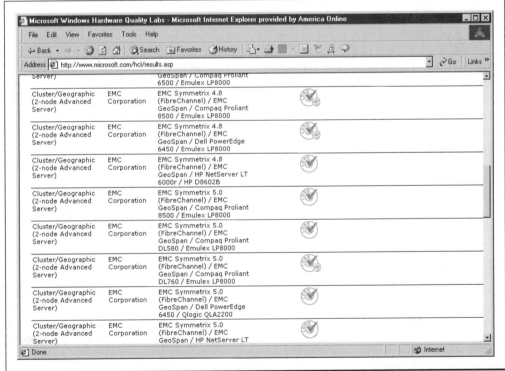

Figure 2-12.   Going to the HCL to verify possible hardware issues

From here on, this is self-explanatory and straightforward. You need to configure a NetBIOS cluster name, which we highlighted in the predesign layout. You can call it whatever you want. I called mine VCLUSTER1 for Virtual Cluster Number 1. As long as a NetBIOS name is 15 characters or less and unique on the network, you can call it whatever you like.

Next, use the Cluster_Service account for the domain you joined. I'm selecting the Rsnetworks.net domain, but you'll use an account from whatever domain is in your production environment. Be careful not to assign this account to any other service. Also be careful not to change the password accidentally or delete the account, or you'll probably disable the Cluster Service. Following this tip is imperative because, if someone accidentally deletes the account, this could give you problems later. I generally have a postproduction meeting and let all the Systems Administrators know this account is "live" and what it does, as well as the ramifications of altering it. I also audit the account for a while (as I do all accounts with anything more than a user group assignment that doesn't have someone's "real name" assigned to it).

Your next steps are to add the quorum device to the cluster and configure the storage. Windows will again remind you that you must be careful with shared storage on a SCSI bus. It corrupts easily and must be managed only by the Cluster Service. You are warned again and you can continue assigning the quorum device (shared storage). This is where all assigned data will be kept and shared between the two-cluster nodes.

Your last grouping of tasks is to configure the network interfaces you diligently prepared in the middle of this chapter. You need to understand how the Cluster Service Wizard views your network interfaces: it calls them private and public networks. I hate this because you're probably putting privately assigned IP addressing on all your interfaces—from the Internet Assigned Numbers Authority (IANA)—which is confusing to someone who doesn't know IP addressing well. I'd say that designing a clustered solution would warrant some TCP/IP knowledge, but the installation of the Cluster Service doesn't.

I could hand you a set of addresses, tell you where to plug them in, and that would be fine, but what about the technician who reads this the wrong way? Regardless, be aware this has nothing to do with true public and private IP addressing. Instead, it stands for the publicly accessible network from which your network clients make requests to the server. The private network would be the cluster management, heartbeat segment, or VLAN.

Configure the Heartbeat Network connection to the private network and assign the Local Area Connection we configured to be mixed, which will also allow for public access from your network clients. You could configure the interface to just be public but mixed enables all communications. Most important is to isolate your heartbeat because you can't afford dropped packets or to have your network card pick up excessive broadcast on the wire and start to process them. You best choice is to keep your heartbeat isolated.

You're almost done. You need to configure an IP address for the entire cluster (finally, that's what the fifth IP address is for) and close the wizard. I'm assigning my cluster to have a cluster IP address of 10.0.0.5 with a 24-bit mask. This should be configured for our public or Local Area Connection network segment, so your clients can access that single address for services. Now, 10.0.0.2 and 10.0.0.3 are meaningless to anything but the internals of the Cluster Service. Congratulations, you're almost done!

Joining a Cluster

Now you need to configure Node 2. You can configure the node the same way, except instead of picking the option to create a new cluster, you want to join a cluster. You'll then be brought to a dialog box, as seen in the next illustration, to produce the cluster name and an account to join the cluster with.

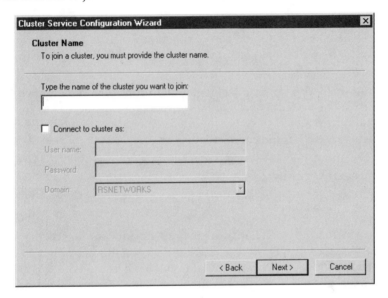

Your final step to join the first node is to use the account Cluster_Service to join the cluster, and then you're finished. If you went back through and followed all the preliminary configuration work you needed to finish before you got to this point, the final step is that easy. Remember, you needed to join the domain and configure your IP addresses accordingly.

Postinstallation Troubleshooting

Did it go without a hitch? I hope so, but you might have experienced some problems. This is where you'll read further to quickly put out any possible problems you might have encountered.

- When doing the install of the Cluster Service, the install is simplistic unless you goofed up the hardware and the shared bus. If you took all the steps listed in the chapter, you shouldn't have had a configuration issue.

- If you have a problem installing the service, check to verify you have enough disk drive space for the service to populate the WINNT/cluster directory.

- This isn't a large install, but it's possible you goofed up the space requirements and need to make some space for the service.

- Make sure you have some form of domain membership with your cluster nodes. The nodes need to be part of the same domain. You can either make the cluster nodes domain controllers or you need to have a nearby domain controller the nodes can join.

- If any of the nodes can't contact the domain controller, you'll have serious problems. The nodes also use remote procedure calls (RPCs) to contact the domain controllers. If this service isn't functional, then you'll also have problems with communication.

- If the Cluster Service won't start (ClusSvc), then you might have many areas you'll need to investigate.

- Although you've heard me say this multiple times, it's probably a hardware problem.

- If you can verify that all hardware is properly functioning, then you can check the service account. If you do change settings on this account, you might have problems with your Cluster Service. If you have issues with this account, you'll most likely get a system event in the Event Viewer from the Service Control Manager. The problem error you may see is that the service doesn't start. Check the Event Viewer for possible clues and check the account if you feel it's been tampered with.

Using Cluster.exe Command-Line Administration

In this section of the chapter, we'll wind down from clustering and slowly move into NLB design. Before we do, though, you need to know some tips on how to configure Clustering Services from the command line. You can perform many administrative tasks directly from CMD or the command prompt, which is sometimes faster and, more important, can be configured in batch and for advanced automation.

Cluster.exe

Cluster.exe is a program that enables you to perform command-line activities. I'll outline some examples of what you can do with the tool. If you type **Cluster /?**, you get the basic syntax for the command, so that would be a great place to start. By using the word "cluster," you can execute the command so everything you put after it is aimed at a specific cluster using the cluster NetBIOS name outlined earlier. You can build on the command by typing **Cluster "Cluster Name"** where "Cluster Name" is the NetBIOS name for your cluster. The last part of the formula is to add an option at the end with the use of a switch. The whole syntax is as follows:

```
CLUSTER vcluster1 /options
```

That's it, but now you need to know what to apply. Test the Cluster.exe program by typing **Cluster /version** to check not only the version of the executable, but also if you have it installed and it's usable.

Listing clusters in the domain is just as easy. If you want to check a cluster contained within a single domain, you need to know both the cluster name and the domain name. In this example, I check the vcluster1 cluster within the rsnetworks domain.

```
CLUSTER vcluster1 /LIST:rsnetworks
```

You can also check on the status of your nodes with the cluster program. To check a node, you need to know the names of your nodes. (Check your documentation.) To check a node, you can use the following commands:

```
CLUSTER vcluster1 NODE cluster-node-a /status
```

This command checks your node's status for any node name to which you direct this command within the cluster group you point out.

Here, the cluster group is vcluster1, the cluster we set up originally. You can also see I specifically named a cluster node (Cluster-node-a) within that cluster to check the status.

You can look up many more commands, but if you need to write elaborate batch files, reference the Windows 2000 Advanced Server help system to get more detail on how to use the Cluster command to construct elaborate batch files. Use the commands I show here to test the two-node cluster we created.

The Test of Failover and Last Tips

You're at the end of the section, so you need to see if all the money, time, and effort invested was worth it. Check to see if your cluster server works as advertised. Have a client access a folder you created on the shared storage and power down one of the nodes. If you failover, then you've achieved victory. If you don't, then you need to backtrack through this chapter and seek clues as to why it didn't work. Do the obvious by checking your logs first, but if nothing jumps out at you, prepare for some detective work. This is where all that documentation comes in handy. Don't be afraid to call the hardware vendor if you're in a jam.

As for other cluster tips, make sure you're also current with all service packs. Check online for new service packs, Windows Update, and any news about possible problems. There's nothing like troubleshooting something for hours only to realize it's a bug that needs to be patched! Although I'm all for new service packs and hot fixes, you should also use caution when installing them. Make sure you have a good backup because service packs have been known to create problems. Don't expect all service packs to improve performance. The best way to prepare for service pack install is to install the pack on a test or lab environment first, and then visit sites like **www.ntbugtraq.com** to get the latest news on possible issues on service packs or hot fixes gone bad. Also, use this site to find problems with the servers you run now, so you can stay current with all the patches for software bugs. This is especially important if you plan on creating a clustered IIS solution for a public Internet connection.

Documentation! You need to take all the notes you just compiled and add them to the network documentation for your company. Your production network needs to be documented, and the more the better. This helps you solve problems quickly and efficiently. In later chapters, we'll go deeper into configuring resources, performance monitoring, logs, and troubleshooting. Now, on to configuring a load-balanced solution with Windows 2000 Advanced Server.

DESIGNING A NLB SOLUTION WITH WINDOWS 2000 ADVANCED SERVER

You now know the finer art of setting up a Windows 2000 cluster. Next, we'll discuss how to configure network load balancing (NLB), which is a different animal in its approach to high-availability networking. NLB is also called clustering, so don't get confused with the use of the name. *Clustering* is a generic term, and you'll find it's used interchangeably over and over again. In case you aren't used to the IT jargon, I'll explain it as NLB or network load-balancing clusters when applicable, so you won't get confused. Let's begin to prepare for NLB-based clusters and more Highly Available solutions with Windows 2000 Advanced Server. An example of a NLB solution using Windows 2000 can be seen in Figure 2-13.

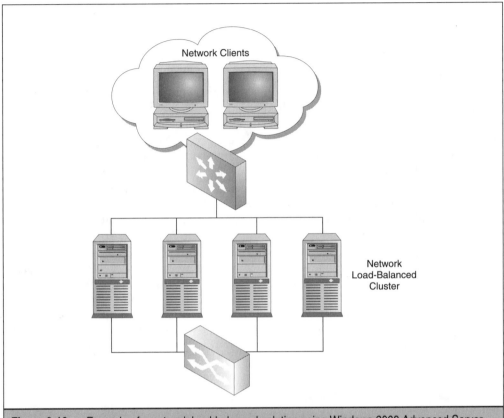

Figure 2-13.   Example of a network load-balanced solution using Windows 2000 Advanced Server

Where to Begin

Load balancing is balancing the amount of work (hence, "balancing the load") that a server must do between two or more computers (up to 32 nodes). You can think of NLB or load balancing as being one of the main reasons for server-based clustering.

Load balancing is mainly used for the web, and all the traffic that comes and goes from what would have been one overwhelmed server. Now, you can have multiple servers in a group that will handle all that traffic and take the load off one single server serving requests.

NLB is usually connected to a failover plan, so you can also have disaster-recovery functionality incorporated into your balanced load. As you see in the previous diagram, you have a server failure, but the server is technically still up for client requests because you have two other servers available.

NLB is just as useful as generic two-node clustering, but it offers some specific features made for specific services. In other words, you might want to put a SQL Server 2000 installation on a dual-node cluster with a shared storage system, but you might want to put four NLB servers in a high-availability cluster running Internet Information Services (IIS) for a web site located across all four servers. You see, a difference in design exists, where one warrants more use than the other. With NLB, you have no single point of failure. If a node fails, then the rest of the available nodes reconverge and take up the load of the failed server. Instead of being locked down to two or four nodes, you can scale out to about 32 nodes with a NLB cluster. This is perfect for web sites that get more hits during holiday months, where you might want to add more nodes to distribute the load and make the single site you're hosting appear able to take on the request, when it's really a group of servers handling the load in an NLB cluster. The configuration is much easier as you see soon. Setting up an NLB cluster takes half the effort it took to set up a two-node failover cluster. NLB clusters are much more scalable than other types of clusters. You can add up to 32 nodes, add nodes at basically any time and with add-on software (discussed when you learn Application Center 2000), and you can monitor the health of all services and applications loaded across the NLB cluster. You can also filter via TCP/IP port for TCP- and UDP-based applications like HTTP, FTP, and others.

Another solution NLB offers over the Generic Cluster Services is the opportunity to manage session states across nodes and manage affinity. We'll discuss this further in its own section. Heartbeats are still used with NLB and machine failure is detected in this fashion, as it was with Cluster Services. You still need to configure a public and a private network segment for your cluster.

Probably the most important things about designing a NLB cluster are lower cost and less-special hardware requirements than in the traditional cluster created with the Cluster Services, which has a demand for a shared bus. This is why most use the service over the other one. If you're clustering SQL or Exchange Server 2000, though, you'll need a shared storage drive, and then you'll warrant using the Cluster Services. People ask me questions about cluster and NLB interoperability, and we can dispel this here: You either use NLB or MSCS. There's no reason to run them both at the same time.

The Design Phase

We've reached the most important step of the NLB rollout. This section of the chapter mirrors the last one as closely in procedure, so you get the subtle (and not so subtle) distinctions between the two services—NLB and MSCS. When planning your NLB cluster, you should consider the following ideas. Remember, planning and preimplementation design goes a long way before the actual roll out.

Hardware Load Balancers and Software Load Balancers

With NLB clustering, you can implement different hardware scenarios because you can either use a Windows 2000 Advanced Server to distribute the packets to other nodes or you can get a dedicated piece of hardware to load balance the packets across the nodes.

Because the hardware requirements are far less stringent than with the Cluster Service in the beginning of the chapter, you'll find this section is a shorter read and this whole cluster hardware solution easier to design. We'll configure the Windows 2000 Advanced Server as the load balancer here because it does the job fine and you'll find it works as advertised. Most of the load balancers used today in large-scale enterprise-level networks are either supplied by Foundry or Cisco and are hardware-based. When planning your design, we'll use the software-based, load-balancing solution (Windows 2000) and continue forward with the design.

Topology Maps

To begin your design, you should have a topology map of your network. No Systems or Network Engineer doing an implementation this important (and somewhat complicated) should be without network documentation. If you don't have it, you either need to get it from another department or create it yourself. You can use anything from paper to MS Paint to something as hi-tech as Visio 2000. Next, you'll want to plan out your server's initial readiness by going through some preparation work on what you'll need to configure this NLB cluster properly. You can see an example of this in Figure 2-14.

Initial NLB Planning and Readiness Assessment

Now that you've designed your network load-balanced solution into the current infrastructure, let's look at some of the preplan requirements you'll need to address before the actual roll out. First, you want to design the use of two network cards in each node. You can only use one, but with the demand you'll be placing on each server (you want this to be as fast as possible) and the price of NICs today, it's almost silly not to set up a dual-homed server. You can get a top-of-the-line NIC card for fewer than $100. Your private Heartbeat network can run on the second grouping of NICs and increase your performance. You'll also want to design the modes to be Unicast mode. We'll discuss all the configurations later as we walk through the installation and configuration of NLB but, before we do that, let's design the cluster first, so you know why to configure the cluster a certain way.

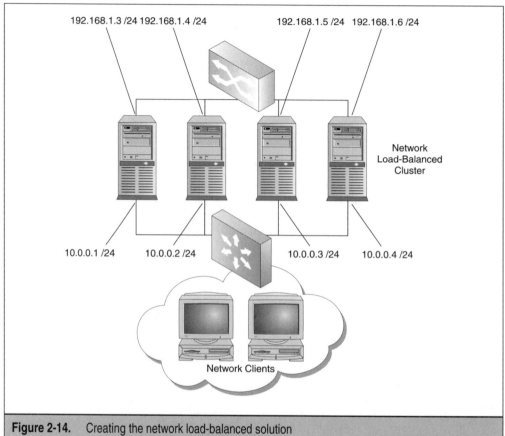

Figure 2-14. Creating the network load-balanced solution

As with MSCS, you also want to have fast access to your NLB nodes. You want to configure 100 Mbps full-duplex access on all network interfaces and, if possible, Gigabit Ethernet. You also want to use network switches where applicable (Cisco is my preferred brand). We'll discuss where you might even want to use a hub, so make sure you read this entire section before buying your network hardware.

At the end of this NLB section, I offer ways to get around known problems with NLB and Cisco switch flooding, so when all these items are mentioned, don't worry about them not being fully explained. This, of course, is the design stage. Make sure you plan for all your NLB nodes to do *only* this function. You don't want these servers tied up with other services that aren't needed. You'll install a service like IIS on it, but limit the services only to what is needed for the cluster. You also only want to configure TCP/IP for each node. Never bind any other protocol to the NIC when implementing this type of solution: TCP/IP bound to the NIC only.

Make sure that if you plan on using Port Rules, they're set for all nodes and are identical. You also want to work with your Security Analyst, Firewall Administrator, or Network Engineer to make sure you know what ports you can use with NLB. We'll configure them later, but you should be aware in preimplementation that you also need to be working with ports. Again, you might need to get other team members involved if you don't have access to getting a block of IP addresses. Planning the usage of IP addressing before the implementation is important. I saw one instance where a client ran out of IPs for the block and had to re-subnet the address to allocate more. You don't ever want to go through this on a production implementation. The IPs you receive will be static and subnetted correctly not using network or broadcasting addresses and not in a DHCP scope. You can't use DHCP for this implementation. Last, you must be using Windows 2000 Advanced Server or the network load-balancing driver won't show up. This changes if you implement Application Center 2000, which allows for the load balancing of Windows 2000 Server Edition, which is discussed in Chapter 6.

Load-Balancing System Requirements

Lets look at what you need for your systems. If you plan out your servers, I would recommend getting a vendor involved to help design what hardware solution you'd need. This isn't as strict as setting up MSCS because you don't have that shared SCSI bus. You can get high-powered servers to do the job and they won't need to share a central storage device.

For this example, we'll be load balancing two servers. In later chapters, this number will grow as we use Application Center 2000. To learn the software installation and configuration, though, we can keep it simple for now. A nice feature with NLB is this: You can add nodes at any time to reduce the load on the other servers. Network load-balancing system requirements needed for your design are the same as small hardware disk drive requirements.

You don't need a lot of space to implement NLB. The service and driver only use about 1MB of space. Your memory requirements are going to vary. I would install what you needed for Windows 2000 (as discussed earlier in this chapter, you would want at least 256MB of RAM on a production system as your minimum and always factor in what your applications will use). IIS uses a lot of memory because it stays memory-resident to increase speed for web site requests. You might want to look at the last chapter to learn how to use system monitor and how to baseline a test system to get accurate numbers on how much RAM you need.

In the last chapter, we also look at using stress test tools in a lab environment to simulate load on your NLB cluster. Other requirements are focused on the network hardware you're implementing the NLB cluster with. If you use a network router for clients to access your NLB solution, you must plan not only for the cluster to operate in Multicast mode (explained later in the section called, "Multicast Support"), but also make sure you plan for the purchase of a router that can take an ARP reply with two different MAC addresses. The two addresses come from the need for the NLB cluster to have one MAC address in the actual data payload and one MAC address in the header. If your router doesn't allot for this functionality, you can add an ARP entry statically within the router you're using. If you use a Cisco router, you'll probably need to add an entry because the router will have a problem resolving a unicast IP to a multicast MAC address. In most cases, if you ever have a problem with this design, by working with Cisco and the TAC (Technical Assistance Center) **www.cisco.com/TAC**, you can have your problems resolved rather quickly. They can help you pick out the hardware you need, the configurations you need to adjust, or show you what to use that's already in your infrastructure. Now that you have what you need, let's install the service.

NLB SOFTWARE ROLLOUT

In this section, I assume you've installed your Windows 2000 Advanced Server on both NLB servers. If so, you'll install NLB by enabling the NLB driver WLBS.SYS on your systems by going to your Network Properties sheet. Go to your Control Panel and select Network and Dialup Connections. Within this dialog box, you find your Local Area Connections. I hope you still have them marked from the last section but, if you don't, go back through the section on clustering in this chapter to learn how to name your connections and identify which ones are which. Then open the Public Local Area Connection by right-clicking it and selecting Properties. In the next illustration, you can see the Local Area Connection Properties sheet. In this dialog box, there's one item of interest to configuring NLB, which is the unchecked Network Load Balancing option within the components section. Checking this box and clicking OK loads the driver: Now you have a NLB server. Easy, right? Well, we haven't configured anything yet; we've only enabled the service to be used. You should still have this property sheet open, so if you clicked OK, you can backtrack and reopen to this General tab once again.

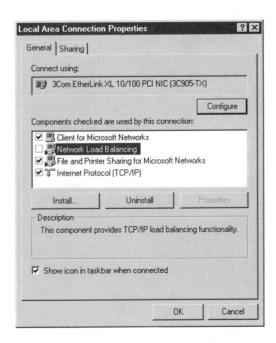

If you open this section and do *not* see the NLB service in the components section, you might have some issues you aren't aware of. If you didn't follow predesign beforehand, you could be using Windows 2000 Server, which doesn't carry the service. You need Windows 2000 Server in its advanced form. If you do have Windows 2000 Advanced Server, you might not have the service installed.

To install the service, click the Install button located on the Network Properties sheet. Then, click Service when you're given the option to select a service. Click add, and then select Network Load Balancing. Once you click OK, the service should appear. Make sure you clicked the check box to enable it. If a check appears in the box then, when you select the service, the Properties button within the Network Properties sheet becomes available. Once you select the Properties button, you're shown a new dialog box with three tabs. I highlight them here, but I describe them in depth in the next sections of this chapter. When you open this new Property sheet, you see three tabs, all of which are configured to allow NLB to work. Although, up to now, the installation has been simplistic, don't be fooled. To get a NLB cluster running properly and optimized isn't as small a task as installing the basics of this service. In the dialog box, you'll be able to configure Cluster Parameters, Host Parameters, and Port Rules.

Installation and Configuration

First, look at the tabs on the top of the NLB Properties sheet, as seen in the following illustration. You can see many items to configure for the success of your NLB cluster. You have the Cluster Parameters, which enable you to specify settings and parameters for the entire cluster. The Host Parameters tab enables you to specify settings that apply to a specific host. The Port Rule tab lets you specify the Port Rules used for your NLB cluster. These settings enable you to control how your NLB cluster will function under load. Let's look at them all in greater detail.

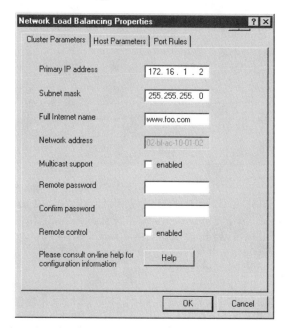

Configuring Cluster Parameter

The first tab you encounter is Cluster Parameters. As mentioned, this tab's settings let you make settings for the entire cluster. You learn how to configure an IP address for cluster use, its mask, or a full Internet domain name, how to enable multicasting instead of unicasting, and how to configure remote access, if needed. Let's take one parameter at a time.

Cluster's IP Addressing and Internet Domain Name

You'll add an IP address (like 172.161.2 or 10.0.0.10) here, which will denote the virtual IP (VIP) address, which is used for the entire NLB cluster. Look at Figure 2-15 to see where this would be used.

The VIP is something you need to set identically without error for every node in the NLB cluster. An error will cause the service of high-availability to become low-availability. This node will be unable to participate properly in the cluster. This address also needs to be something you can resolve via DNS to the full Internet name you place in the fields below the IP address. Enter the subnet mask for the IP you selected. For this exercise, I'm using a 24-bit mask, but you can use whatever you selected for the IP range you blocked off. Make sure the DNS name you're using is resolvable or you'll experience problems with your NLB clusters functionality.

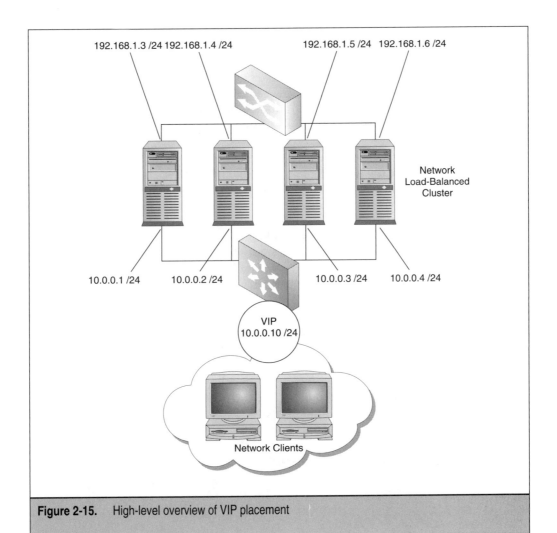

Figure 2-15. High-level overview of VIP placement

Multicast Support

This is, by far, the most confusing of all configurations you can make for a NLB cluster. You need to think about many factors if you enable multicast support.

First, let's quickly review the difference among your three main functions: broadcast, unicast, and multicast. For *broadcasting,* a node will send a request to every node it can reach with an address set to all 1's in binary or a 255.255.255.255 address in decimal. If a broadcast is used, you can expect every node to receive a packet you transmit whether or not it was meant for them. A *unicast* is a point-to-point transmission between two nodes. *Uni,* or *one* is a transmission meant for a single node. When you implement multicasting, you're allowing a transmission of data to an addressable "group," based on a specific class of addressing. This way, you can get your message to a group of listening nodes, instead of inundating the entire segment with a broadcast.

When you configure this parameter, you need to take into account the MAC address to be used for your NLB cluster. When you enable this parameter, it allows the NLB service to change the cluster node's MAC address into a multicast-based MAC address. This parameter makes sure your primary IP address resolves this multicast MAC via ARP.

The configuration is quite simple until you have to deal with a router connection that might not automatically allow for this conversion. I mentioned before what you need to do, depending on what router you have. If you can't find the configuration details, call your router vendor's support line for some support to get the ARP feature configured properly.

The only problem you might have is deciding to use an old NIC (I mentioned in presales design to order only the newest and best NICs because they're cheap) and the NIC doesn't allow you the functionality for having the MAC address modified against the NLB multicasting function. This will be hard to determine and should be thought of as a last ditch guess on what a problem is by updating the vendor's drivers, or buying and installing a newer NIC card. To play it safe, get new NICs and check the documentation for possible incompatibilities against NLB and multicast support.

When configuring NLB, you need to understand that you can't mix and match your multicast and unicast nodes. If you plan to add more nodes in the future, now is a good time to jot down all your settings for documentation. I make a template for work and, when the need arises to add nodes, I look at the Word template to cover the settings that must be identical for the newly added nodes. Don't mix the multicast and unicast option because, if you do, the cluster won't operate correctly.

Remote Control and Remote Password

Moving down on the Properties sheet, you can see an option to set a Remote Control option and password. When you use the Remote Control option, you're using the Windows Load Balancing Service (WLBS) executable program called wlbs.exe. This functionality is disabled by default because the use of this function is dangerous, unless it's protected properly. The password is sent over the wire in cleartext and is a security risk when used.

As stated earlier in the chapter, there are ways to create strong passwords and this is another password you'd want to make hard to guess or crack. If you do enable this function, you'll also need to know that any router access list or firewall Port Rule needs to allow UDP ports 1717 and 2504 through. This is what the remote control service uses to communicate with. To change the password, you can use the wlbs.exe command line tool, and then use the /PASSW switch to change the passwords. As a recommendation, I wouldn't use this at all. Instead, use either terminal services or go to the server console for security reasons.

Configuring Host Parameters

We just finished working on the actual cluster parameters and those settings were for the entire cluster. Because they're for the entire cluster, you might wonder where you would set the individual host parameters. Set those up by using the Host Parameters tab, as seen in the next illustration.

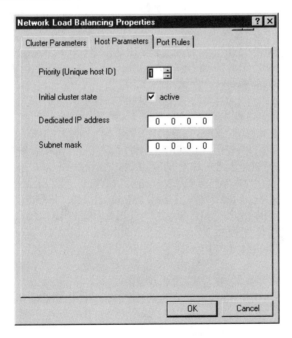

Let's look at each setting and what each one does for the host you're configuring.

Priority (ID)

Priority or unique host ID is your first configurable setting. This parameter enables you to change this node's priority for handling incoming traffic. A priority of 1 is the highest available priority and this is how they are all set by default to make them all equal.

If you want to change this ID, you would have to do a little detective work on your servers. Say you have a four-node NLB cluster, and you have three lower-quality servers and one high-quality server with better hardware that handles traffic faster. You can make this better server a priority of 1 and make the others lower priorities to handle less traffic. You want to adjust this for all your NLB cluster nodes to make them all unique within your cluster.

Again, do some detective work and see what host is better than the others when setting priority IDs. Also, you want to read the last chapter in the book to learn the finer art of true analysis and detective work, so you can accurately make that judgment call on which node is higher quality than the others.

When configuring IDs, make sure you don't add a new node to the cluster (which most companies do to decrease the load as needed) without first making the newly added node a unique priority ID. This is (again) where documentation won't fail you. Documentation and design planning are keys to the success of any production cluster. If you do make the mistake of adding a node with the same ID, the node won't be accepted into the NLB cluster. You can find this problem occurring (and recorded) within the Windows event log. You'll want to check the Event Viewer constantly within the early stages of configuration to make sure you have all the bugs and configuration mistakes corrected. Then, you won't have to backtrack too far when something doesn't work.

Initial State

The *Initial Cluster State* tab is where you can instruct your clustered node to start NLB-based services upon bootup of the system. If initial state is turned off (check box empty), then you'll have to start the nodes manually from the command line. By typing **wlbs stop** and/or **wlbs start** at the command prompt, you can start and stop the NLB services. At the end for this section, I list more wlbs commands but, for now, you can easily use these. If you get an error, make sure you have either administrative privileges or that you installed the NLB services in the network Properties sheet. Leave this checked unless you have a specific reason for altering it.

Dedicated IP Address and Subnet Mask

When you configure the NLB node's dedicated IP address and subnet mask, you're essentially configuring the uniqueness of the node against the entire cluster for which you set an IP address within the Cluster Parameters tab. This IP address (and mask) is used to address each node individually within the entire cluster. Normally, this address is the original one assigned to the node within the TCP/IP protocol properties. You don't want to make this the same IP address as the actual Cluster Address. That is why it's important to look at the design phase of the project where you pick out and assign your IP addresses before you even install the service. It makes this part of the implementation easier to do, less confusing, and even less prone to error or mistake. Make sure you assign IP addresses, subnet makes, and default gateways and other pertinent IP addressing information to your nodes correctly or communication won't take place. If you select the IP address you placed in the TCP/IP properties here in the dedicated address field, make sure the IP addresses are the same in both areas. Finally, as with any operations and services configured up until now, you can't use DHCP and you must provide a static IP address for this service to function properly.

Configuring the Port Rules Tab

One of the greatest features with NLB clustering is the use of Port Rules. A *port* is what TCP/IP uses for services-based communication. If you have to connect to a web server hosting a web site, you'll most likely (by default) attach via port 80. This can be changed but, by default, it's via 80. The IANA, found at **www.iana.org**, is the keeper of such port numbers for your review. The port numbers are divided into three ranges: the Well Known Ports, the Registered Ports, and the Dynamic and/or Private Ports. The System (Well-Known) Ports are those from 0 through 1023. The User Registered Ports are those from 1024 through 49151. The Dynamic and/or Private Ports are those from 49152 through 65535. There are 65,535 of them and 0–1023 (the first 1,024) are earmarked for commonly used specific services, such as SMTP (port 25) and HTTP (port 80).

The combined use of a TCP/IP address and a port creates a socket connection between nodes. For example, if you want to connect to a web server using HTTP and the web server's IP address is 10.1.1.10, you would enter the DNS name that resolves to that IP address or enter **http://10.1.1.10**. Because port 80 is well known (and hasn't been altered), you should immediately connect to the web server via port 80. The ports can, however, be altered. If the port is changed, say, to port 8080, then you need to create a socket connection manually by specifying the port. You could then enter the following to make a connection with the web server: http://10.1.1.10:8080. Although you needn't know all this for setting up this feature, I hope this helps you understand what a port is. Next, you learn how to configure rules for these ports and their use with the NLB Port Rules Parameters tab.

Port Rules, Port Range, and Protocols

To configure Port Rules, you need to click the Port Rule tab within the Network Load Balancing Properties sheet. You'll automatically recognize the port range explained in the previous section.

You can configure all ports for both Transport Layer protocols UDP and TCP. (You can duplicate ports if they're for the same protocol. Using a different transport protocol, such as TCP or UDP, for instance, DNS will use port 53 for both TCP and UDP, but Zone Transfer will only go over the TCP 53 port.)

The reason for setting up these Port Rules is so you can instruct how each node in the cluster will respond to and handle each protocol-based port. This allows for great amounts of flexibility if you want to load balance HTTP traffic specifically to a web server. In the following illustration, you can see the Port Range allowable for this NLB cluster node and which Transport Layer protocol will differentiate the ports across one of them if not both.

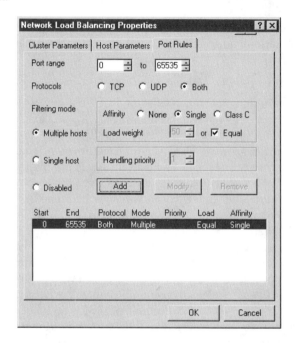

Within the Port Rules section, you can configure a Filtering mode for your network traffic. You can set the filtering mode in three ways: Multiple hosts, Single host, and Disabled. Each of these options is explained in greater detail in following sections.

When configuring the Port Rules tab, be aware of a few items that will either spell success or defeat of your NLB cluster implementation. When you configure the port numbers and rules for your NLB cluster, make sure they're exactly the same for each node in the cluster. If you don't set this exactly right, when you try to add a node to the NLB cluster with a different set of rules, it won't become part of the NLB cluster. You'll notice this doesn't work because we already discussed how frequently I want you to check the Event Viewer after making any changes on the cluster or its nodes. In the Event Viewer, you find entries of the node's failure to join the cluster because it isn't set properly. Make certain the rules entered on each node have matching ranges, protocols, and modes. Now, in the next and final sections of working with this property sheet, you learn all the ways you can configure your filtering modes.

Filtering Mode

As mentioned, you have three modes and, we look at them all in detail here. With *multiple hosts,* you can allow multiple nodes in the NLB cluster to handle network data traffic in a specific way. It filters across multiple nodes, which allows for fault tolerance and the adjustments in load weight across each node. You can specify different weights per node or have the weight equally set across them all.

If you set your filtering on *single host,* you're telling your node you want it to handle network traffic distributed across the NLB cluster based on its Priority ID. The Priority ID (Handling Priority) is adjustable and closely resembles the Priority ID we set within the Host parameters.

You can also set the filtering to disabled. Setting your node to *disabled* means all network traffic coming to that node (and set for the associated Port Rule) is blocked. To build a Port Rule, modify the setting with one of the three filtering modes, and then click the Add button on the bottom of the Properties sheet. You can modify and remove a Port Rule at anytime within the Properties sheet. If you don't click Add after you adjust the Port Rule, the new setting won't take effect.

Client Affinity: None, Single, and Class C

Affinity, the natural drawing of services to one node over another, is set by selecting Single, Class C, or None. Affinity settings exist because, in today's web culture, business is done over the Internet with millions of customers coming to your web sites (or better yet, e-commerce sites) to shop and do business with you.

A shopper enters a credit card number or wants to make a transaction with your web server. The hope is that you're using highly available architecture. If not, what happens when the server has a hiccup (the server locks up, and so forth), crashes, or if there's a flapping WAN route from your shopper to the server? How does that session pick back up?

Session state is what's kept when shopping, so when you do have these common problems, ways exist to adjust how the client's session state (held with cookies) is handled based on the following settings.

If you set your client affinity to single, then you're selecting the option to have many client requests come to the same clustered node. If you put a web site on a server with an IP address of 220.1.1.1 /24 and want your clients to access the same node each time, then you would set a single affinity.

This would only have an affinity for a single IP address, but what if you want to have multiple web sites with multiple IP addresses? You could then set your affinity to Class C. With Class C affinity, you can set affinity to a class of addresses, so you can specify different IP addresses and affinity will be drawn to any node in that class range, instead of a single IP address.

This is especially helpful when you use proxy servers that might cause the appearance of requests coming from different computers that could disrupt the network load-balancing solution. If this is the case, you also need to make this part of your design, hence, the calling for a topology map and an overview of your infrastructure when preparing the NLB design. Make sure the proxy server(s) are in the same Class C subnet.

Finally, if you set your affinity to None, then you won't use client-based affinity at all. The recommendation is that you use single, unless the need arises to use Class C. Be aware that Class C affinity on an intranet can cripple a NLB machine because all requests will come from the same Class C subnet.

Load Weight and Equal Load Distribution

Load weight is set within the Multiple Hosts Filtering mode. After you decide on what affinity setting you want to use, you can set the load weight if you need it to be equally distributed or skewed differently across nodes in the NLB cluster.

You can either set the load weight to equal (explained in a moment) or to a numerical range you select. You can set the load from 0 to 100. If you select 0, you disable the node from handling any traffic, so don't set it to 0.

The only thing that's confusing about setting the load is you don't have to set it equally across the nodes to equal 100 percent. If you had four nodes, you might be apt to set them all at 25 percent. What would you do if you then added another node to the cluster? Would you reset them all to balance out to 100 percent? The nodes will handle their fraction of the load based on the percentage you set, so each of them will handle 25 percent of the whole load.

This is a little confusing, but if you start setting this, then you'll have to understand the specifics on what to do. For this example, you can leave it to equal and that's usually the best way to set it. When you set the load to equal by checking the box in the Property Sheet, you're essentially saying that all hosts (multiple hosts) will handle an equal amount of traffic that makes up the whole.

If you set the single host option, then you only have one parameter you can adjust, which is the Handling priority. When you create a Port Rule, you'll want to adjust this single node on how to handle it. When you set the handling priority to the highest available handle (which is 1), the node with the highest handle will handle all the traffic associated for this Port Rule. For this reason, you must set each ID to be unique because another node in your cluster could have a different Port Rule, which you want to set, and it would require a different handling ID number to function.

Last, you can disable filtering. This is useful only if you want to block traffic, which would essentially make the server into a port firewall. This isn't recommended unless, for some reason, you want to start blocking incoming traffic on a NLB cluster node.

If you make a mistake on any of the previously mentioned settings, there's a good chance that newly added nodes won't be allowed to participate. The only way to get clues on why this is so would be in the Event Viewer.

WINDOWS 2000 ADVANCED SERVER NLB INSTALLATION AND ADVANCED SETTINGS

Now, you have all the power you need to configure network load balancing with a Windows 2000 Advanced Server solution. You know what hardware you need, what to install, how to install it, and all the configuration settings needed to control your NLB cluster. There are, however, some tricks of the trade and tips that can make your life much easier when rolling out your solution. In this section of the chapter, we look at problems you might have with network switches when using NLB, why clustering could appear to be slow, and some advanced configurations.

NLB Cluster Performance Is Slow

Consider the following nightmare: You sell your management team on a faster solution and it slows it down. Although I've had many experiences with clustering and load-balancing solutions, my favorite is this one. I've seen this many times where resources have been made "highly available" and almost turned into a denial of service! This happens, so let's look at some of the most common problems with why NLB might slow your servers or services down.

Again, the last chapter of this book teaches you the finer details of network and performance analysis, so you can tweak your solutions and make them quicker, more reliable, and put them on an even higher level of availability. Here, we cover some configuration-based issues that can slow down your solution.

With NLB, there's a common problem when using network switches. Because NLB operates by sharing a single IP address—the VIP—there's a phenomenon of unicast flooding on a network switch. This is by no means the fault of either the NLB service or the switch because it's expected behavior.

You might ask why this is such a big deal because a switch should be able to handle massive amounts of traffic. While that assumption is correct, not all switches can handle such a flood. This can be so bad it has been known to cause Spanning Tree (STP) Problems. Because the flooding was bad, the switch was dropping updates coming from other switches via Bridge Protocol Data Units (BPDUs).

When the requests for the VIP come in, the first one that comes across the switch is learned and the MAC-to-switch port table is kept in memory. If this switch learns the cluster's MAC addresses and maps it in memory to one of its designated ports, the load-balancing service can't balance traffic correctly. Ways exist to prevent these problems, which we outline in the next section.

MAC Source Configuration

If you set the settings to unicast, you can mask the Source MAC address. Masking the cluster MAC Address forces the NLB cluster nodes to use a "dummy" MAC address while they send data requests through the switch. The way this works is by tricking the switch into mapping the fake MAC to a port, while sending the frame to all ports on the switch to which they're destined to go. When configuring this workaround in Unicast mode, open the Registry Editor (Regedit.exe) and navigate to the following Registry key:

HKEY_LOCAL_MACHINE\SYSTEM\CurrentControlSet\Services\WLBS\
Parameters

You can change a value called the MaskSourceMAC, as seen in the next illustration.

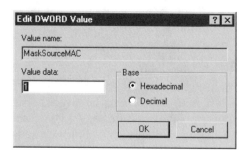

When you use unicast, and your NLB host is plugged into a switch, keep the MaskSourceMAC registry value set to 1, which is the default. If you decide you want to use a hub, then you can change it to 0 on all nodes.

So why use a hub? A hub won't function on Layer 2 and memorize MAC addresses. A hub is basically a multiport repeater that regenerates signals and forwards them to all ports. If you then uplink this hub to a single switch port, you'll only worry about the switch memorizing the hub uplink and the MAC addresses from the hub.

Not to confuse you, but you must also be aware of which NIC card you're uplinking to the hub or switch. If you remember our original design, we were to have all the primary public NICs, which take client requests on one segment, and then all the Internode traffic will be on a private network segment. You can connect all the cluster network adapters to the hub you have uplinked to the switch. You can then connect all the other adapters to another switch, a separate VLAN, or another hub. Because this NLB solution is scalable up to 32 nodes, you won't be using a crossover cable, which you might have used when configuring MSCS.

If you do all the previously mentioned steps, you have a good chance at eliminating port flooding. One item you might notice is the hub could be a bottleneck if you haven't appropriately purchased what you need in terms of speed: Make sure it's a 10/100 hub if you're using Fast Ethernet or you could bottleneck your servers on the hub.

Router ARP Configuration

Adjusting the Source MAC in your configuration will lead to a few different problems from what you configured when using the Unicast option. You might also find you could have potential communication problems when you "dummy" the MAC, so as mentioned much earlier in the chapter, you'll want to add a static ARP entry in the router if you find that router can't communicate properly with the cluster using a VIP. The router will want to do an ARP to find the cluster-based VIP's MAC address. If you mask the source MAC address, as you learned to do in the last section, you might confuse the router, so adding the static ARP command will enable you to do that. To add a static ARP command to a Cisco Router, enter the following:

```
router#configure terminal
router(config)# arp 10.0.0.1 0070.b3cd.0343
```

The syntax is as seen in the following:

```
arp ip-address mac-address
```

Make sure you save your configuration with a Write Terminal command.

Virtual Network Adapter Confusion

If you're an old timer who has experience setting up clusters (or trying to) with Windows NT 4.0 Enterprise Edition, then you might think your configuration isn't correct because there's no virtual adapter made with Windows 2000 Advanced Server. If you configure Microsoft Windows 2000 Advanced Server NLB service, you won't see the creation of a virtual adapter within the network properties or in the Network Connections dialog box. NT made a WLBS Virtual NIC entry, so don't get thrown off if you don't see it.

Exam Fundamentals

If you decide to take some of the Microsoft Certified Professional Exams to obtain your MCP or MCSE, you'll find that Microsoft offers quite a few for you. In this book, I take the liberty of adding some sections toward the end of the chapter to highlight areas for you to study. Although this isn't a study guide (it's more of a handbook for design and implementation), I suspect some readers will either want to take the exam or might be stimulated to take one of the exams from reading this book. In that case, it would be a waste not to offer at least a paragraph to you on what and where you should focus your studies. In each chapter, where applicable, I'll add a section at the end of the chapter where an exam topic might come into play.

In this chapter, we covered quite a few topics that can be found on the following two exams:

- Exam 70–223: Installing, Configuring, and Administering Microsoft Clustering Services by Using Microsoft Windows 2000 Advanced Server
- Exam 70–226: Designing Highly Available Web Solutions with Microsoft Windows 2000 Server Technologies

- Exam 70–232: Implementing and Maintaining Highly Available Web Solutions with Microsoft Windows 2000 Server Technologies and Microsoft Application Center 2000

Both exams cover clustering in depth. For Exam 70–223, be prepared to know nearly everything in the chapter to include the installation and configuration of the MSCS and NLB solutions. You're tested in great detail on preparation and implementation of these services. For Exam 70–226, you must incorporate *all* chapters in this book and use an overall design approach to study. This was the hardest Microsoft exam I've ever taken because the amount of information you needed to remember (even more than contained in this book) all revolved around proper design and implementation of all high-availability services. This chapter can help prepare you for both of them. Exam 70–232: Implementing and Maintaining Highly Available Web Solutions with Microsoft Windows 2000 Server Technologies and Microsoft Application Center 2000 is another exam covered in this book, but not until we get to the chapters that focus on Application Center 2000. I feel this exam was fair in its content, which only revolves around the Application Center 2000 product, but concepts such as affinity and load balancing are covered. If you want to prepare, most of this chapter (relating to NLB) can help you get ready for it.

CONCLUSION

Congratulations! You've just learned how to design, plan out, configure, and implement both Windows 2000 Clustering Services (MSCS) and Windows 2000 load-balancing services (NLB or WLBS) with ease. Although you're at the end of this chapter, you'll continue to build on your theories and discuss even more advanced topics as you move along into Windows Server 2003 cluster and load balancing, as well as other types of high-availability solutions.

The most important thing I expect you to get out of this chapter is the fundamentals and the methodology of determining what's unique to your environment. No book could be written to cater to any one reader because, as we all know (or should know), each network is different and it isn't easy to add new functionality and solutions to old networks. Most networks are poorly documented and in need of serious upgrades. Some aren't and these are state-of-the-art. One thing is contiguous about all these different networks: they all need to be up all the time when clients need resources from them.

This chapter showed you options you have and things to think about when trying to create that Highly Available network solution. In upcoming chapters, you look at implementing actual system and network services of one the clusters to include WINS, and Server 2003 enterprise servers like SQL Server 2000. This chapter should have been the framework for those upcoming chapters. In the next chapter, I show the transition to Server 2003 and we'll cluster and load balance Server 2003 as well.

CHAPTER 3

Designing a Clustered Solution with Windows Server 2003

In this chapter, you walk through the start-to-finish process of designing, installing, and configuring all aspects of a Windows Server 2003 Enterprise Clustered solution in a failover design. The cluster will contain two nodes, both running Windows Server 2003 Enterprise edition. Just as in the last chapter, the nodes are set in an Active/ Passive configuration. In this chapter, however, you look at upgrading the previous cluster you created in Chapter 2. This type of upgrade comes in the form of a *rolling upgrade,* which is a fully functional cluster that's operational and you upgrade it completely without disrupting your clients. A rolling upgrade is effective and we discuss it in great detail within the chapter. With the rolling upgrade, your cluster should already be configured from the last chapter, so we'll look at the planning and design for the upgrade, highlight the major differences between configuring Windows Server 2003 in a Highly Available solution, and then perform the upgrade. After performing the upgrade, we'll look at rolling out Windows Server 2003 in a clustered solution from scratch—without the upgrade process. Last, we look at the design and implementation of rolling out a Windows Server 2003 highly available NLB or network load balanced solution. In this chapter, you'll find many of the same ideas discussed in Chapters 1 and 2, but contoured to a solution using Microsoft's new flagship operating system (OS): Windows Server 2003.

WINDOWS SERVER 2003 ROLLING UPGRADE

In this section, you learn how to perform a rolling upgrade. This can save you time and will keep your clients up and running, and connected to resources while you perform the upgrade. Why not schedule an outage and simply upgrade the servers in the allotted time frame? While this might seem most logical, remember, the whole point of clustering is high availability. If you schedule an outage, then you won't be able to provide resources to clients. How can you achieve 99.999 percent uptime if your servers are down? You can't and that's why the rolling upgrade exists. A rolling upgrade can upgrade your servers with a new service pack level (most common) or it can upgrade the entire OS to something new, which we discuss next.

Planning a Rolling Upgrade with Management

A rolling upgrade must be planned carefully before you do it. If not, you jeopardize the smooth functioning of your production systems. Planning, research, testing, and a solid back-out plan are highly advisable. A *back-out plan* is a detailed list of steps that will bring you back to the original system state befopre any changes were made. When performing any maintenance on systems, you should always follow this methodology anyway. It gives you reassurance (your management team will also be reassured) in performing high-level maintenance routines on large scale production environments. In this section, you learn about the planning stage for the upgrade.

Reasons for Upgrade

When performing a rolling upgrade, you're taking a functional system that has served you well and changing it to something different. To plan for this change, you should have the new product you're moving to on a test system, so you can learn the interface, the differences, and how to smoothly execute the same functions you were performing on the old systems. Most often, you'll want to have a team meeting with management to discuss "why" you're going to the new platform in the first place. Remember, you aren't rolling out a new cluster solution from scratch. You're upgrading the current one, so you'll want a good reason to perform this upgrade. We discuss all the benefits you get from moving to Windows Server 2003 later in the chapter, but I'll mention one now. We perform the rolling upgrade to take advantage of Windows Server 2003. This is because the new Server 2003 maximum-supported cluster size has been increased from two nodes in Windows 2000 Advanced Server to eight nodes in Windows Server 2003. Your upper management has expressed a need to scale out the current clustered solution to support more traffic-based requests from the clients because they're acquiring a new company and roughly 1,000 more clients will be accessing the current servers. Because you've baselined the servers (you learn about this in Chapter 8), you know a problem exists with the current solution at peak periods during the day. Adding more users could surely create a problem. You need to upgrade, but what's the best solution? You decide not to go with Datacenter Server for three reasons:

- Microsoft's newest platform will put you ahead of the end of life (EOL) support on Windows 2000

- Benefits added by Windows Server 2003 outweigh what's offered by Datacenter Server

- With Windows Server 2003, you can scale out to eight servers, an improvement over Datacenter, which is locked down to four servers, so you have a wider scaling range to work with

Let's look at the actual rolling upgrade plan, which is your biggest challenge. Later in the chapter, you see a design again but, for purposes of an upgrade, you need to make sure your new solution "fits" into your already designed solution of Windows Server 2003.

Other Reasons to Upgrade to Windows Server 2003

With Windows Server 2003, you get many new benefits that you might be interested in implementing. Look at Table 3-1 to view all the new options.

Now, you should have enough reasons to perform this upgrade or any upgrade for that matter. Be aware, though, because quite a few "gotchas" are along the way, which we'll expose!

Easy Setup and Configuration	The Cluster Service has been changed from the Windows 2000 Advanced Server and is preinstalled with Windows Server 2003. You can see that when you get ready to do a fresh cluster installation from scratch, you no longer need to install the Microsoft Cluster Services, which was necessary in Chapter 2. While configuring the Cluster Service, all defaults are used to get you up and running quickly. You can use Cluster Administrator at a later time to customize your cluster administration.
	Third-party software vendors now have access to the cluster-based open interface. This is a first for Microsoft toward working with vendors to make better solutions, especially Highly Available solutions.
Larger Clusters Now Supported	In Windows 2000 Advanced Server, you could only make two node clusters. Now you can make up to eight-node clusters in Windows Server 2003, which gives systems engineers more flexibility to scale out for more redundancy.
Integrates with Active Directory Service	Windows Server 2003, when used with clustering services, now has full active directory integration where the cluster becomes a computer object within the directory. This is a solution that benefits those who want to take advantage of delegation and Kerberos authentication.
64-Bit Architecture	Windows Server 2003 64-bit Edition has support for server clusters. You can use the extended architecture to take advantage of larger memory spaces.
	If you plan to move to 64-bit support, Windows Server 2003 only supports Fibre Channel to shared storage on your shared storage bus. Plan accordingly if you're going to move to Windows Server 2003 64-bit Edition and use clustering.
Increased Manageability	You can increase manageability with Windows Server 2003 with a new in-the-box tool called DiskPart (covered in depth in the upcoming section titled "DiskPart").
Easy Resource Configuration	Windows Server 2003 will allow configuration information replicated to other nodes like clustered printers and the Microsoft Distributed Transaction Coordinator (MSDTC).
	Also, Microsoft Message Queuing (MSMQ) has been enhanced to allow trigger support if needed while clustering SQL Server. We will look at clustering SQL Server later in Chapter 5.
Network Enhancements	Windows Server 2003 has highly increased failover protection in a few forms. The quorum ownership decision after failure is made much quicker in Server 2003.
	A multicast heartbeat is now used by default with a failover to unicast, if it's needed.
Improved Storage Capabilities	Windows Server 2003 storage capabilities have been enhanced in many areas. The distributed file system (DFS) now supports multiple standalone roots, independent root failover, and has outstanding support for multiple file shares on different machines to be aggregated into a common namespace. DFS now also has support for Active/Active-clustered configurations.
	If vendor support is available, you can add support for Storage Area Networks (SANs).
Streamlined Operation	Windows Server 2003 provides for better operation, such as rolling upgrade support (which we do in this chapter). You can also delete clustered resources without having to take the cluster offline. You can use cluster administrator as well as Cluster.exe. (We look at these commands in the following sections).

Table 3-1.   Viewing Windows Server 2003 Benefits

Easier Troubleshooting and Failure Recovery	Windows Server 2003 has made troubleshooting much easier though better logging facilities, as well as a new resource kit tool called *ClusDiag*, which enables you to compare logs and events on the cluster. *ClusterRecovery* is also a resource kit tool that enables you to rebuild a disk resource, as well as the cluster state.
New Cluster Topologies	Windows Server 2003 uses a *Majority Node Set*, which is a new quorum resource that uses something other than a shared disk as a quorum device. The nice design feature enables you to create topologies that don't have shared disks that need to span multisite configurations.
EFS Is Supported on Clustered Disks	Windows Server 2003 now supports the Encrypted File System (EFS) on clustered or shared disks.

Table 3-1.   Viewing Windows Server 2003 Benefits *(continued)*

Planning a Rolling Upgrade

In this section, you see the steps of performing a rolling upgrade and all the things you need to consider before you do the upgrade. Because every server platform you might work on can be different and so many factors exist, I invite you to practice this on your own lab systems as well. Rehearse the process first. You might also want to get training or have your staff get training in weak areas of this evolution. Many times, you could find you aren't up to speed on OS issues or certain aspects of new technology. Take risks in a lab that you would never take in real-life production. Be cautious and test, test, test!

Running a Test Lab

A test lab is simple to build. You can use the same test solution we're using in Chapter 2. If you recall, we set up a two-node cluster in an Active/Passive state. This is the same cluster we'll upgrade in the test lab: a two-node cluster with a shared storage device on a shared SCSI bus. You perform the rolling upgrade on this lab, so you know how to use Windows Server 2003 in your production environment, how to eliminate any compatibility problems you might encounter, and how to practice your arranged blackout plan if needed.

Planning with Your Vendors

As discussed in Chapter 2, you know about presales support wisely to help your planning and rollout stages—and this is where you should use it again. When you plan with your vendors, you can help to eliminate many problems before they occur in the test lab.

The four most common problems are the following:

- Vendor doesn't support Windows Server 2003
- Vendor hasn't certified Windows Server 2003
- Vendor hardware doesn't support Windows Server 2003
- Vendor software doesn't support Windows Server 2003

Each problem warrants its own explanation. If you purchased Server 2003 from Microsoft and you have a maintenance contract, you'll have the support of Microsoft. But, when Microsoft deems your problem a direct result of your hardware vendor, then what? Make sure your hardware vendors support the new OS completely by inquiring if its staff has certified and experienced Microsoft Certified Systems Engineers (MCSE) who can assist you with this upgrade.

Make sure your vendor has certified Windows Server 2003 with its equipment. How annoying to hear an OS and software giant like Microsoft isn't certified to run on a hardware platform! Luckily for us, hardware vendors usually make sure Microsoft products are tested and certified first. You can find this out by looking on the vendor's web site and seeing if its products (hardware and software) and support are certified on Windows Server 2003.

Make sure your vendor software does run on and support Windows Server 2003. This takes the form of hardware drivers as well but, more important, check your vendor's management software that comes with servers. With some vendors, such as Dell and Compaq, you can use their proprietary management software to manage your server. Test that, too. Last, test every single application you'll run on your new Windows Server 2003 Cluster and make sure each one runs as advertised. Make sure the vendors also support and certify their applications, and you have a number to call when a bug or problem appears.

Saving Settings on Current Systems

Get a book, a spreadsheet, or any other type of information recording device and record every single setting you have on your servers that could get misconfigured or altered if a major meltdown occurs in the upgrade process and you can't get the server back online or—worse yet—the backup has a problem and you need to rebuild a server completely from scratch.

Make sure you have all the old software on hand in case you need to restore the old system completely to its original state from scratch (Table 3-2 describes information you should record in case of a disaster).

Disk Configuration	Open the Disk Management utility with the Computer Management MMC and record your volumes, names, sizes, volume types, file types, drive letter assignments—everything. If you need to re-create your disks, you'll need this information.
Computer Name	Make sure you have your computer name recorded for replacement when needed.
IP Addresses	You can record all your IP address information to include interfaces, and all services available like DNS and WINS.
Domain Information	Make sure you fully record all domain connection information. You might have multiple domains and you'll need to know which servers are authenticating to which domain controllers. Also, record the account used to connect the Cluster Service to the domain.
Local Administrative Password	Know all your password and local account information. If you write this down or store it on a server share, make sure it's secured, so no one can break into it and hack your servers with this information. You'll need it, however, when you need to re-create your servers.

Table 3-2. Information You Need to Record for a Disaster Scenario

Current Backups

Make sure you back up your system before you do the upgrade. Remember, the only way to know if a backup works is to do a sample restore and make sure you can get your data successfully. I also recommend you have two tapes and you store one off-site. Here are some tips to help you establish a backup plan:

- Develop backup and restore strategies with appropriate resources and personnel, and then test them.

- A good plan ensures you can quickly recover your data if it's lost.

- Give the responsibilities of backup and restore to a designated backup administrator.

- Back up an entire volume to prepare for the unlikely event of a disk failure. This lets you restore the entire volume in one operation.

- Back up the directory services database (Active Directory) to prevent the loss of user account and security information. This must be done locally.

- Keep two copies of the backup media. Keep one copy off-site.

- Perform a trial restoration at times to verify your files were properly backed up.

Your backup strategy will be tailored to your organization, but you must have one, *especially* if you're clustering and saving every piece of company data to a shared storage solution. Make sure you have a plan to back up and restore this data in an emergency. Also, make sure that your back up software is cluster friendly.

Software and Hardware Plan

You need to obtain any application patches. You'll also want to ensure that you have every piece of hardware checked out and drivers ready to go if the upgrade calls for it. Make sure your NICs are supported, as well as your input devices and anything you have attached to the servers.

As for Microsoft, make sure you also have its support. If you're upgrading a server and have to fall back to the original configuration of Windows 2000 Advanced Server, make certain you have disks, service packs, and drivers specific to Microsoft supported hardware on hand.

If you're upgrading a cluster that has a Server 2003 Solution on it, such as SQL 2000 or Exchange 2000, make sure you've thoroughly checked with Microsoft to make sure it's supported, service packed, and/or hot fixed, if needed. As a final reference, you'll always want to check the Hardware Compatibility List (HCL), but Windows Server 2003 is too new to have many, if any, listings.

The Back-Out Plan

Your back-out plan is all the ideas mentioned in this entire section that relate to a successful contingency plan in case of disaster. The person or department responsible for change management or disaster recovery generally handles a back-out plan. You might not be afforded the luxury of having this in your company. If you don't, then it's your responsibility to make sure you've thought of every possible problem and how to get back to a working solution if your upgrade doesn't work. You might want to find the answers to the following questions for your plan:

- What steps are you going to follow to change the system?
- What changes are you going to make to the system?
- What is your planned fallback routine?
- How will you know the upgrade or fallback has been a success?
- What were the reasons for failure?

Your back-out plan should detail changes you make to the system. If a change involves replacing an application that's incompatible with Window Server 2003, then record this in your back-out plan.

Your failback routine is simply a list of steps you'll perform to restore the system to its previous (working) state. If you were unsuccessful with a portion of the upgrade where you had a problem with basic upgrade installation, an example could be the following:

- If installation/upgrade doesn't work, then cancel upgrade and return to the previous installation of Windows 2000 Advanced Server.
- Check to make sure the installation program didn't make any changes to the system, check the event logs, and make sure no system files were changed.
- Plan to reinstall Service Pack 2 for Windows 2000.

How do you know if you had a successful upgrade? If you had a problem, you need to document when it occurred and why you think it occurred. Get in touch with a vendor or Microsoft if you believe the problem was on their end, and then document their replies and possible solutions.

Preparing Windows 2000 for Disaster

Make sure you know how to prepare your Windows 2000 Advanced Server for a possible disaster. You're going to be upgrading it and, if you aren't careful, you'll damage the original installation if you need to back out. Be cautious and follow these pointers to prepare your current systems for possible disaster.

When working with Windows 2000 Advanced Server, you have some options to help its recovery, if needed. Here's a brief overview of some of the most important things you'll either want to do or investigate further, depending on your organization's systems configurations.

To cover every detail of Windows 2000 disaster recovery could span an entire publication. Make sure you look even deeper into this if you're going to take this out of the lab and apply it to a production system. Let's review some items you might want to look at for the disaster recovery of Windows 2000 Advanced Server.

Windows Backup and ERD   Windows Backup (Figure 3-1) includes Backup and Restore Wizards, property sheets for media pools, and direct access to My Network Places via Active Directory.

Backup lets you perform the following tasks:

- Back up selected user files and folders located on your hard disk.

- Back up your computer's *System State,* which are the files central to system operation.

- Restore backed-up files and folders to your hard disk or to any other disk you can access.

- Schedule regular backups to keep your backed-up data current.

- Create an Emergency Repair Disk (ERD), which helps you repair your system if it becomes corrupted.

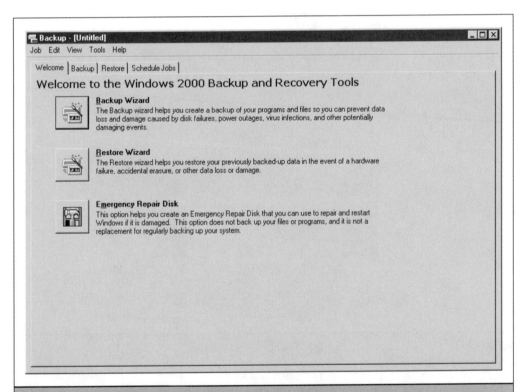

Figure 3-1.   Using NTBACKUP to back up your system before the upgrade

Detailed Step-by-Step Rolling Upgrade Plan

In this section, you look at the basics of what you must follow to finalize your planning stage. The next stop is the rolling upgrade. In the next few diagrams, you see the process to follow while trying to upgrade your servers from Windows 2000 Advanced Server to Windows Server 2003. This takes place in four steps:

Step 1 evaluates the initial cluster, as seen in Figure 3-2. This two-node cluster is currently running Windows 2000 Advanced Server across two nodes and uses a shared storage solution. This is also an Active/Passive two-node cluster. As you can see, a public network with clients is accessing the cluster you plan to upgrade.

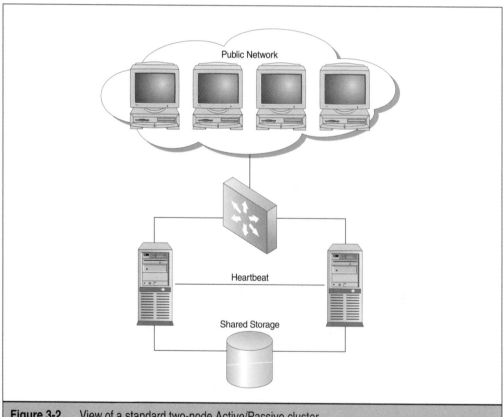

Figure 3-2.   View of a standard two-node Active/Passive cluster

Now look at Figure 3-3. The next step is to make sure the Active node is online and working properly. You want to perform the upgrade on the Passive node first, but you'll be taking it offline. You don't want a failover situation while you're performing the actual upgrade, so the plan is to 'down' the Passive Server, upgrade it, and then begin working on the Active node.

After you upgrade the Passive node to Windows Server 2003, you can then upgrade the Active node, as shown in Figure 3-4. The Active node is taken offline after you make the Passive node active. Your clients will only be disrupted as you move the Passive node to the active state. Once you make the Passive node active, you can 'down' the now Passive node and upgrade that to Windows Server 2003.

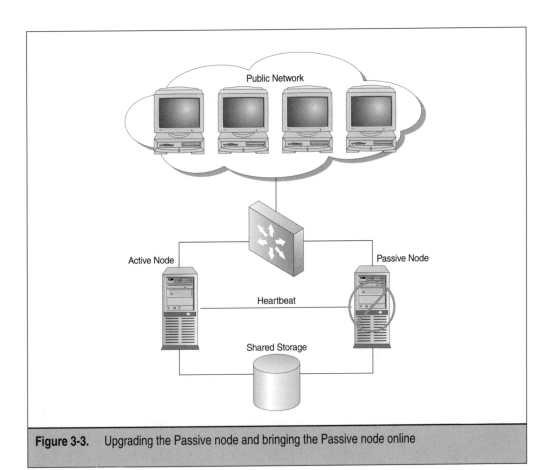

Figure 3-3.   Upgrading the Passive node and bringing the Passive node online

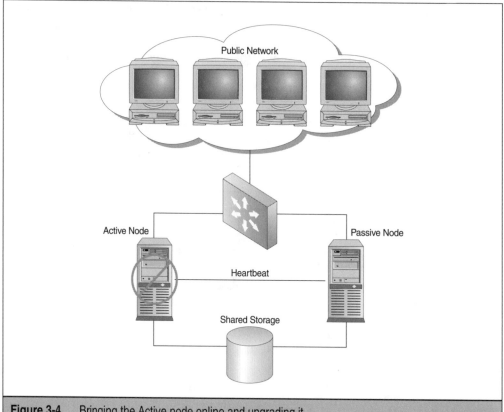

Figure 3-4. Bringing the Active node online and upgrading it

In Figure 3-5, you can see both servers are now running the Windows Server 2003 Enterprise Edition and are clustered in an Active/Passive configuration. Your network clients only had a slight disruption when you 'failed' the Active node over to the Passive node.

Rolling Upgrade Going Live

Now it's time to go live with the actual upgrade. Make sure everything is documented, so you can check off every step, and then check for problems during that step. This way, you can quickly identify where a failure occurred, if one occurred. In the appendix located in the back of this book, you'll find a sample project plan and checklist for doing a rolling upgrade from Windows 2000 Advanced Server to Windows Server 2003. Before we start, I want to discuss the ramifications of doing the rolling upgrade.

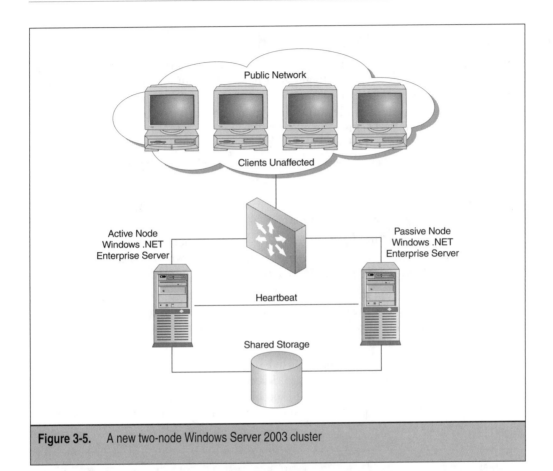

Figure 3-5.   A new two-node Windows Server 2003 cluster

A rolling upgrade isn't as disruptive as a regular upgrade, but remember, it requires the applications to be moved between nodes and does cause minimal disruption in services. When an application is moved from one node to another, it must be stopped. Once the application is stopped, Cluster Service moves all the resources the application uses—disks, Internet Protocol (IP) addresses, or network names—to another node, and restarts the application on another node. Any sessions between clients and the server application are cancelled during this process. Database transactions are aborted and file handles are invalidated. Client applications can retry and, eventually, reconnect and recover once the server application is restarted on the second node. While the impact could be minimal, it shouldn't be ignored.

Windows Server 2003 Rolling Upgrade

Now, we can do the rolling upgrade step-by-step. You've done all the proper planning and documentation. Now it's time to get your hands dirty. In this section, I'll number the installation steps, so you can follow the process easily.

This is a step-by-step upgrade and should get you from a two-node Windows 2000 Advanced Server two-node cluster to a Windows Server 2003 two-node cluster. Take advantage of trying this in a lab environment before applying it to your production Windows 2000 Server Cluster. You could run into issues concerning hardware or software application incompatibility. Let's begin.

1. TimeSync the nodes with the domain controller. Do this by going to each node and applying the Net Time command, as seen in Figure 3-6.

2. To complete the TimeSync, go to Start | Run, and then type **cmd** in the Run dialog box. You can also use the entire string found when you use the time command: *net time help: Net time /domain:<your domain> /set*

3. Any resources you might have must be brought offline. You can do this in multiple ways, but the easiest way with Server 2003 is to bring resources offline. Your clients will experience an outage to the resources when you do this, so be prepared.

4. Begin the upgrade on the first Passive node. Put the Windows Server 2003 disk in and run the installation program. Select upgrade and run through all the upgrade steps. In the lab, this worked like a charm on both nodes, so you shouldn't have any problems. Take step-by-step notes anyway, just in case.

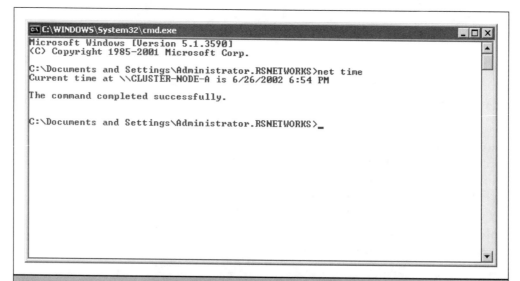

Figure 3-6.   Viewing the Net Time command in the command prompt

5. After you upgrade the Passive node to Windows Server 2003, then proceed to upgrade the Active node. The Active node is taken offline after you make the Passive node active. Your clients will only be disrupted as you move the Passive node to the active state. Once you make it active, then you can down the now Passive node and upgrade that to Windows Server 2003.

6. Both servers are now fully upgraded to Windows Server 2003. You have much more customization to do but, for now, you're upgraded and your clients can access the resources.

7. Bring any resources that are offline back to the online state, download any needed service packs and, of course, activate the license on your new Windows Server 2003.

Congratulations, you just completed the rolling upgrade to Windows Server 2003 from Windows 2000 Advanced Server. Let's move on to learn how to implement a Windows Server 2003 Cluster from scratch.

DESIGNING A CLUSTERED SOLUTION WITH WINDOWS SERVER 2003

In this section, we look at designing and installing a two-node cluster with Windows Server 2003 from scratch. Earlier in the chapter, you performed an upgrade from a previous Windows 2000 Advanced Server cluster. This won't always be the case, so here you learn how to design, implement, and configure a brand new cluster with Windows Server 2003 from start to finish.

This section covers two important areas of your high-availability design: hardware and software. This is broken up because, as you'll see by the end of the chapter, it's important to plan out, purchase, and configure your hardware properly before you start with the Windows Server 2003 Cluster configuration, which is software-based.

Where to Begin

You must consider a few new things, other than what you learned in Chapter 2, when you think about planning out a Windows Server 2003 cluster. The following is a short list of the most important things to take into consideration:

- Increased hardware requirements
- Hardware compatibility
- Firmware and driver compatibility
- Vendor support
- Application compatibility and support
- Training and on-site staff knowledge
- Product activation

Let's look at each one within the preplanning and design phase of the cluster rollout.

The Design Phase

Clustering must be planned and designed before it's implemented. As you learned in the last chapter, the design phase of any project is one of the most important pieces of the project because it outlines the budget dollars needed to buy what you need and the resources you need to allocate to the project tasks. Resources aren't simply servers and cables; resources are also people. You need to configure a switch with a VLAN . . . do you know how to do that? You might know how, but you might not have access to those systems and you could need to get another department in your organization involved. My main objective here is to get you to think about all the work you need to lay out and accomplish before you even get on the server console to configure the Cluster Services. This holds true no matter what you roll out, especially when you want to implement the bleeding edge of technology, namely Windows Server 2003 Cluster Services. Let's look at what you must consider for high-availability solution success.

Increased Hardware Requirements

Windows Server 2003 is different than Windows 2000 Advanced Server and you need to consider the difference when you want to implement a Windows Server 2003 solution. In Table 3-3, you can plan your server hardware to Microsoft specifications.

As previously discussed, never go with the bare minimum specified by Microsoft or you'll be unhappy with the performance of your servers. Make sure you plan out your hardware well, using tips learned in Chapter 2 about scalability and redundancy, and always overshoot the hardware requirements by a long shot. For any production server running in a cluster, you should double, if not triple, the minimum requirements.

Requirement	Windows 2000 Advanced Server	Windows Server 2003
Minimum CPU Speed	133 MHz for x86-based computers	133 MHz for x86-based computers
Minimum RAM	128MB	128MB
Recommended Minimum RAM	256MB	256MB
Maximum RAM	8GB	32GB
Multiprocessor Support	Up to 8	Up to 8
Disk Space for Setup	1.0GB	1.5GB

Table 3-3.   Hardware Requirements for Windows 2000 Advanced and Server 2003

Hardware Compatibility

Windows Server 2003 is brand new. You need to contact your vendors and triple-check the fact that they're going to support it on their hardware platforms. Never roll out an unsupported solution. Make sure you have vendor support. *Hardware compatibility* is the security of knowing that when you install Windows Server 2003 on your servers, it won't have any compatibility problems that will result in blue screens, stop errors, memory leaks, and system freeze ups. Nothing would be worse than implement a solution to be highly available for increased speed and reliability, only to have it run slower than the original solution.

Firmware and Driver Compatibility

Windows Server 2003 must have full driver support from all your network hardware resources to include NICs, SCSI cards, and anything else you can install in your server. This is important because if something isn't supported, incorrectly written drivers for a platform will also result in blue screens, stop errors, memory leaks, and system freeze-ups. Contact your hardware vendors and ask them about their compatibility progress about getting drivers designed, tested, and digitally signed for Windows Server 2003.

Vendor Support

Windows Server 2003 is an operating system (OS) that's just being released. Find a hardware vendor who has a support system that knows, understands, and has test experience with Windows Server 2003. Knowing this about your hardware vendor can help you to make a solid decision about who your hardware vendor will be when you decide to go to Server 2003.

Application Compatibility and Support

Windows Server 2003 must be tested in a lab with all the applications you plan to run on your cluster. With Windows 2000 Advanced Server, you have over two years of application testing, hot fixes, and application development on your side. With Windows Server 2003, you might not have support for your current application set. This means extensive testing must be done by you or your staff to fully plan and implement your current applications on Windows Server 2003 in a clustered solution.

Training and On-Site Staff Knowledge

Windows Server 2003 has to be supported by your staff. While some of your staff could be struggling with understanding and troubleshooting a clustered solution, you've just added another learning curve into the mix: a new OS interface, new system tools, and other new features on which the staff might need to be trained. This is something to take into consideration before you implement a clustered solution with Windows Server 2003.

Product Activation

Windows Server 2003 must be activated online. This is something that can trip up many administrators when trying to roll out a Server 2003 solution. Here are some of the reasons why:

- You now have to purchase the software for real (not run it for a year before you license it). Windows Product Activation (WPA) is now in full effect and will become even more important in the future when Server 2003 is fully released.

- You might be able to use a volume-licensing activation solution and/or a Microsoft Select solution where you pay for what you use.

- You have to give your cluster nodes Internet connectivity to register them, which is something you normally don't do (usually, you wouldn't configure Internet access on your servers in your server farm for security reasons).

You may need to configure Internet connectivity to the clustered nodes. I suggest you connect the server to the Internet by configuring them to go through a proxy server, configuring Windows Update to get the latest patches and updates, and then activating Windows Server 2003 after that. Your last step would be to remove Internet access from the server once you finish.

Other Infrastructure Design Concerns

Now, let's walk though all the hardware installation and preliminary configuration you need to accomplish prior to and during the installation of the Windows Server 2003 Clustering Services. In Chapter 2, you got Windows 2000 Advanced Server up to speed to handle a Clustered Service solution. Here, we look at getting Windows Server 2003 ready for the installation and the configuration of the Cluster Service. The following is a short list of what you need to do.

1. Spec out all the hardware your need for you solution (use Chapter 2 as your guide). You need to determine your requirements (shared storage, and so forth) and get all applicable hardware for the solution you need. You need a shared SCSI bus and two network cards per server.

2. Have the Windows Server 2003 OS installation media on hand and have any licensing information / configuration information you might need ready.

3. All drivers you might need must be standing by and ready.

4. Install the OS per specified requirements.

5. Name the First Server **Cluster-Node-C** and name the second Server **Cluster-Node-D**.

6. Cluster-Node-C uses an IP address of 192.168.1.2 /24.

7. Cluster-Node-D uses an IP address of 192.168.1.3 /24.

8. The default gateway for both servers is 192.168.1.1 /24.

9. The Private network is configured on the second set of NICs.

10. Cluster-Node-C uses an IP address of 10.0.0.1 /24 (Heartbeat).

11. Cluster-Node-D uses an IP address of 10.0.0.2 /24 (Heartbeat).

12. The cluster name is DOTNET-CLUSTER and it has a virtual IP of 192.168.1.25 /24.

13. Install the OSs with all drives created and formatted with the NTFS file system.

NOTE   These IP addresses are a guide. You can configure the node any way you need to use the addresses you procure.

You should be able to install the server OSs one at a time while using these configuration settings. Remember the following when you install to a shared SCSI bus:

- Don't have both servers powered on at the same time, so you don't corrupt the shared drive.

- Document every setting along the way for future troubleshooting reference.

- In Windows Server 2003, you won't need shared storage, so make sure you configure a drive for storage within one of the cluster nodes for an alternative.

The approach I took here while writing this was to remind you of common pitfalls technicians blunder into while planning a clustered solution. Believe it or not, most of the pitfalls are in ordering and configuring the appropriate hardware.

Take a trip to Microsoft's web site at **www.microsoft.com/hcl** and review the HCL to verify all hardware you're going to implement.

Clustering Services Install Preinstallation Checklist

I created a quick checklist for you to run down, so you can verify all the preplanning you did was completed and all the tasks are done. These are, by far, the most important high-level tasks that must be done before you install the Cluster Service on the nodes. Before you install the Windows Server 2003 Cluster Service, you should do the following:

- Design your cluster for your infrastructure, have appropriate support, resources, and budget.

- Have a log of all the details of your implementation to be transferred to documentation later.

- Configure all your hardware properly using only items listed on the HCL.

- Install the hardware properly for your clustered solution. Take your time to step through every section of this chapter to make all the hardware settings appropriate to your solution.

- Verify the shared SCSI bus: termination, cables, and IDs.

- Prepare all your drivers, licenses, software, firmware, and anything else you need before your installation begins.

- Install Windows Server 2003 one node at a time. Go through all the details listed in this chapter to make all needed setting's adjustments and changes.

- Install all necessary service packs and hot fixes.

- Configure the shared storage, NTFS files system formatting, and drive letter assignment from one Windows Server 2003 node.

- Be certain your NICs are configured properly and IP addressing is configured correctly. Test your NICs with ping.

- Make sure an available domain controller is on the segment where your cluster nodes will reside. Your nodes need to be part of a domain.

- Check your Event Viewer logs to ensure they're clean of any big problems. You'll always have informational events and possibly warnings, but you should be concerned about critical errors that can be caught and fixed now.

- Have a NetBIOS name set aside for the cluster. This name should be something meaningful and easy to understand.

Configuring Network Properties

You need to configure the Windows Server 2003 Network Properties before you configure the Cluster Service. Make sure you look at Figure 3-7, which shows the new server look and feel. In this figure, you can see it uses a slightly modified GUI, but closely resembles Windows 2000. You can customize this but, for purposes of this

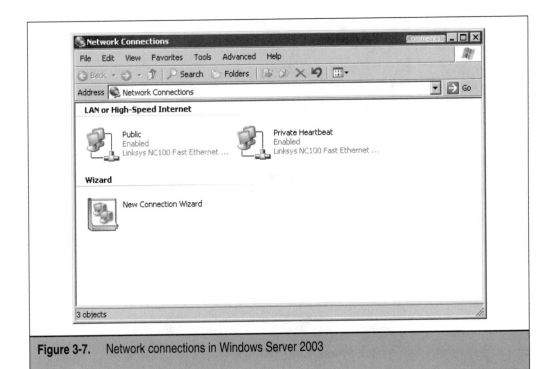

Figure 3-7.   Network connections in Windows Server 2003

book, we'll work with it as-is. Take this time to rename your interfaces accordingly to denote whether they're for your private Heartbeat network segment of for your publicly accessible LAN segment. I named them accordingly: Public for the client access and Private Heartbeat to denote the segment where heartbeat traffic will traverse.

Our next task is to configure our network bindings. As in Chapter 2, we configured everything in much more detail. I'll point you to the right areas (which are virtually the same) and I'll explain what to configure and why. And, I'll point out any differences where applicable. (Remember, on each node, you want to configure a Public Network Interface and a Private Heartbeat Interface.) You'll also want to ensure that you optimize communications as much as possible by configuring 100-Mbps full-duplex communication, if possible. You can configure full-duplex by going to the network interface you want to set (see the following illustration), opening the Properties Sheet and, when you view the field named Connect using, select the Configure button. Select the Advanced tab and change the Media Type to full-duplex at 100 Mbps.

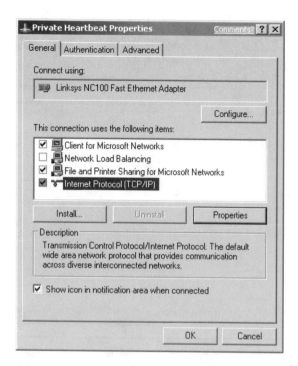

NOTE   If you hard code these settings, you'll also need to hard code the network switch you're attached to. Failure to do so will result in possible loss of communications.

Domain Connection and Client Access

Before you begin the Cluster Service configuration, you also need to make sure your two-node cluster is connected to a domain controller. Remember what you learned in Chapter 2: you must have both nodes logged into a domain and it must be the same domain. In Windows Server 2003, the steps are nearly identical to Windows 2000 Advanced Server. Go to the System Applet in the Control Panel, and then click the tab called Computer Name.

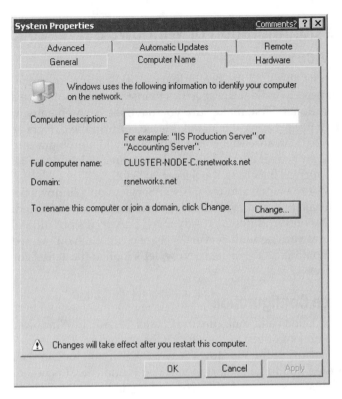

You must have a computer account on the domain controller. Without one, you'll probably run into connectivity problems when you try to add Server 2003 to it. Note, you needn't upgrade your domain Controllers at this time to Server 2003 to take advantage of the Server 2003 Clustering Service. You can log your nodes into a Windows 2000 domain and it will work. Eventually, you'll want to upgrade to Windows Server 2003 to take advantage of the newer version of Active Directory.

In the previous illustration, you can click the Change button to begin the process of adding the node to the domain. As mentioned before, the steps are identical to Chapter 2. The only thing I want to reiterate is your accounts.

User Accounts and Security

You also need to set up your cluster account on the domain controller. Using the administrator account isn't recommended. You might need to change this account, change the password, or something else, which will, essentially, disable the entire cluster. Make a service account (we used Cluster_Service in Chapter 2) and use that account instead. You'll use this account to log your Windows Server 2003 server into the domain and to connect to the domain.

Installation and Configuration of Windows Server 2003 Cluster Services

Now that you know about all the preliminary work leading up to the actual installation, you need to look at the specifics to installing the software and getting your cluster operational. First, make sure you have the licensed software and any drivers you might need during the install. Please confirm the drivers are certified for Windows Server 2003 because that could also cause you a problem during the install. In this section, I won't cover every detail on how to install Windows Server 2003 Cluster Services, such as installing the Server 2003 OS.

When you want to launch and use Cluster Services on Windows Server 2003, you'll find the installation and configuration different than what you did to install Clustering Services on Windows 2000 Advanced Server. It's not difficult, just different. Most of the changes you see with Server 2003 are cosmetic. You can see the difference immediately on booting up the system. Now, let's look at the actual configuration of the Cluster Services.

Cluster Service Configuration

In this section, you launch and configure the Cluster Service. In Windows Server 2003, you'll notice you no longer install the service for clustering. This is, by default, already installed when you install the Windows Server 2003. If you look in the Administrative Tools folder located within your Start menu, you'll find the Cluster Administrator Console already installed. Launch this icon and begin to configure the Cluster Service:

1. The Cluster Administrator (as seen in the next illustration) opens as a dialog box with nothing in it. This will remind you of the old Cluster Administrator, but this one is different. In the File menu, you'll find the Open Connection... menu option. (You can also use the only available toolbar icon.) Go ahead and click the Open Connection selection.

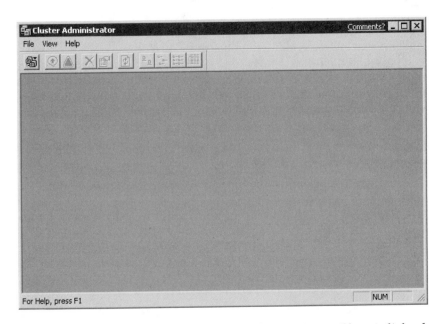

2. In the next illustration, you see the Open Connection to Cluster dialog box. This dialog box enables you to do multiple things, such as create a new cluster, add a node to a cluster, or open a current cluster. Because you're creating a new cluster, select the default and select to create a new cluster.

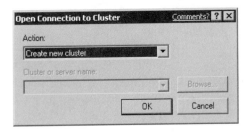

3. Once you select to create a new cluster, you'll launch the New Server Cluster Wizard, as seen in the following illustration. In the New Server Cluster Wizard, you have much more flexibility than you had with Windows 2000 Advanced Server, as you soon see. You need to provide the domain the cluster is joined to, the cluster name that's unique to the domain, the name of the first node you'll add to this cluster, and one static IP address that's unique and will be used for the entire cluster as the virtual IP address (VIP). You also need the account you were asked to make on the domain controller, which will be used as the Cluster Service Account.

4. Now add all the information you were just asked to obtain to the Cluster Wizard. In the next screen, provide the domain name, which is RSNETWORKS. The cluster name I chose for the entire cluster is DOTNET-CLUSTER. You can make this anything you want, but make sure it's 15 characters or less (NetBIOS restriction) and, if you can, stick with what I provided because I change the name later to force errors on the cluster, as shown in the next illustration.

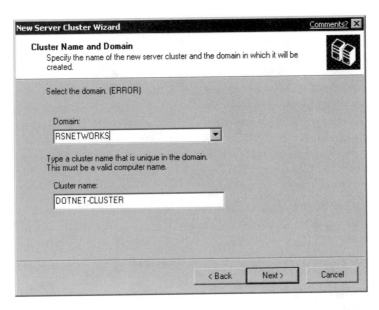

5. Once you click the next button, you begin the domain confirmation search seen in the following illustration. If you don't have the proper credentials and prior configurations set up correctly, your Cluster Service configuration will fail every time. Misconfiguration is the number one reason cluster server solutions don't work, can't be installed, or break down.

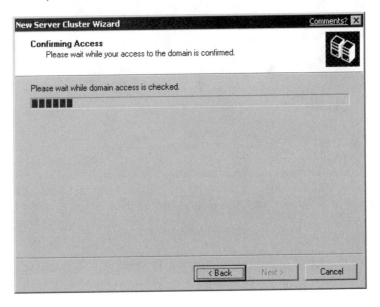

6. After domain access is confirmed, you can add the first node to the cluster. You must have your nodes joined to the domain and you might need to verify on the domain controller that your nodes have computer accounts on them. At times, this isn't added automatically and you have to add them manually. To add a machine account manually to a domain controller, you need to log in to the domain controller and open the Active Directory Users and Computers MMC. Once opened, open the Computers folder located in the left-hand navigation pane of the MMC and in the right-hand contents pane, you should find your nodes as computer accounts on the domain controller. If you don't find them, right-click the Computers folder and add them. If you had trouble adding the node to the domain, this will solve your problems.

7. In the next illustration, you can see I added a totally new cluster node to the entire new cluster I'm building called DOTNET-CLUSTER. Click Next to continue.

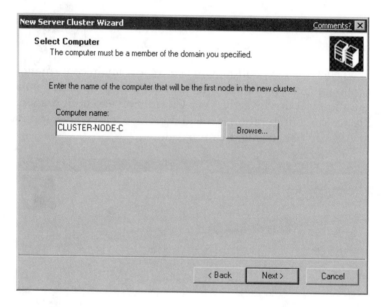

8. Once you select your node, you can click Next to continue. The following screen is a tremendous help to any administrator trying to determine what's wrong with a service configuration. It gives you a nice way to view the errors, have a log you can save to your desktop to analyze, and a Details tab to troubleshoot problems immediately without having to open any other consoles to view the Event Viewer or any other logs. If the screen in the following illustration is successful, you can continue with your cluster configuration. If not, you have many ways available to you to troubleshoot why it didn't work.

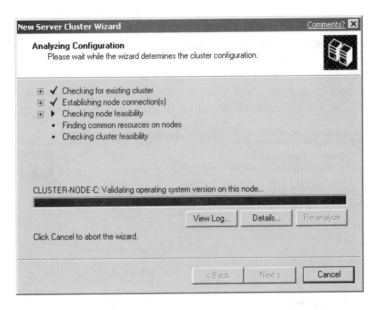

9. You look at the log when the installation is completed but, for now, click the Details button. This produces the dialog box. This is a new add-on for Server 2003 and it's extremely handy. If you look at the previous illustration, you can see check marks next to plus signs. These plus signs can be expanded (you see this in the next section) to reveal information about the configuration the wizard performed. When you click Details and open the dialog box, you can see the information in a more detailed manner with time stamps and other useful information.

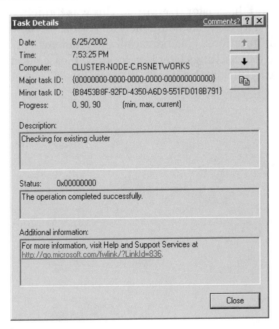

10. Close out of Details and go to the plus signs. Expand them and look at the contents of the configuration dialog box. The check marks let you know everything was configured correctly and you could move on, but if you want to look into the actual steps and find more details about the configuration, you can inspect them here. Once you finish analyzing the configuration in the next illustration, click the Next button to continue the cluster configuration.

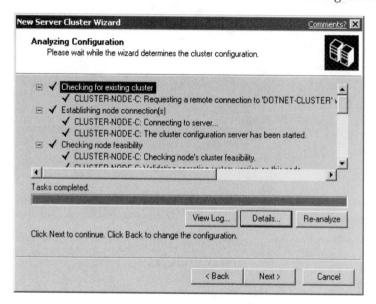

11. Once you click the Next button, you can see in the following illustration that you have to add the cluster IP address. This was thought out in the redesign plans. This IP address must be publicly accessible or you won't have proper cluster communications. We analyze all the problems you might have if you misconfigure these settings later but, for now, please add the proper IP address and continue by clicking Next.

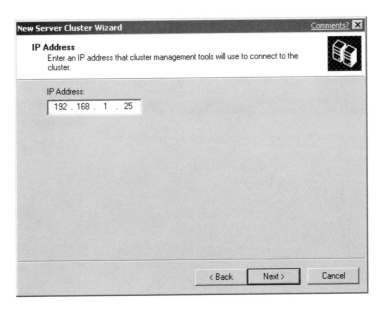

12. After you add the IP address, you can click Next to continue. The next dialog box, as shown in the following illustration, lets you use the Cluster Service account. The Cluster_Service account is what you created on the domain controller specifically for the Cluster Service. You can now log the node into the domain with this account, the password, and the domain name. Click Next to continue.

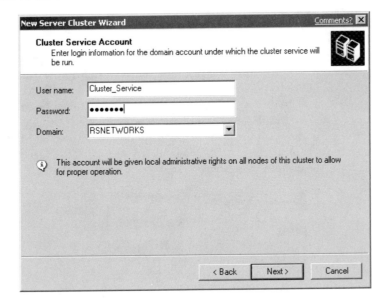

13. Once you click Next, you'll finish the Cluster Wizard with a "proposed" Cluster Configuration dialog box as seen in the following illustration. This is where you must pay strict attention to what kind of quorum device you want configured. In this dialog box, you have the option to click the Quorum button.

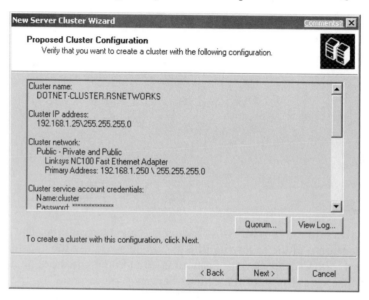

14. Click the Quorum button to open a smaller dialog box. Previously, I mentioned one of the advancements you would see is the addition of a locally placed quorum or a majority node set if you didn't want to configure a shared SCSI bus. The Cluster Service can now be configured without a shared device, but with a separate drive on a single server where resources can be pooled together. Because you already did a rolling upgrade on the other nodes from Chapter 2, let's configure a brand new two-node cluster with Windows Server 2003 with the use of its new features, including selecting the local quorum and the Majority Node Set. In the following illustration, you can see the local quorum configuration and, if you drop the arrow down, you can see the Majority Node Set. Select either Local Quorum or Majority set, and click the OK button. For this exercise, please use Majority set.

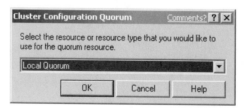

NOTE   When you switch back and forth between the quorum configurations, your proposed configuration re-creates itself to apply the change to the quorum you select.

Another note from the beginning of the chapter is a Majority Node Set (as seen in the following illustration), which is a new quorum resource that enables you to use something other than a shared disk as a quorum device. This new service enables you to create topologies that don't have shared disks and/or need to span multisite configurations.

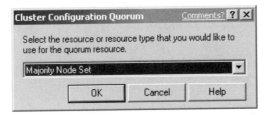

15. Now, the final steps of configuring the cluster are underway. The next screen you see is the New Server Cluster Wizard, in the next illustration, attempting to finalize your proposed configuration. Everything should run smoothly and no errors should be seen because you've read nearly three chapters on how to preplan your design! You should see the status bar run straight through and you can click Next to continue.

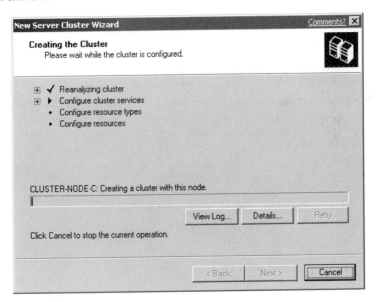

16. Let's look at a common problem. In the next illustration, I forced the cluster configuration to create an error, seen in the expanded errors within the dialog box. You can see the final error was a logon failure, which was caused by my going over to the domain controller and disabling the Cluster Service account. If you set the Administrator account for this task, and someone changes a password, this error (and many more of its kind) can become a harsh reality. Let's put things back the way they were and continue with the cluster configuration.

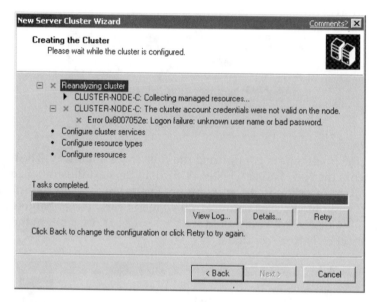

17. As you move forward (and past this error), you can see in the next illustration a nice, clean, fully installed cluster configuration. I expanded all the positive acknowledgements to see what was done. The quorum device and the resources were configured correctly. Remember, you can click the Details button to get more information about any wizard event you highlighted (I have Configure Resource Types highlighted here). After you examine the configuration completion, click Next.

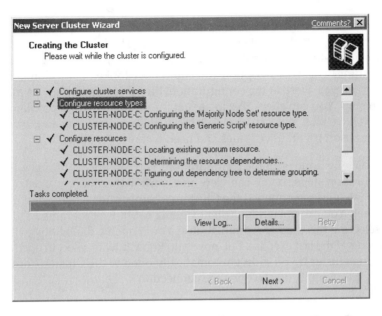

18. Congratulations! You successfully created your new Windows Server 2003 Cluster. You still have much more work to do, such as add a node, create resources and groups, and so on but, for the most part, your work here is completed as far as the basic cluster configuration goes. In the following illustration, the wizard is finalizing the cluster completion. Click the View Log.

19. Once you select the View Log option, you can see the log referred to earlier in the exercise, which is called the ClCfgSrv log. The log (as seen in Figure 3-8) takes a step-by-step snapshot of your entire cluster configuration from the beginning. This was an option you could have looked at all along, depending on where you were in the configuration, but all it was doing was recording each step. You can check this log to get information on any problems you might have had. You can also save these files for archiving and/or submittal to Microsoft if you have issues and need technical support.

You're officially done with the configuration. You can now continue with the rest of the configuration steps so you can view and work with your new cluster node.

In Figure 3-9, you see I opened the Cluster Administrator where we'll now manage our new cluster. You can open this cluster by going to Start | Programs | Administrative Tools and selecting the Cluster Administrator. You'll open a dialog box, which you saw in the beginning of the last exercise. But, now, you know how to select to open a connection to a preexisting cluster if you didn't automatically open to the Cluster Administrator. Go to File | Open Connection to open the connection.

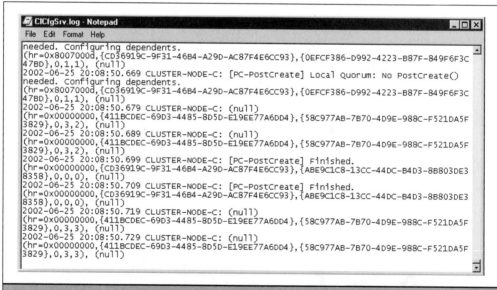

Figure 3-8. Viewing the ClCfgSrv log

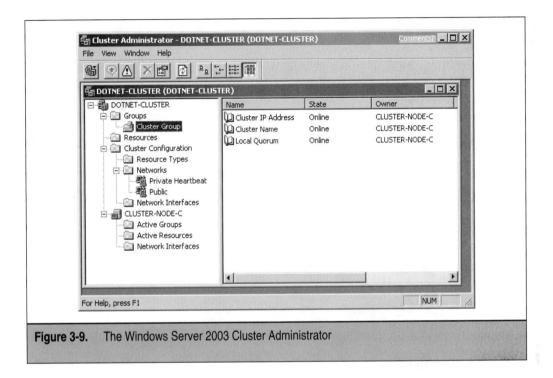

Figure 3-9.   The Windows Server 2003 Cluster Administrator

Windows Server 2003 has many different configuration settings within the Cluster Administrator to work with. We'll get to them but, first, we have to add a cluster node to the cluster, so we can have an Active/Passive two-node cluster. Let's add another cluster node.

Configuring and Troubleshooting the Cluster Service

In this section of the chapter, we'll look at the advanced configuration you can perform on the cluster you created. We look at adding another node and all the problems you can encounter along the way.

Adding Nodes

Now that your cluster is up and running, you only have one node connected to it. This is where we add another node to the cluster to make it a two-node cluster. In the next exercise, we build up the cluster you already have by adding another server. To add another server, start by opening the Cluster Administrator.

1. To add nodes, you need to open the Cluster Administrator, as seen in Figure 3-9. Once opened, you can right-click the Cluster Name icon at the top of the left-hand side navigation pane and select New from the menu. Once New is selected, choose Node.

2. When you choose Node, the Add Nodes Wizard is launched to help you in the process of adding nodes to your cluster, as seen in the next illustration. The wizard is helpful in pointing you to requirements to add a node, such as the computer names of the nodes you want to add and the password for the Cluster Service account.

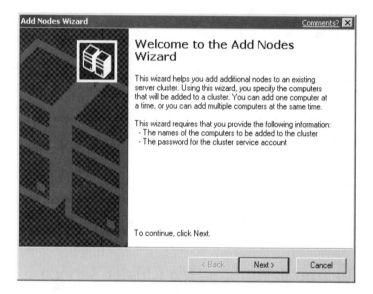

3. Once you click Next, the wizard quickly confirms access to a domain. If the domain is available, you're shown a dialog box to select the names of the node you want to add to the cluster. Click Browse and you'll open the dialog box you see in the following illustration.

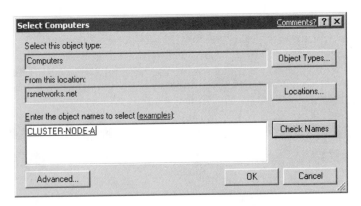

4. In the Enter the object names to select section of the dialog box, add the name of the cluster node you want to join the cluster. You can click the Check Names dialog box to verify it does exist, and then click OK.

5. In the next illustration, you can add the cluster node you selected by clicking the Add button. You can also remove it if you want to select a different node. Click Next.

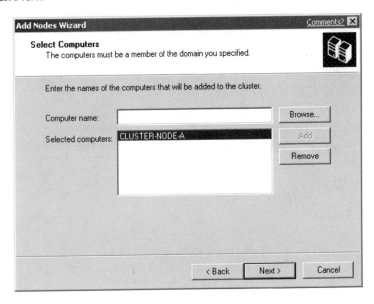

In the next three scenarios, I show you problems you can have while adding a node. To add a node, all you need to do is click Next, the wizard will finish, and you'll have added the node. In the following illustration, I created a situation where the resolution for the cluster name DOTNET-CLUSTER wasn't available (from being taken offline) and the name couldn't be resolved, so the node couldn't be added.

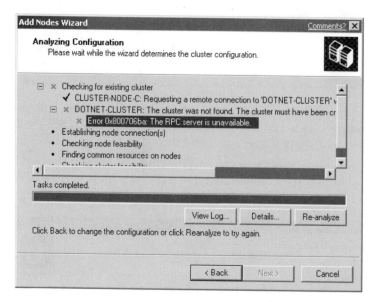

6. In the next illustration, I disabled a NIC connection to the cluster node we're trying to add. Because the connection was disabled, the cluster couldn't be contacted. If you are unable to contact the cluster, it won't let you add a node.

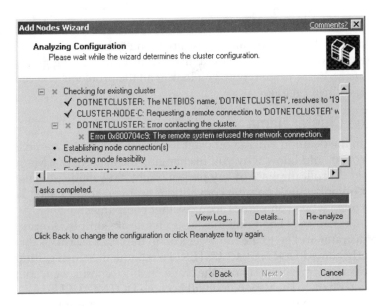

7. In the next illustration, you see many errors relating to cluster networks (192.168.0.0) not being found. While the wizard was checking feasibility, I changed the IP address subnet. This caused errors based on TCP/IP.

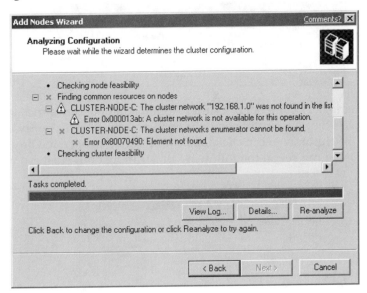

As you can see, the error information is a bit cryptic and didn't exactly explain the problem that caused the error. Because these are going to be the most common errors you'll see, I re-created them here for you to use as a troubleshooting guide to adding nodes to the cluster. In the next section, you look at all the problems you can experience while changing a cluster name.

Changing the Cluster Name

If you're ever in the position where you want to change the cluster name, remember these points. You should know why you're changing a cluster name. Many times, organizations in the rollout phase of any project might have made up a name that wasn't in your organization's naming conventions and you could have to change it. (This happens often when companies acquire other companies.)

The actual mechanics of changing the cluster name are simple. Simply open the Cluster Administrator and go to the top-level icon in the console. This is the cluster root and it's currently named DOTNET-CLUSTER. To rename the cluster, simply right-click the icon and select Rename. Now change the name. In this scenario, we want to remove the dash in the cluster name. The new name will become DOTNETCLUSTER. Once you finish the change, you're prompted to take the cluster offline for it to be known as the new name, as seen in the next illustration, or simply close the Cluster Administrator and reopen it.

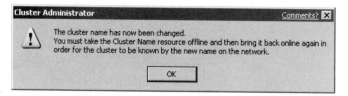

In this scenario, let's close out of Cluster Administrator and relaunch it, so you can be prompted with the new cluster name through browsing. Once you try to open a connection to the cluster, you can click the Browse button to open the Browse Clusters dialog box. As you can see in the following illustration, both cluster names are maintained.

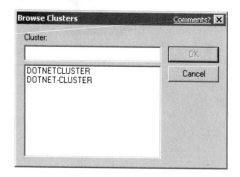

A problem exists, however. You don't have the old cluster anymore because you renamed it. Windows Server 2003 has a glitch that it will retain a renamed cluster name as if it's another cluster on your network, instead of a renamed one. It does this because it holds the name in the Registry. The key is

HKEY_CURRENT_USER\Software\Microsoft\Cluster Administrator\
Recent Cluster List

As you can see in the Registry (go to start | Run | type **REGEDIT**), your Recent Cluster List has the old DOTNET-CLUSTER as a second cluster when it isn't the second cluster. I don't recommend you try to remove it because there's no recommended Registry hack for it at this time.

Let's see how the new cluster name appears in the actual browse list. Open My Network Places and browse to the domain to which you're currently attached. Once you open the domain, you'll see, as shown in the following illustration, the DOTNETCLUSTER cluster name appears in the browse list. If you recently changed the cluster name, remember that the name change can take up to 45 minutes or so to disappear from the browse list and change the new name because of browser-based updates.

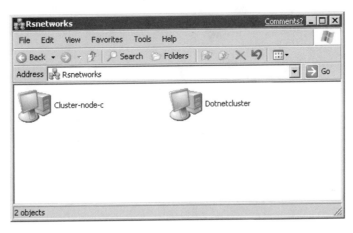

In the next illustration, you're shown a Cluster Administrator error that you might experience if you have poor NetBIOS resolution on your network. For example, NetBIOS is disabled, WINS isn't configured properly, or NetBIOS is being blocked on the network somewhere. If you see this informational error, you might want to start looking at possible networking-related issues with NetBIOS resolution.

In this section, you saw possible issues you might experience while trying to rename a cluster node. In the next section, you learn how to take a node offline and correct offline errors you could experience.

Taking a Cluster Offline

To take a cluster offline, you can either go at the group level or at the node level. This is important to note because you might only need to take a node offline and not the entire cluster. Let's review the differences.

If you take the cluster offline, you need to right-click your cluster group in the left-hand pane of the Cluster Administrator. You can choose to put the group in offline status, which makes the whole group inaccessible, but this creates a red mark up on the cluster group to make you aware the group is offline. You can also select a single node to go offline in much the same way, except by right-clicking the node you want to make unavailable temporarily. This won't affect the whole group. When you take Cluster Services offline and online, you can see a state column when you're looking at the cluster group in the right-hand Contents pane in Cluster Administrator. You should see it online. (In Figure 3-10, you can see "Unknown" which means that you are having

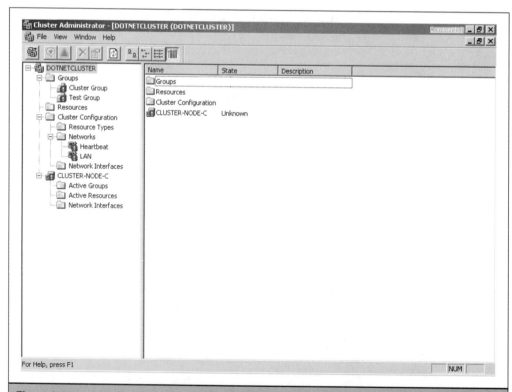

Figure 3-10. A similar offline error relating to network connectivity

a problem with it, is as previously mentioned.) You might see online pending if you're waiting for the service to start, but you want to see it in the online state for it to be functional to network clients.

Don't be mistaken by what you see in Figure 3-10, where all I simulated was lost network connectivity (I shut the switch ports to which the cluster is connected) and it showed blue exclamation marks. This isn't the same as the red marks the offline cluster shows you. Be aware of this because you might think your cluster is offline but, instead, you've lost network connectivity.

Now that you know how to take a node or the whole group offline, let's start to look into the more advanced configurations you can perform with your new cluster.

Advanced Cluster Configuration Settings

In this section, you see how to make configuration settings to your new two-node cluster. You look at the configuration settings you can make after everything is operational from configuring with wizards.

In the following illustration, the actual quorum configuration is available from the cluster. To get to this Properties dialog box, right-click the cluster object itself within the Cluster Administrator and select Properties. You can now configure the settings for the entire cluster itself. Here, in the next illustration, you can change the settings once again for the quorum. Note, for most of the settings changes you make, you're forced either to restart the Cluster Administrator or to take objects offline and online, so the settings changes can take place. Here, you can change the quorum log size to be larger or smaller. I recommend either keeping the log the size it is or increasing it (in the preplanning stages, you should have made sure you acquired a server with plenty of disk space available).

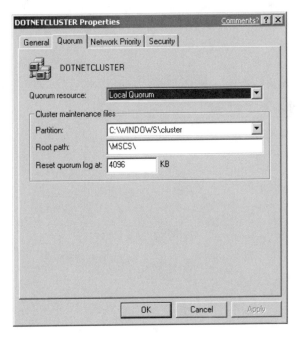

While you're still looking at the Cluster properties, you can click the next tab to look at the Network Priority. The Network Priority tab enables you to set which interface should be given priority. In this case, you can see I set the external, publicly accessible interface (LAN) to be given priority. In the following illustration, you can move the priorities up and down (up being the highest priority), and you can also set the properties on each interface. Change the properties by clicking the Properties button on the interface which you want to configure. You might or might not see both interfaces in the Network Priority tab. If you don't, then you have an interface configured as external only. Later in the section, you see how to set internal/external and mixed interface values. Be aware, this is only looking at the internal interface or interfaces that are mixed, as in both internal and external.

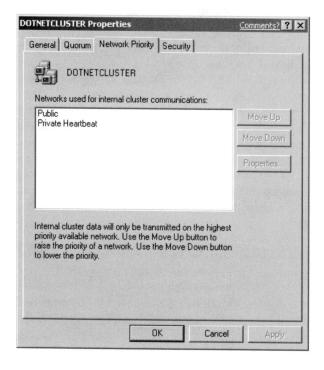

In the next illustration, you can see the Cluster Group properties where you can set thresholds and periods for failover and failback. To get to the failover and failback settings, right-click the actual cluster group in the Cluster Administrator console. Right-click cluster group | Properties | Failover tab. Failover is set by default. You can adjust the threshold, which defaults (and is recommended) at ten and the period of six hours, which you can also leave at default level. Most important here is to notice failover is configured by default, as you see shortly, failback is not.

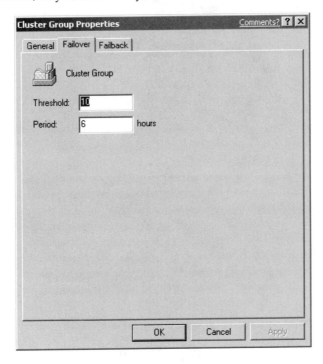

In the next illustration, you moved to the Failback tab and now you see that failback is configured by default. As you learned in Chapter 1, a failover is what happens when one node goes down or offline and the other node in the cluster takes over. Failback is when the other node that failed attempts to take over automatically as the primary and active node on the group when it comes back online. This can be prevented, as seen in the following illustration, or it can be configured either to failback immediately or within an hourly range.

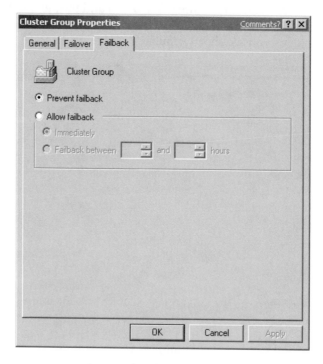

Let's move to some actual cluster group resources to configure. In the left-hand side of the Cluster Administrator, you find your cluster group. If you left-click it once, you can see in the Contents pane (right side) a cluster IP address. This is, by far, the most important setting you can view because it's the IP address by which the cluster will be referenced by your client. Look at this setting. In the right-hand side Content pane, right-click the Cluster IP address and select Properties. You'll open a dialog box, as seen in the following illustration. Here, on the General tab, you can find the possible owners of the IP address and they're set to be both nodes in the group. Make sure you select the Modify button on the General tab and add all cluster nodes to the Cluster IP address.

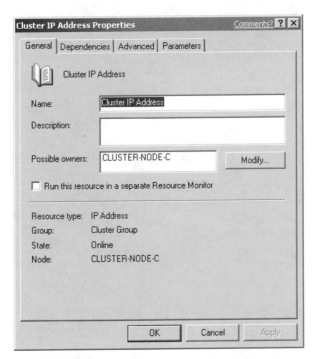

Next, click the Parameters tab to set the actual interface, so the cluster, as well as the IP address of the cluster itself, is accessible by clients. This IP address was referred to as the VIP in Chapter 1 and is the IP address clients use to connect to the cluster. In the next illustration, you can add the IP address and switch the interface. It's configured as accessible from the LAN interface (which isn't my Heartbeat interface) and to have an IP address unique to the cluster itself, not one carried currently by any nodes. You need to know how to configure this IP address in case you configured it wrong during the initial setup with the Create New Cluster Wizard. Here's where you can now make those specific setting changes.

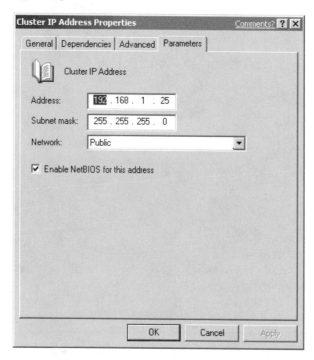

Before moving to the next topic, which is to configure the NIC connections, I want to mention taking advantage of new Server 2003 Cluster Service features within the cluster group. In the same section (the Contents pane) where the cluster IP address is located, you can also find a Cluster Name object. Right-click it and go to Properties | General tab | Parameters tab. Within the Parameter tab, you can also rename your cluster here. I showed you the easy way to do it earlier—this is simply another way to rename the cluster itself. In the Cluster Name Properties box, with the advanced tab, look at the Enable Kerberos Authentication check box.

This is what you can select to make sure Kerberos is used for authentication for the Cluster Service. Table 3-1 mentioned that Windows Server 2003, when used with clustering services, now has full active directory integration where the cluster becomes a computer object within the directory. This is a solution that benefits those who want to take advantage of delegation and Kerberos authentication. Here's where you can force the cluster to use Kerberos.

Next up in advanced configuration is setting the NIC properties. If you look at Cluster Administrator and expand the Navigation Pane folders down to the Cluster Configuration level, you'll find a Networks folder. Left-click the Networks folder and, in the Contents pane of the Cluster Administrator, you'll find the NIC interfaces configured for this cluster. As previously mentioned, when looking at the network priority within the Cluster properties, you can now set the interfaces on how they will listen for client traffic.

In the next illustration, we selected the properties of the Heartbeat interface connection. In these properties you will enable your interfaces for cluster use by putting a check in the Enable this network for cluster use check box. Once you do, you'll next be asked to specify which interfaces you want to enable for specific communications. Because you named your interfaces properly (denoting what they are) you won't have a problem configuring this role. In the three radio button selections, you have the following:

- Client Access only (public network) is the setting for your publicly accessible client access network interfaces. Because you named your interface (this one is the heartbeat) that would not be proper for this connection.

- Internal Cluster communications only (private network) is perfectly accessible for your heartbeat connection. This will keep communications optimized for the private heartbeat connection.

- All communications (mixed network) is what you can use if you have all your connections plugged into the same device (hub, switch, and so on) and you are uncertain of what connection goes where exactly. This (as you can see from the next illustration) is the default selected for enabling this function. You can either leave it here, or you can set it to private internal use.

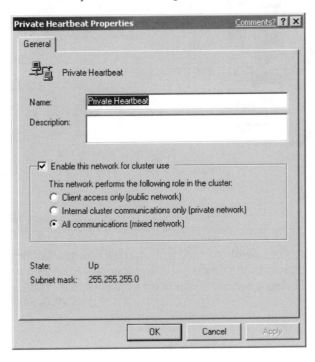

We have now gone over some of the more obscure settings changes you can make on your cluster, and ones that will definitely keep your cluster from working if set incorrectly. Lets now look at creating a new cluster group.

Creating a New Cluster Group

At times you may want to configure new cluster groups to be managed within the same console such as Cluster Administrator. Here you are setting new groups for new clusters. In this case, you may want to add a cluster group name for clusters based on what you are clustering. You should name it something meaningful to you. Lets begin by creating a new group.

To add a new group, right-click the Groups folder within the Cluster Administrator, go to New, and then to Group. In the following illustration, you can see the new Group Dialog box where you're asked to add a new name and description. Click Next and you're asked to provide the nodes available for the new group. Select the nodes you want to add, and then click Next.

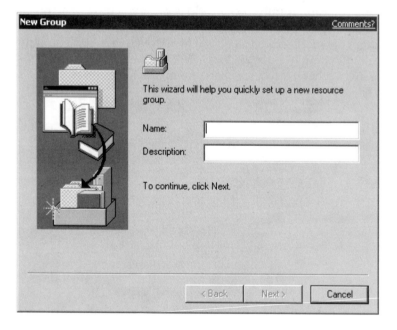

You can now see your newly formed group in the Cluster Administrator. Notice, however, that it's created in the down or offline state. All you need to do is right-click the new group and bring it online. If you want to remove the group, right-click it and select Delete.

Although you can do more tweaking, this is enough to get the Cluster Service installed and functional. In the next section, you set some of the command line tools you can use to configure and manage your cluster.

New Command Line Tools

Command line tools are enhanced on Windows Server 2003. In this section, you see the new DiskPart command line tool for Server 2003. As discussed in Chapter 2, command line utilities are useful for quick manipulation of the Cluster Service so you can write scripts in batch for management and automation. Let's look at the new Windows Server 2003 tool: DiskPart.

DiskPart

DiskPart is a new tool in Windows Server 2003 that enables you to add disk partition manageability from the command line for your Cluster Services. To enter DiskPart, open a command prompt and type **DiskPart**, and then press ENTER. Notice this is a lot like the Windows FTP utility where you're within a command line program, instead of just executing programs for the command prompt. You see the following prompt open:

Microsoft DiskPart version 5.1.3590

Copyright (C) 1999-2001 Microsoft Corporation

On computer: CLUSTER-NODE-B

DISKPART>

Once you're at the DISKPART command prompt, you can execute the following commands, as seen in Table 3-4.

DiskPart is most useful when you want to do disk partition operations from the command prompt. You can bring disks online and offline at will from the command prompt. You can also add, delete, convert, and configure drive letters to drives, all at the prompt. As a final note, you must be careful when using DISKPART because any mistake made here will render your server useless. Practice using this command in a lab server before using it in production.

Windows Server 2003 Cluster Tips

In this section, I would like to add a tip or two to your arsenal of pre-deployment items to look for either while testing or going into production.

You might be unable to reconnect with a cluster you know is operational. While testing the Server 2003 cluster, change the name of the cluster and take it offline. Shut

ADD	Add a mirror to a simple volume
ACTIVE	Activate the current basic partition
ASSIGN	Assign a drive letter or mount point to the selected volume
BREAK	Break a mirror set
CLEAN	Clear the configuration information or clear all information off the disk
CONVERT	Convert between different disk formats
CREATE	Create a volume or partition
DELETE	Delete an object
DETAIL	Provide details about an object
EXIT	Exit DiskPart
EXTEND	Extend a volume
HELP	Print a list of commands
IMPORT	Import a disk group
LIST	Print a list of objects
ONLINE	Online, a disk currently marked as offline
REM	Does nothing; used to comment scripts
REMOVE	Remove a drive letter or mount point assignment
RESCAN	Rescan the computer looking for disks and volumes
RETAIN	Place a retainer partition under a simple volume
SELECT	Move the focus to an object

Table 3-4.   DISKPART Command Line Options

off the Cluster Administrator and try to reopen the cluster via the old cluster name. The cluster name wasn't found, so close the Cluster Administrator again and try to reopen the cluster by its new name. This also wouldn't connect. Well, now that you can't connect to both, what do you do? Did you notice the Cluster Service isn't something you install through the Add/Remove Programs Control Panel applet? The Cluster Service comes already installed with the Server 2003. So, how do you get around this mess? To reenter the Cluster Administrator, go through the Computer Management MMC, found within the Administrative Tools folder in the Control Panel. You can also find the cluster management utility Cluster Administrator available for management within the Computer Management MMC under the Services and Applications icon within the MMC. Expand it to reveal the Cluster icon. Right-click the Cluster icon and select Manage…, so you can reconnect to the Cluster Service. It opens right up and is accessible.

You should know you can't create a new MMC (go to Start | Run, and then type **MMC** and press ENTER), and then add the Cluster Administrator to it. This isn't a valid snap-in, so you can only access it from Administrative Tools or from the Computer Management MMC.

Let's step away from our two-node cluster with Windows Server 2003 and look at the network load balancing features within Server 2003 and how to configure them.

DESIGNING A NLB SOLUTION WITH WINDOWS SERVER 2003

Now you've learned the finer art of setting up a Windows Server 2003 Cluster. Next, you learn how to configure NLB, which is a completely different animal in its approach to high availability networking. As you previously learned, NLB is also called clustering, so don't confuse it with the use of the name. "Clustering" is a generic term and you'll find that it's often used interchangeably. I'll explain it as NLB clusters when applicable. Let's prepare for NLB-based clusters and more Highly Available solutions with Windows Server 2003.

Where to Begin

Load balancing is balancing the amount of work a server must do between two or more computers. When applied to network available resources, we use the term "network load balancing." Before we jump into working with NLB in Windows Server 2003, let's step back and look at what Microsoft has done with NLB in the next generation of Windows Servers—this is quite an improvement over Windows 2000. Table 3-5 has a quick rundown of some points about moving to Windows Server 2003 NLB.

Bidirectional Affinity	Using Bidirectional Affinity enables you to cluster Internet Security and Acceleration (ISA) servers together for use as proxy and firewall load balancing. You typically use NLB with an ISA server for web publishing and server publishing. Although web publishing doesn't require Bidirectional Affinity, server publishing does, so this is a great improvement for those running an ISA server in a NLB cluster. Bidirectional Affinity solves the server-publishing problem by creating multiple virtual instances of NLB on the host, which then work together to ensure the responses from each published server are routed through the appropriate ISA servers in the NLB cluster.
Internet Group Management Protocol (IGMP) Support	When NLB is configured in multicast mode, you can use Internet Group Management Protocol (IGMP) support to limit the switch flooding caused by the NLB algorithm, which requires all hosts in the NLB cluster be able to see every incoming packet addressed to the cluster IP address. IGMP support can greatly conserve network resources by preventing switch flooding from occurring, except on those switch ports that have an NLB host connected to them.

Table 3-5.   Server 2003 NLB Features

Network Load Balancing Manager	Network Load Balancing Manager is a new utility in Windows Server 2003, which provides you with a single configuration point for the configuration and management of your network load balancing clusters. You can use the NLB Manager to perform the following tasks, plus several others such as: Create new NLB clusters Add and remove hosts to and from NLB clusters Manage existing clusters by connecting to them Configure NLB to load balance multiple web sites Configure NLB to load balance multiple applications Troubleshoot and diagnose improperly configured clusters
Multi-NIC (Network Interface Card) Support	Windows Server 2003 NLB can now be bound to more than one NIC in a single host. This enables you to host more than one NLB cluster per server now, while still segregating them on to entirely separate networks.
Virtual Clusters	The Virtual Clusters feature works similarly to Virtual Servers under IIS and enables you to perform tasks that, traditionally, you couldn't perform when using NLB, such as: Configure different port rules for different cluster IP addresses, where each cluster IP address corresponds to a web site or application being hosted on the NLB cluster Filter out traffic sent to a specific web site or application on a specific host in the cluster

Table 3-5.   Server 2003 NLB Features *(continued)*

A quick rehash of some of the general discussion related to Network Load balancing from Chapter 2 is appropriate, as you may have missed it if you skipped Windows 2000 network load balancing.

Typically, you use NLB for web-based traffic coming into your organization, splitting this load between more than one machine to improve response times and reliability. NLB is almost always configured with a failover plan, so you can also have disaster recovery functionality incorporated into your load balancing solution. As you see in Figure 3-11, if you experience the failure of one server in the NLB cluster, you can still service user requests on the remaining three NLB cluster members. This transition occurs behind the scenes, completely unseen by the user.

Unlike with clustering, NLB isn't appropriate for solutions that require a shared storage device, such as an SQL server implementation on the back-end of an e-commerce web site. NLB would, however, be an appropriate solution to enhance the performance and availability of those front-end IIS servers serving up our web site to users. The determining factor why one solution is better than another is directly tied to the type of application being run. Clusters typically share a storage device, whereas NLB clusters don't. Also, NLB is much more robust when it comes to reacting quickly to sharp changes

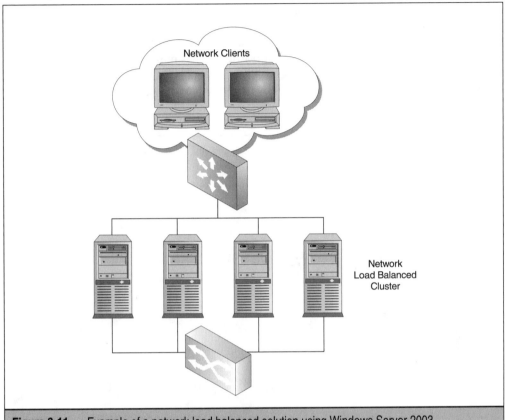

Figure 3-11. Example of a network load balanced solution using Windows Server 2003

in network loading. New members can be easily "dropped" into an existing NLB cluster with little preparation ahead of time—the same isn't true of clustering, as you know now. Also, NLB members can quickly react to the loss of a member server via the process of convergence, reassigning the load based on what servers remain after the casualty occurs. This makes NLB perfect for use with IIS applications, where fluctuations in load can occur sporadically, such as during the busy shopping period around the holidays.

Another area where NLB shines over standard clustering is managing session state and client affinity across members of the NLB cluster. These will be discussed in the upcoming section, "Multiple Host." Another management tool you can leverage in NLB is port filtering.

NLB clusters make use of heartbeat traffic, just the same as Cluster Service clusters do. As you can see in Figure 3-12, a typical NLB cluster has one network segment for the front-end (public) traffic and another, separate segment for the back-end (heartbeat) traffic. The heartbeat traffic is what makes convergence work.

The last thing you should know about NLB clusters is they almost always have a lower cost to set up and maintain, and they also have much less stringent hardware

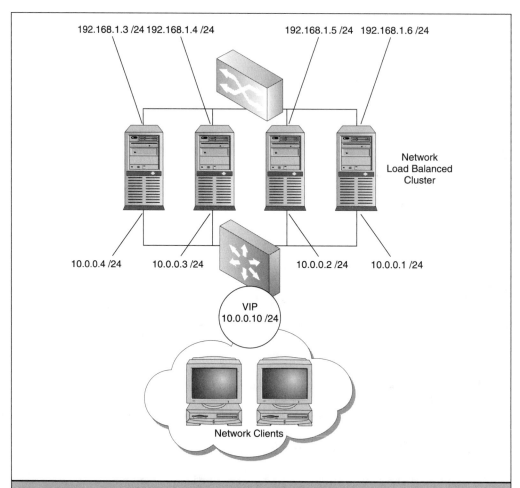

Figure 3-12.   Example of a network load balanced solution using Windows Server 2003

requirements. These factors can be directly attributed to the lack of need for a shared bus and storage device as in Cluster Services clustering. Remember, though, some applications absolutely require a shared storage device, such as SQL Server or Exchange Server (Enterprise Editions). Make sure you know what your storage requirements are ahead of time, so you can use this to help you decide which way to go when you design your Highly Available solution.

The Design Phase

We've reached the most important step of the NLB rollout. This section of the chapter mirrors the last one as closely in procedure, so you get the subtle (and not so subtle) distinctions between the two services—NLB and MSCS. When planning your NLB cluster, consider the following ideas. Remember, planning and preimplementation design go a long way before the actual roll out.

Windows Server 2003 as a Load Balancer

When you plan your NLB solution using Windows Server 2003, you can opt to use either Windows to perform the load-balancing distribution or a hardware appliance built specifically for that purpose. Because we're focusing on Windows-based solutions in this book, we'll configure Windows Server 2003 to serve as our load-balancing device. I think you'll find this solution works as advertised and delivers good results in all but the largest scenarios. In those large scenarios, you'll be using a hardware device, such as one from Foundry or Cisco to perform your load balancing. Either way, Windows Server 2003 will provide superb NLB performance.

Topology Maps

You wouldn't go out and implement a new network without diagramming it first—correct? Getting it right would be difficult the first time without taking the time to plan the layout of the physical and logical layout of the network. The same is true for your NLB cluster. Although it's much smaller than an entire large scale network, the NLB cluster still deserves your time and attention when it comes to planning the layout, both physical and logical.

Although larger organizations will probably use Visio to perform the diagramming tasks, you can perform this task using nearly any technology you have at your disposal, whether it's graph paper, MS Paint, or even Visio. Looking back at Figure 3-12, you can see exactly what you plan to implement, down to the IP address assignments. Everyone knows a picture is worth a thousand words, and when it comes time to implement your plan, your picture can prevent a thousand mistakes as well. Still need an incentive to plan your design on paper? Managers like to see pictures. Pictures make it easy to digest your solution and visualize how it will provide the desired results.

Once you have a clear idea of how your new NLB solution will be laid out, you can move on to assessing your readiness to implement that solution, which is the topic of the next section.

Initial NLB Planning and Readiness Assessment

Once you determine how your NLB solution will be laid out—both physically and logically—you can go about the process of addressing some additional planning and readiness assessment issues. Some of the more typical items you should give consideration to include the following:

- Use two network interface cards in each server node. You could use only one NIC in each server, but with the low price of high-quality NICs and all the benefits gained by using two NICs, it would be foolish to use only one NIC per server.

- When deciding what type of NIC to install in your servers, remember the golden rule: faster is better. Don't settle for anything less than a 100-Mbps, full-duplex–capable NIC. If both your budget and your network infrastructure support it, you might want to consider placing 1000 Mbps (gigabit) NICs in your servers. The extra money spent now will pay off over time with increased network throughput.

- One last point about NICs. Spend the extra money and get a good brand that you know and trust. To make things easier, consider using exactly the same NIC in all machines . . . and buy a few extras to have as a spare for that rainy day.

- Buy high-quality, name-brand switches and hubs, as required for your NLB solution. Although some problems exist with Cisco switches and switch flooding, refer to Chapter 2 for the discussion on how to get around flooding issues with NLB.

- Plan for your NLB hosts only to perform one function of your network. Putting other network services, such as DHCP, DNS or file and print shares, on a NLB node is a recipe for disaster. Just say no! Of course, this probably doesn't include IIS, which could be the reason you're setting up the NLB cluster in the first place.

- As TCP/IP is the heart and soul of Windows Server 2003 communications, plan on having only TCP/IP and NLB bound to your NICs. This can provide better performance by removing unnecessary protocols from the NIC and also provide enhanced security.

- If you plan on using port rules (discussed in the upcoming section "Port Rules"), know that you must configure them identically for all nodes in the NLB cluster. This is much easier now in Windows Server 2003 because of the availability of the NLB Manager. If you don't control the port opening and closing on your firewall, you might want to get the appropriate people involved with your project.

- If you haven't already determined your IP addresses to be used during the diagramming phase of your design, do that now. Again, this could be one of those areas where you need outside assistance from another group within your organization if you don't directly control the assignment of IP addresses. This is a critical point: You must get the IP address assignment right the first time. Failure to do so could both have catastrophic results and cost you much more time and money down the line when you're faced with reconfiguring your solution. Also, know that you can't use DHCP-allocated addresses for your front-end network. You could get by using DHCP-allocated addresses for the back-end (heartbeat) network, but this isn't recommended. Stick with static, manually configured IP addresses and you'll be safe.

Load Balancing System Requirements

As you might suspect, before you can even get into setting up Windows Server 2003 NLB, you must first have met the hardware requirements to run Windows Server 2003. These requirements were outlined previously in Table 3-3. I recommend you go back and review the table again quickly before proceeding.

Once you know what hardware requirements you must meet, you can safely begin the process of shopping for hardware to build your NLB solution. The best (and safest) way to do this is by working with a reputable vendor and walking through your requirements point-by-point. By doing this, you can be reasonably assured that you're not only going to get high-quality hardware that meets your needs, but also a good level of technical support and assistance should things go south. For the purposes of this chapter, we'll configure a simple two-node NLB cluster, although your solution could easily call for a larger number of servers. In later chapters, we explore larger NLB cluster solutions and also dive into additional Microsoft products, such as Application Center 2000, which transform NLB management into a fine art.

The actual system requirements of the network load balancing components are relatively minor. As long as you met (or, hopefully, exceeded) the hardware requirements of Windows Server 2003, then you should have no problems getting NLB up and running. Be aware, however, the application you're designing for this NLB solution, such as IIS serving your e-commerce web site, might need to meet some high requirements for your systems. Again, with the relatively low prices of computer hardware, you'd be wise to max out your NLB servers with as much RAM and hard drive capacity as they can handle. On the topic of hard drives, give consideration to using faster SCSI drives configured in some sort of RAID array, such as RAID-5 or RAID-10. Chapter 1 discussed RAID in some detail if you need to review it.

IIS uses a lot of memory because it stays memory-resident to increase speed for web site requests. Look at Chapter 2 to learn how to use system monitor and baseline a test system to get accurate numbers on how much RAM you need. Chapter 2 also tells you how to use stress test tools in a lab environment to simulate load on your NLB cluster. Other requirements are focused on the network hardware with which you're implementing the NLB cluster.

If you use a network router for clients to access your NLB solution, you must plan to use the cluster to operate in Multicast mode, explained in the upcoming section

"Cluster Operation Mode," and make sure you plan for the purchase of a router that can take an ARP reply with two different Media Access Control (MAC) addresses within the entire packet. The two addresses come from the need for the NLB cluster to have one MAC address in the actual data payload and one MAC address in the header. If your router doesn't allot for this functionality, you can add an ARP entry statically within the router you're using. If you use a Cisco router, you'll most likely need to add an entry because the router will have a problem resolving a Unicast IP to a Multicast MAC address. In most cases, if you ever have a problem with this design, by working with Cisco and the TAC (Technical Assistance Center **www.cisco.com/TAC**) support center, you can have your problems resolved rather quickly with their help picking out the hardware you need, the configurations you need to adjust, or by using what you already have in your infrastructure. Now that you have what you need, let's install the service and get our NLB cluster up and running!

WINDOWS SERVER 2003 NLB SOFTWARE ROLLOUT

I assume for this section that you have, by now, installed Windows Server 2003 on your two (or more) servers that will be set up as the NLB hosts. Once you have Windows installed, the rest is fairly simple. This will become obvious during the next few sections as we walk through configuring network load balancing for your servers.

The process of configuring NLB is started by enabling it on your NIC. Note, I said NIC instead of NICs. We'll walk through a standard implementation here, not taking advantage of the more advanced features Windows Server 2003 brings to the table. Once you have the basics down, then you can safely get to work using the more advanced features. To enable the NLB driver, open the Network and Dialup Connections window by clicking Start | Settings, and then double-click Network and Dialup Connections. I hope you already renamed your NICs, so you know which one is to be configured as the front-end (load balancing) one and which is to be configured as the back-end (heartbeat) one. If not, you might need to experiment by removing and reinstalling cables until you know which one is which. Open the Properties window for your public adapter by right-clicking it and select Properties. The following illustration shows the Properties page of a typical public adapter with NLB enabled.

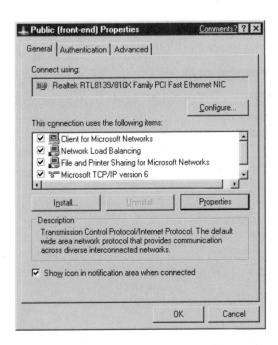

To enable the NLB service, simply put a check in the box next to it, as shown in the previous illustration. That was easy, right? It was. But we haven't gotten down to the real work of configuring NLB yet and that's where the real work of NLB comes into play. Don't worry, though. If you can set up a cluster using the Cluster Service, you can set up a NLB cluster with your eyes closed! To begin the configuration, highlight the Network Load Balancing option and click Properties. Now you'll get into the task of configuring NLB, examining each item, tab-by-tab.

Cluster Parameters

The Cluster Parameters tab is the first tab you need to get your hands dirty in configuring your NLB cluster. As you can see in the following illustration, a few items on this tab absolutely require your attention for the NLB cluster configuration to be successful. And some new features are in Windows Server 2003 that you didn't see when (if) you configured a NLB cluster using Windows 2000 Advanced Server. One important point that can't be overemphasized is this: all the configurations you make here must be identical across all NLB hosts or the NLB cluster won't function properly.

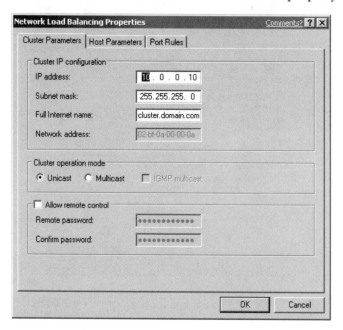

Cluster IP Configuration

The Cluster IP configuration area is where you configure the basic cluster information for the NLB host.

- In the IP address box, enter the cluster IP address in standard dotted notation. This IP address is the Virtual IP (VIP) that corresponds to the entire cluster. So, in our example, you'll use the value of 10.0.0.10/24, as previously determined when we mapped out the new design.

- In the Subnet mask box, enter the required subnet mask that corresponds to your VIP entered in the IP address box. Because you're using the 10.0.0.1/24 range for your NLB cluster, you'll enter 255.255.255.0 here.

- In the Full Internet name box, enter the full Internet name that corresponds to the NLB cluster as a whole. This is the name that maps to the VIP entered previously and it must be resolvable to clients either through a DNS server or a Hosts file. As you can see, we have a cluster named Cluster, which belongs to the DOMAIN.COM domain.

- Although the Network address box isn't a configurable option, it displays the MAC address of the adapter being configured for NLB clustering. The NLB service automatically generates the MAC address based on the given cluster VIP address. This address also serves as a multicast address when multicast support is enabled. Because the overriding of the network adapter's built-in MAC is automatic and controlled by network load balancing, as long as it's bound (enabled) to that adapter, you needn't configure the adapter to recognize this MAC address. If your network adapter doesn't support overriding the MAC address, you'll need to get one that does.

Cluster Operation Mode

From the Cluster Operation Mode area, you'll configure the operation of the cluster, either unicast or multicast. A *unicast* transmission is a point-to-point transmission between two nodes. *Uni* or *one* is a transmission meant for a single node. When you implement *multicasting,* you allow a transmission of data to an addressable group, based on a specific class of addressing. This way, you can get your message to a group of listening nodes, instead of inundating the entire segment with a broadcast.

- Selecting the Unicast Mode radio button specifies your NLB cluster is operating in Unicast mode. When the cluster is operating in Unicast mode, the NLB service assigns and controls the MAC address for the network adapter, assigning it the MAC address of the cluster. This network adapter doesn't retain the built-in MAC address while NLB is bound to it, but regains it if NLB is removed from the adapter. While in Unicast mode, no communication is possible between hosts unless each host has two more network adapters. In Unicast mode, network load balancing assigns the cluster's MAC address to the network adapter. The network adapter to which the network load balancing driver is bound doesn't retain its original MAC address. For this example, we're going to configure Unicast mode for our NLB cluster.

- Selecting the Multicast Mode radio button specifies your NLB cluster will operate in Multicast mode. When an NLB cluster is operating in Multicast mode, NLB converts the cluster MAC address into a multicast address. NLB also ensures that cluster IP (the virtual IP) address resolves to this multicast MAC address via Address Resolution Protocol (ARP). In Multicast mode, the network adapter retains its built-in MAC address. The problem with using Multicast mode is some routers don't support ARP resolution. If you run into a case like this, you need to make manual entries in the ARP table of the router to correct the problem.

- If you select to have your NLB cluster operate in Multicast mode, you have a new option in Windows Server 2003 available to you: IGMP Multicast. If you enable *IGMP Multicast*, NLB attempts to prevent switch flooding by limiting multicast traffic to only those ports on a switch that have a NLB-bound network adapter connected to them. So, when you use IGMP Multicast, traffic is designed to flow only to those switch ports connected to NLB cluster hosts, thus preventing all other switch ports from being flooded by the multicast traffic. This is a major improvement for multicasting in an NLB cluster and it goes a long way toward making switches function smoothly in this environment.

Allowing Remote Control

The last area of the Cluster Properties tab is fairly straightforward. If you plan on using remote control to control the nlb.exe executable, then you want to enable support for remote control, as well as provide the password required to initiate the remote control session.

- Placing a check in the Allow Remote Control box will allow other network (remote) computers running Windows to control cluster operations using the nlb.exe cluster control program. As a security measure (and a recommended way of doing business), remote control is disabled by default. I recommend you leave it this way.

- If you enable remote control, then you need to specify a password to be used to allow remote control access in the two password field boxes. Ensure that the password selected is a strong one. This password won't be subject to any of the password policies that might be in effect via Group Policy for your organization.

If you decide to enable remote control of your NLB cluster, you need to make certain you blocked UDP on ports 1717 and 2504 on your external firewall, thus preventing someone from taking control of your NLB cluster from outside the organization. Again, the password you choose should be complex and it should consist of a combination of letters, numbers, and characters. If you're concerned about security by enabling remote control of your NLB cluster, then you're better off administering it via Terminal Services, which has the capability to authenticate user requests against Active Directory.

Host Parameters

Up to this point, you've only been configuring options that apply to the entire cluster. From the Host Parameters tab, shown in the next illustration, you can configure those options that apply to only the specific NLB host you are working with.

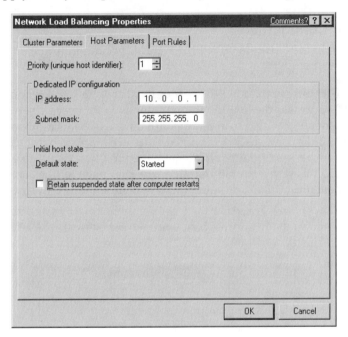

Priority

You configure the Priority (unique host identification) to specify a specific host's unique priority for handling the network traffic for those TCP and UDP ports that are not otherwise accounted for on the Port Rules tab. Each NLB cluster member is assigned a unique number, ranging from 1 (highest priority) to the maximum of hosts in the NLB cluster (lowest priority). In the event a cluster goes offline or is otherwise lost (that is, becomes unresponsive), the priority setting is used to determine which host within the NLB cluster will now become responsible for handling this traffic. Each host within the NLB cluster must have a unique priority number configured.

When attempting to join a new host to the NLB cluster, ensure that the priority setting for it is unique and does not conflict with any existing settings. The new host will not be allowed to join the cluster if its priority setting conflicts with any other already existing host and will cause an entry to be written to the event log describing the error.

Dedicated IP Configuration

The information in the Dedicated IP address space specifies information applicable to this particular host only.

- In the IP address box, enter the cluster IP address in standard dotted notation. This IP address is the IP address that belongs to the specific network adapter you are dealing with. So, in our example, we will be using the value of 10.0.0.1/24 as previously determined when we mapped out the new design. This IP address is typically already assigned to the network adapter before getting to this step from the TCP/IP Properties page for the adapter, as shown in the next illustration. The value you configure must be the same in both places.

- In the Subnet mask box, enter the required subnet mask that corresponds to your VIP entered in the IP address box. Since we are using the 10.0.0.1/24 range for our NLB cluster, we will enter 255.255.255.0 here.

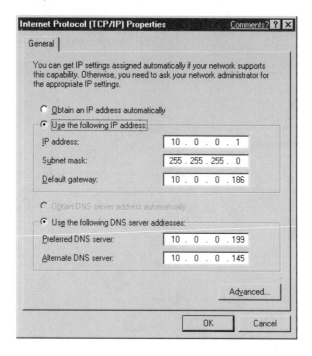

2-Node Active Passive Cluster

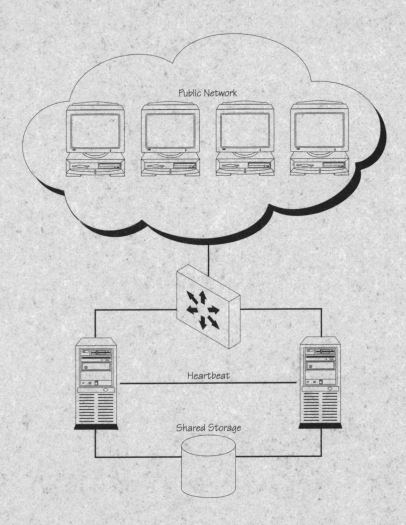

Basic NLB Cluster

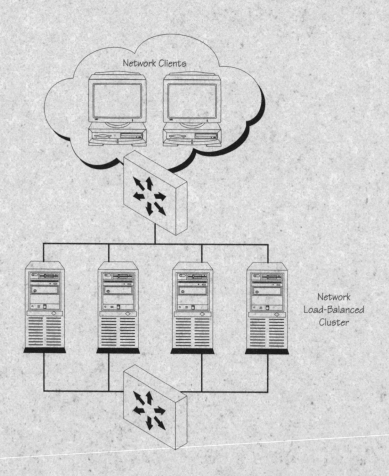

Network Clients

Network
Load-Balanced
Cluster

Detailed Load Balancing Cluster

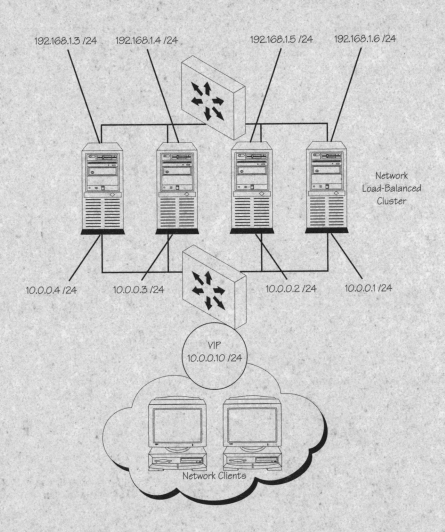

192.168.1.3 /24   192.168.1.4 /24   192.168.1.5 /24   192.168.1.6 /24

Network
Load-Balanced
Cluster

10.0.0.4 /24   10.0.0.3 /24   10.0.0.2 /24   10.0.0.1 /24

VIP
10.0.0.10 /24

Network Clients

Basic Database Cluster Design

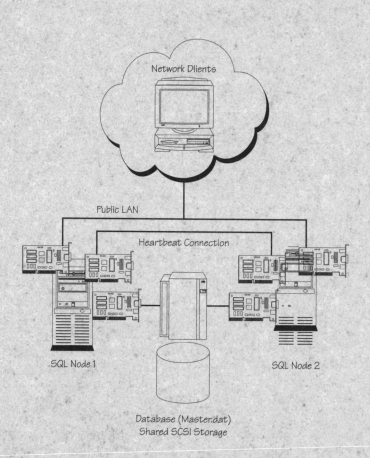

Network Dlients

Public LAN

Heartbeat Connection

SQL Node 1

SQL Node 2

Database (Master.dat)
Shared SCSI Storage

N-Tier Architecture Model

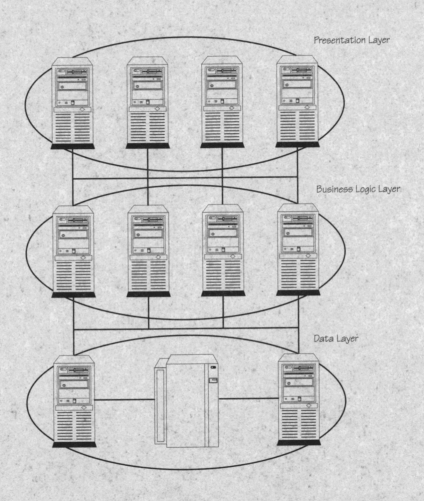

Presentation Layer

Business Logic Layer

Data Layer

5

Advanced NLB (Network Load Balancing) Design

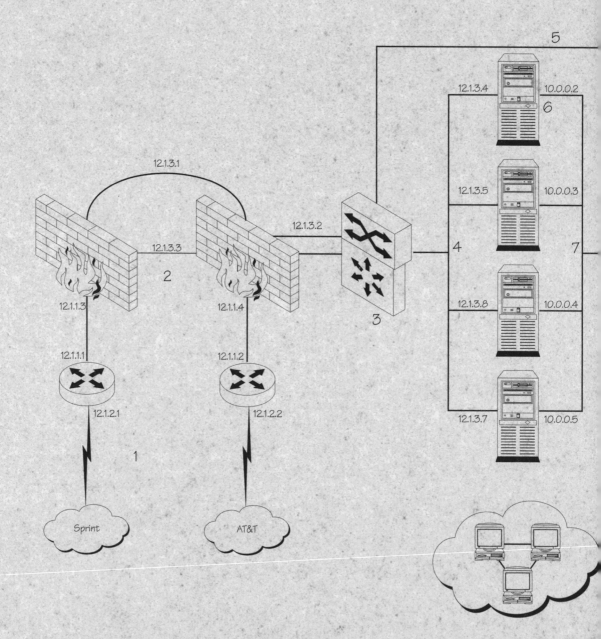

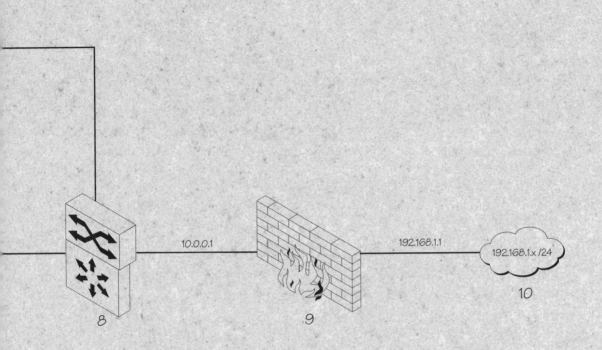

10.0.0.1

192.168.1.1

192.168.1.x /24

8

9

10

Implementing Security with NLB

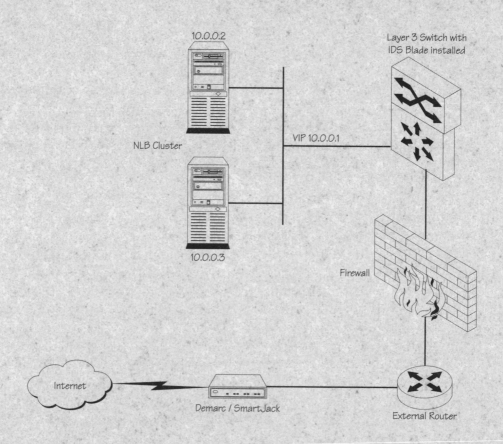

10.0.0.2

Layer 3 Switch with
IDS Blade installed

NLB Cluster

VIP 10.0.0.1

10.0.0.3

Firewall

Internet

Demarc / SmartJack

External Router

Initial Host State

Using the Default state configuration, you can determine what happens when the NLB host starts up.

- If you want the host to immediately join the cluster when Windows starts up, then you should select the Started option.

- If you want the host to start and not join the cluster until you manually join the cluster, then you should select the Stopped option.

- If you want the host to start without joining the cluster and enter a suspended state, then you can select the Suspended option. Note that when the host is suspended, it will not take part in any clustering operations until you issue the resume command; all other cluster commands will be ignored by the host with the exception of the query command. You can instruct the host to resume NLB cluster operation from either the command line or by using the Network Load Balancing Manager, one of the new features in Windows Server 2003.

If you enable the Retain setting, the host will start up in a suspended state if it was in a suspended state at the time of shutdown. For the purposes of our example here, I am going to configure the host with the Startup option selected so the host can immediately become part of the NLB cluster upon startup. In most cases, your configuration should be the same. One reason why you might not want to have the host immediately join the NLB cluster is after the hardware installation where you want to monitor performance before putting the host back into the cluster.

Port Rules

One of the greatest features with NLB clustering is the use of port rules. A *port* is what TCP/IP uses for services-based communication. If you have to connect to a Web Server hosting a web site, you'll probably (by default) attach via port 80. This can be changed but, by default, it's via 80. The Internet Assigned Numbers Authority (IANA), found at **http://www.iana.org**, is the keeper of such port numbers for your review. The port numbers are divided into three ranges:

- Well-Known Ports—port 0 to 1023. These ports are usually marked for specific services, such as HTTP on port 80 or SMTP on port 25

- Registered Ports—port 1024 to 49151

- Dynamic and/or Private Ports—port 49152 to 65535

The combined use of a TCP/IP address and a port creates a socket connection between nodes. For example, if you were going to connect to a web server using HTTP and the web server's IP address is 10.1.1.10, then you would enter the DNS name that resolves to that IP address or enter **http://10.1.1.10**. Because port 80 is a well-known port, you should immediately connect to the web server via port 80. The ports can be altered, so if it's changed to port 8080, then you'll need to create a socket connection manually by specifying the port. You could then enter the following to make a connection with the web server: **http://10.1.1.10:8080**. Although you don't need to know all this for setting up this feature, I hope this helps you understand what a port is because now you'll learn to configure rules for these ports and their use with the NLB Port Rules Parameters tab, shown in the next illustration.

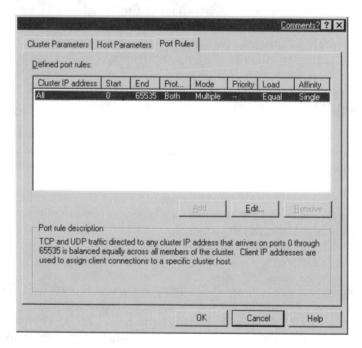

Defined Port Rules

The Port Rules tab has undergone some changes from Windows 2000 Server to Windows Server 2003. In the previous version of Windows, you could use the Port Rules tab to perform the configuration and editing of port rules. In Windows Server 2003, you only see a listing of the currently configured port rules. I think this is a much cleaner approach that makes working with port rules easier and more efficient. As you saw in the previous illustration, a default port rule is configured. From the Port Rules tab, you can click the Add button to define a new port rule, click the Edit button to edit a selected port rule, or delete the selected port rule by clicking Remove. Active port rules are sorted by the port range they cover by default, but you can change the sort by clicking the column you want to sort by.

Adding/Editing Port Rules

If you decide to add new port rules or to edit an existing port rule, you'll be working with the new (and improved) Add/Edit Port Rule page, as shown in the next illustration. When you work with port rules, always remember the number and type of rules must match across all the hosts in the NLB cluster.

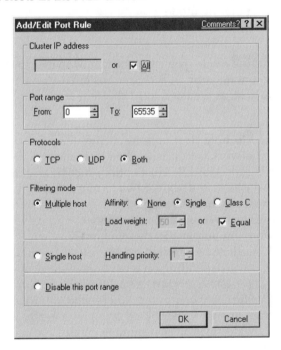

Cluster IP Address

If you're configuring a port rule for a specific machine, enter the IP address for that host. If the port rule is for all members of the NLB cluster, leave the IP address blank and place a check in the All box. By selecting the All box, the port rule is configured as a global port rule and covers all VIP addresses associated with the NLB cluster.

Port Range

Port range lets you specify the starting and ending port numbers for the port rule. The default range is all ports (0 to 65535). If you're configuring a port rule for a single port, then you simply need to enter the same port number in both the starting and the ending box.

Protocols

This enables you to specify the IP protocol the port rule is for—TCP or UDP, or both. By configuring a protocol, only network traffic for that protocol(s) is affected by the rule. All other traffic not affected by this port rule (or any other existing port rules) is handled per the Default Filtering mode.

Filtering Mode

By configuring the Filtering mode, you can choose how to distribute the network traffic for the port rule among your NLB cluster hosts. You have two major choices: Multiple host or single host, as well as a third choice that won't be used often: Disable this port range.

Multiple Host Selecting Multiple Host option specifies that multiple hosts in the NLB cluster can handle the network traffic associated with the specific port rule. Many advantages exist to using the Multiple Host option, such as fault tolerance and scalable performance as the load is distributed over two or more cluster hosts, instead of being applied solely to one host as when the Single Host option is selected. Loading can be applied equally to all hosts or it can be manually configured for each host as desired (and as hardware limitations dictate sometimes).

Incoming network traffic to be handled by this rule is distributed to each of the NLB hosts in different ways, depending on what type of traffic it is. If the traffic is TCP, then it's distributed on a *per-connection basis,* which means a specific NLB host maintains a connection with a specific client computer. You see the importance of this shortly. If the traffic is UDP, though, then it's distributed on a *per-datagram basis,* either way, the source IP address and the destination port number creates a unique client request. You can further configure the behavior of the load distribution algorithm by configuring affinity options, as discussed next.

Webster's Dictionary defines affinity as "An attractive force between substances or particles that causes them to enter into and remain in chemical combination." While we aren't dealing with chemical combinations and reactions here, the term affinity is still quite relevant. In simple terms, *affinity* is the attraction one item feels for another item. In network load balancing, affinity can be configured to control how NLB hosts distribute incoming client requests.

- Selecting None specifies that NLB doesn't need to direct multiple requests from the same client to the same NLB host. This usually isn't the preferred option, as explained in the following discussion of the Single and Class C affinity options.

- Selecting Single specifies that NLB should direct multiple requests from the same client (by IP address) to the same NLB host until the session is closed or timed out. These requests can be either TCP connections or UDP datagrams. Using Single affinity ensures that one, and only one, cluster host handles the entire session from a specific client, which is vital if an application running on the server requires the maintenance of a client session state—such as an ecommerce application that maintains cookies between connections. In this way, the Single affinity setting can be quite useful. However, a benefit exists to disabling Single affinity and resorting to None for affinity: disabling affinity will improve performance of the entire NLB cluster by allowing multiple connections from a single client to be distributed to multiple hosts. Single affinity is best used for intranet-accessible web sites that require the maintenance of session state between connections.

- Selecting Class C affinity specifies that NLB should direct multiple requests from the same TCP/IP Class C address range to the same cluster host. These requests can be either TCP connections or UDP datagrams. When you implement Class C affinity, you safely ensure that the use of multiple proxy servers within the requesting client's domain don't cause a session state to be lost—a single NLB host would end up being responsible for all the domain's proxy servers, assuming they all share the same Class C address range. In this way, Class C affinity works similarly to Single affinity. The only difference is in the scope of the IP address—each will still maintain the client's session state between connections. As with Single affinity, disabling affinity altogether and using the None setting improves the overall cluster performance, but at the expense of session state data. Class C affinity is best used for Internet-accessible web sites that require the maintenance of session state between connections.

If you're using the Multiple Host option, then you have the option to configure the load weight setting. The *load weight setting* specifies the percentage of the load-balanced network traffic the host should handle for that port rule. You can change the load weight setting to any value from 0 (prevents the host from handling any of the network traffic associated with the port rule) to 100 (sets the host to handle all the network traffic associated with the port rule). A point often misunderstood about configuring the load weight is this: the total load weight setting of all the NLB cluster hosts doesn't have to add up to 100. The actual percentage of traffic a specific host will handle is computed by dividing its load weight setting by the sum of all the load weight settings across the entire NLB cluster. So, if you had five NLB hosts with a total load weight of 150, and one specific host had a load weight setting of 60, then it would receive about 40 percent of the total distributed load.

If you don't need to manually configure the load weight for each cluster host, then you can simply place a check in the Equal box to specify that all network traffic associated with this port rule should be equally divided among all active cluster hosts per the distribution algorithm in use.

Single Host Selecting the Single Host option specifies the network traffic associated with the port rule should all be handled by one specific host, as determined by the Handling priority. In this way, the Handling priority serves a similar (but not the same by any means) purpose as the Priority setting by determining which server will handle the network traffic.

The *Handling priority* is used to specify the local NLB host's priority for handling the network traffic associated with the port rule being configured. The host with the highest priority (which would be the lowest settings) handles all traffic associated with this rule first by default. If that host becomes unavailable; the next highest priority host takes over the role of handling network traffic associated with the port rule. The allowable values range from 1 to the number of hosts in the NLB cluster and each cluster host must have a unique value configured.

Disable This Port Range The last option available when configuring a port rule is to block all traffic in the port range you have configured from passing. When this option is selected, the NLB driver filters all traffic that corresponds to the port range configured and prevents it from passing. The *Filtering* mode helps you build a firewall to prevent unwanted network access to a configured range of ports on your NLB cluster hosts.

MANAGING NETWORK LOAD BALANCING

Now that you've configured your first NLB cluster host, you want to ensure that you've documented everything at each step of the process. You could have been doing this along the way or you can go back and do it now. I prefer to take screen shots of each area requiring configuration, print them, and then place them in a notebook. In this way, you can easily see what gets configured if you need to add another host or change a specific setting. On the topic of adding another NLB host, you'll probably want to do that now because an NLB cluster isn't an NLB cluster until you get two or more hosts up and running the NLB service. You can add additional hosts by following the same process you went through for configuring the first one or by using the Network Load Balancing Manager. One caveat for using the NLB Manager to add new cluster hosts: you must have already configured the IP address for the host from the Internet (TCP/IP) Properties page.

In the next few sections, you look at managing NLB clusters and performing more advanced operations with NLB clusters.

Using the Network Load Balancing Manager

As mentioned previously, the Network Load Balancing (NLB) Manager is a new feature to Windows in Windows Server 2003. Using the NLB Manager (nlbmgr.exe), you can easily perform the most common NLB cluster control and configuration options from within an easy-to-use GUI. Figure 3-13 shows what the NLB Manager looks like after completing the configuration of your first NLB cluster host.

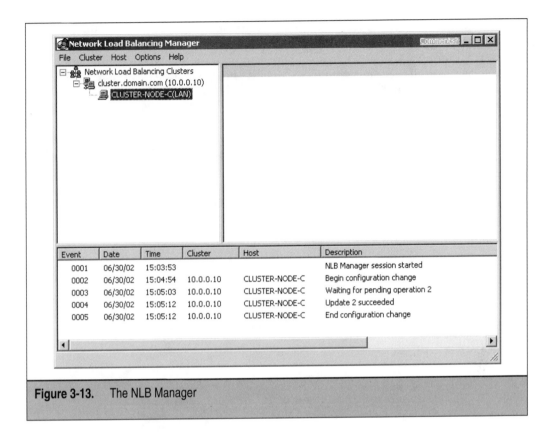

Figure 3-13. The NLB Manager

Some of the tasks you can perform with the NLB Manager include the following:

- Connect to existing clusters
- Create new clusters
- Delete clusters
- Add hosts to a cluster
- View the properties for a cluster
- Issue the Query, Start, Stop, Drainstop, Suspend, and Resume commands to a cluster
- Delete a host from a cluster
- View the properties for a host
- Issue the Query, Start, Stop, Drainstop, Suspend, and Resume commands to a host
- Specify the credentials to use when connecting to a host
- Specify logging to occur

Let's look at how you can add a second host to your NLB cluster using the NLB Manager. After Windows Server 2003 is installed and properly configured, you must ensure the Internet (TCP/IP) Properties are configured for the new host. In this example, you use all the same settings for the first host, with one exception: the IP address will be set as 10.0.0.2. Once this is done, you can add the host to the NLB cluster by right-clicking the cluster name (in this case, cluster.domain.com), and then selecting Add host to cluster, as seen in the following illustration.

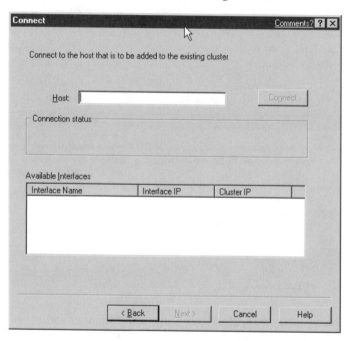

After you enter the name or IP address of the host to add to the cluster, click Connect to connect it to the cluster. The list of available adapters appears at the bottom of the page: select the adapter you want and click Next. All you must do now is configure the Host Properties page with the correct information. Ensure that you use the correct IP address—the one that matches what you configured previously on the Internet (TCP/IP) Properties page. If all went well, you should have another node in your NLB Manager. You can continue to add any remaining NLB cluster hosts in the same fashion.

Using the NLB Command

After you enable Network Load Balancing on an adapter, you'll find a new executable file, nlb.exe, has appeared in your %systemroot%/system32/ folder. The nlb.exe command replaces the wlbs.exe command previously used in Windows NT 4.0 and Windows 2000 Server. The context for the NLB.exe command is

```
nlb <command> <remote options>
```

Table 3-6 lists the commands available for use with the nlb.exe command.

Command	Description
help	Displays the help listing all commands.
suspend [*<cluster>*[:*<host>*] | all *<local>*|*<global>*]	Suspends all cluster operations until the Resume command is issued. Using suspend prevents remote control commands from being carried out by the cluster. The Suspend command can be targeted at a specific cluster, a specific cluster on a specific host, all clusters on the local machine, or all global machines that are part of the cluster.
resume [*<cluster>*[:*<host>*] | all *<local>*|*<global>*]	Instructs a suspended cluster to resume cluster operations. Using the Resume command doesn't restart clustering operations but, instead, allows the use of Cluster Control commands, including those sent remotely. The Resume command can be targeted at a specific cluster, a specific cluster on a specific host, all clusters on the local machine, or all global machines that are part of the cluster.
start [*<cluster>*[:*<host>*] | all *<local>*|*<global>*]	Directs that cluster operations on the specified hosts should start. This enables all ports that might have been previously disabled. The Start command can be targeted at a specific cluster, a specific cluster on a specific host, all clusters on the local machine, or all global machines that are part of the cluster.
stop [*<cluster>*[:*<host>*] | all *<local>*|*<global>*]	Directs that cluster operations on the specified hosts should stop. The Stop command can be targeted at a specific cluster, a specific cluster on a specific host, all clusters on the local machine, or all global machines that are part of the cluster.
drainstop [*<cluster>*[:*<host>*] | all *<local>*|*<global>*]	Instructs the specified hosts not to add any new network traffic. The specified hosts drain (servicing existing connections, while not allowing new connections) and stop all cluster operations when all active connections have terminated. You can cease draining by issuing the Stop command or the Start command. The Drainstop command can be targeted at a specific cluster, a specific cluster on a specific host, all clusters on the local machine, or all global machines that are part of the cluster.
enable [*vip*[:*port*|:all] | all[:*port*|:all]] [*<cluster>*[:*<host>*] | all *<local>*|*<global>*]	Enables traffic handling for the port rule, which contains the specified port in its port range. Using the first set of optional parameters, the Enable command can be targeted at every VIP, a specific VIP on a specific port rule, or all port rules. Using the second set of optional parameters, the Enable command can be targeted at a specific cluster, a specific cluster on a specific host, all clusters on the local machine, or all global machines that are part of the cluster. All ports specified by the port rule are affected. If all is specified for the port, then the Enable command is applied to the ports covered by all port rules. If the hosts specified in the command haven't yet started cluster operations, the Enable command is ignored.

Table 3-6.   NLB Commands and Remote Control Options

Command	Description
disable [*vip*[:*port*|:all]	all[:*port*|:all]] [<*cluster*>[:<*host*>]	all <*local*>|<*global*>]	Issuing the Disable command immediately disables and blocks all traffic handling for the port rule whose port range contains the specified port. Using the first set of optional parameters, the Disable command can be targeted at every VIP, a specific VIP on a specific port rule, or all port rules. Using the second set of optional parameters, the Disable command can be targeted at a specific cluster, a specific cluster on a specific host, all clusters on the local machine, or all global machines that are part of the cluster. All ports specified by the port rule are affected. If all is specified for the port, then the Disable command is applied to the ports covered by all port rules. If you want to maintain existing active connections, use the Drain command instead. If the hosts specified in the command haven't yet started cluster operations, the Disable command is ignored.
drain [*vip*[:*port*|:all]	all[:*port*|:all]] [<*cluster*>[:<*host*>]	all <*local*>|<*global*>]	Disables new traffic handling for the rule whose port range contains the specified port. Using the first set of optional parameters, the Drain command can be targeted at every VIP, a specific VIP on a specific port rule, or all port rules. Using the second set of optional parameters, the Drain command can be targeted at a specific cluster, a specific cluster on a specific host, all clusters on the local machine, or all global machines that are part of the cluster. All ports specified by the port rule are affected. If all is specified for the port, then the Disable command is applied to the ports covered by all port rules. All new connection requests will be refused, but all active connections are maintained until the session is terminated. If you want to disable existing active connections, use the Disable command instead. If the hosts specified in the command haven't yet started cluster operations, the Disable command is ignored.
query [<*cluster*>[:<*host*>]	all <*local*>	<*global*>]	Provides a display showing the current cluster state and the list of host priorities for the current members of the cluster. There are four possible states: Unknown—The host hasn't started cluster operations, so it can't determine the state of the cluster. Converging—The cluster is attempting to converge to a consistent state. If the cluster remains in Converging status for a long time, a problem with cluster parameters is usually to blame. Investigating the event logs for messages related to NLB could offer an indication of the problem. Draining—The cluster is converged, but the host had initiated draining to drain all active existing connections. This state is caused by issuing the Drainstop command. Converged as default—The cluster is fully converged and the responding host is the current default (highest active priority host). The default host handles network traffic for all the TCP and UDP ports not covered by the configured port rules. Converged—The cluster is fully converged and the responding host isn't the default host. The Query command can be targeted at a specific cluster, a specific cluster on a specific host, all clusters on the local machine, or all global machines that are part of the cluster.

Table 3-6.   NLB Commands and Remote Control Options *(continued)*

Command	Description
reload [*cluster*	all] (local only)	Instructs NLB to reload the current parameter set from the Registry. If required to complete the process, cluster operations are stopped and subsequently restarted. Any errors that exist within the parameters prevent the host from joining the cluster and also cause a warning dialog box to be displayed.
display [*cluster*	all] (local only)	Displays information about the current NLB parameters, cluster state, and past cluster activity. The Display command also displays the last several event log entries produced by the NLB service, including any binary data attached to the log entry. The Display command is typically used for troubleshooting cluster operations.
ip2mac <cluster>	Displays the MAC address corresponding to the specified cluster name or IP address. The ip2mac command is useful when creating a static ARP entry in routers.

Table 3-6.   NLB Commands and Remote Control Options *(continued)*

The following table lists the Remote Control options:

/PASSW *password*	Supplies the remote control password to initiate a remote control session.
/PORT *port*	Specifies the cluster's remote control UDP port.
/local	Performs the operations only on the local machine.

CONCLUSION

In this chapter, you learned the start-to-finish process of designing, installing, and configuring all aspects of a Windows Server 2003 clustering as well as NLB services you'll need to know to have a Highly Available solution. In this chapter, you began by looking at a rolling upgrade from a Windows 2000 Advanced Server two-node cluster to a Windows Server 2003 Enterprise two-node cluster. Next, you saw all the design work that goes into planning for a Windows Server 2003 cluster from scratch and how to implement it. Once you had the cluster operational, you looked at advanced configurations and troubleshooting. Finally, you examined the design and implementation of rolling out a Windows Server 2003 Highly Available NLB or network load-balanced solution. In this chapter, you also learned how to take Microsoft's newest platform and create Highly Available solutions using Microsoft's new flagship OS: Windows Server 2003.

CHAPTER 4

Designing a Clustered and Load-Balanced Solution with Application Center 2000

In this chapter, you learn about Microsoft's Server 2003 solution called Application Center 2000. In previous chapters, you learned the fundamentals of clustering, network load balancing, and high availability in Windows 2000 Server and Windows 2003 Server. Now you're going to examine a product designed solely for creating large, robust, and easy to manage server farms using clustering or load balancing (both network load balancing and component load balancing). In this chapter, you learn about how to plan, design, configure, and install Application Center 2000. This chapter also sets the stage for future chapters that will cover the more advanced configurations with Application Center 2000.

PREDESIGN PLANNING

Application Center 2000 is the Server 2003 solution used for building and managing Web applications, and managing high availability and load balancing, as well as enabling you to "scale out" your load-balanced solution over many more nodes for a much more robust NLB solution. Application Center 2000 also offers you more manageability (which you learn about in great detail throughout this chapter.). Another benefit to appreciate is rolling out and deploying content to a load-balanced cluster using Application Center 2000.

The Purpose of Application Center 2000

Microsoft Application Center 2000 is the management and deployment tool that enables you the ultimate in management and deployment of content of your web and COM+ applications.

So what's at the core of this product? Quite simply, Application Center 2000 leverages your preexisting load-balanced cluster solution. You don't just install Application Center 2000 on a machine and load balance it. You install NLB clusters with Windows 2000, and then install Application Center 2000 on top of the nodes to create a more manageable cluster. Remember in Chapter 2 when you installed network load balancing from Windows 2000 Advanced Server? We covered many settings you can configure, but you never had total control over all your nodes. You never had the capability to send content to the entire cluster from one location. Now you can, as you'll see when we take a critical look at Application Center 2000.

I want to explain the terminology for this chapter quickly. We already covered the differences in terminology when discussing building a cluster with Microsoft Clustering Services, instead of building a load-balanced cluster with NLB Services. In Application Center 2000, you build Application Center 2000 clusters. Figure 4-1 shows a basic topology map with Application Center 2000 in use.

Application Center clusters are designed for stateless, middle-tier applications, such as web sites and COM+ applications. They don't require a shared disk (or any special

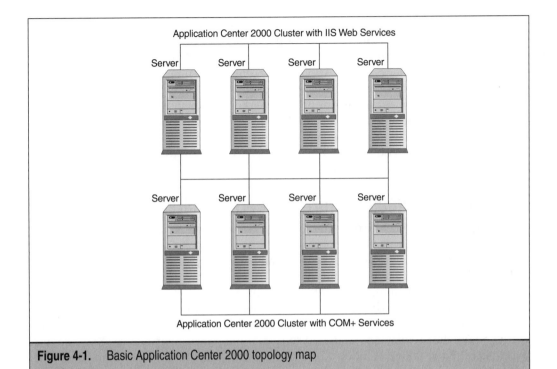

Figure 4-1.   Basic Application Center 2000 topology map

hardware). You wouldn't want to use Application Center 2000 for Exchange 2000 or for SQL clustering because these are considered stateful applications. If an application is *stateful,* this means it's one in which some information about a connection between two systems is retained for future use: state is maintained. A *stateless* connection is one in which no information is retained by either sender or receiver.

You can use Application Center to manage availability and application deployment on stand-alone servers or servers that aren't running web sites. Also, be aware for design purposes that you can build Windows 2000 Server Application Center 2000 clusters because you aren't locked into using Windows 2000 Advanced Server to use NLB. Installing Application Center 2000 on a Windows 2000 Server installs the drivers that enable you to use NLB.

Application Center 2000 comes with a great management tool-based console (you'll see this later), which is a Microsoft Management Console (MMC) snap-in. This console does something unique: it enables you to monitor the state of the cluster with a view of how every node is doing, as well as their combined health. From this console, you can even manage Internet Information Server (IIS) and deploy content to it.

Availability with Application Center 2000 is top of the line. Because all nodes balance together, no single point of failure exists for the cluster. This also works for maintenance because you can easily take a node offline and repair it while all other nodes take the brunt of the load. This also makes Application Center 2000 a powerful tool for repair and troubleshooting purposes.

The true reason for installing Application Center 2000 is to enhance the product you currently use: Windows 2000 Server. Windows 2000 Server with IIS installed on it is a powerful tool by itself, but add the power of high availability and extended management to it, and you have an even more powerful formula. Let's look at how this fits into your current environment.

Application Center 2000 Feature Set and Requirements

Application Center 2000 is hard to deploy if you don't understand how it benefits you, the purpose of the rollout, what preparations you need to make, and so on. Just like every other technology we've discussed, it's all about the plan and design. Anyone can install software and get something to work eventually but, without a solid plan and meeting good prerequisites, most high-availability designs won't perform well during implementation. Let's step back and review the specifics before we get to the installation.

The feature set behind Application Center 2000 is light on the surface, but gets dense when you use the product. The heart and soul of Application Center 2000 revolves around the cluster. You're taking Windows 2000 Servers and providing yourself (or your staff) with a better way to implement and manage the cluster. Application Center 2000 isn't cryptic like NLB on Windows 2000 Advanced Server. With Windows 2000 Advanced Server there is no central console and no Deployment Wizard. Application Center 2000 is scaled down. If you were asked by management to give an accurate assessment of the load on a four-node Windows 2000 Advanced Server NLB cluster, this would be difficult to do. Once Application Center 2000 is installed, you have the benefits of Health Monitor (explained later) to use for this purpose alone, as well as its many other uses.

Application Center 2000 also supports both NLB for network load balancing (NLB) and component load balancing (CLB). Be aware that the Application Center 2000 product is key to successful web site deployment, content deployment (which uses the load-balancing feature for all components within the web sites), and management of its high availability within many tiered environments.

Application Center 2000 also plays a major role in the synchronization, replication, and deployment of nodes—up to 32 in total. When you make a system's settings change, this change is quickly replicated to all other nodes within your cluster. This makes deployment of changes easy (and quick) to do.

Application Center 2000 allows you to apply more control over affinity as well. We discussed affinity and how to configure it with Windows 2000 Advanced Server NLB in Chapter 2, but as we move forward with Application Center 2000, you'll see it's more easily managed and configured.

Application Center 2000 is feature-rich and builds your infrastructure to allow your servers to be managed and monitored better. You now have a tool to deploy content. Let's look at the requirements.

System Requirements

With Application Center 2000, you need to have Windows 2000 Server or Windows 2000 Advanced Server installed. You could also use Windows 2000 Datacenter Server, but we won't discuss it specifically here. In Chapters 1 and 2, you learned you must have Windows 2000 Advanced Server installed to take advantage of any clustering services. With Application Center 2000, you can now set up a cluster of Windows 2000 Servers (which saves you money on licenses), and install Application Center 2000 on top of Windows 2000 Server to get the network load balancing feature and drivers installed. Note, you can also mix and match, so if you already have a cluster of two servers running Windows 2000 Advanced Server in an NLB cluster, you can install Application Center 2000, and then start adding nodes using Windows 2000 Server into the preexisting cluster as new nodes. We'll drill down deeper into specific hotfixes and Service Packs you need later, but first look at the fundamentals of what you need to get started.

First, you need to know the requirements listed in the following tables, Table 4-1 and Table 4-2, for the server and the client. When you first read this, you might become confused because the "client" almost seems as if you need to install a software package on your network clients. This isn't the case. The client portion of the install is the PC you'll install the console on to manage the cluster through Application Center 2000.

Processor	Pentium-Based 400 MHz or Higher CPU
Operating System	Microsoft Windows 2000 Server Windows 2000 Advanced Server Microsoft Windows 2000 Service Pack 1 or later Microsoft Internet Information Services 5.0 must be installed
Memory	256MB of RAM minimum and 512 or above recommended, especially if running IIS
Hard Disk	100MB of available space
Other Devices	One network interface card (NIC) (two recommended) If using Windows 2000 Network Load Balancing (NLB), two NICs are required CD-ROM, mouse, and compatible display

Table 4-1.   Server-Based Requirements

Processor	Pentium-Based 266 MHz or Higher CPU
Operating System	Microsoft Windows 2000 Professional Windows 2000 Server Windows 2000 Advanced Server operating system (OS) Microsoft Windows 2000 Service Pack 1 or later
Memory	128MB of RAM minimum
Hard Disk	20MB of available space
Other Devices	Network adapter card, CD-ROM, mouse, and compatible display

Table 4-2.   Client-Based Requirements

The server portion of the install is the actual package you place directly on the server, so it becomes Application Center 2000. You can also, if needed, manage Application Center from a console directly on the server. Microsoft Application Center 2000 Server requires the following minimum system configuration, as seen in Table 4-1.

Microsoft Application Center 2000 Client requires the following minimum system configuration, as seen in Table 4-2.

Make sure you never settle for only the minimum requirements and always figure you could be running other services (such as IIS), which cache much of their services in RAM for improved performance and speed. If you try to skimp on resources, your system may be impacted. If you plan on installing Application Center 2000 Service Pack 1, you need an additional 110MB of disk space available. In addition, you need to ensure that servers to be updated with Application Center 2000 SP1 have been updated already with Windows 2000 SP2.

Application Center 2000 Installation Summary

This is a breakdown of the most essential items you need to pay attention to while preparing an installation and deployment of Application Center 2000.

- To install Application Center on the Windows 2000 Server and Windows 2000 Advanced Server OSs, you must install the Windows 2000 Service Pack 1 (SP1) and Pre service Pack 2 (SP2) components. If you fail to adhere to these strict requirements, Application Center 2000 installation will fail every time.

- IIS 5.0 must be installed as part of your Windows 2000 solution, see the following illustration. If you need to reapply the service, follow this path: Start | Settings | Control Panel | Add/Remove Programs. Click the Add/Remove Windows Components Icon, then add the IIS Service.

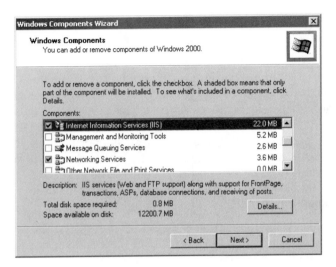

- Application Center 2000, when installed on Windows 2000 Server (not Windows 2000 Advanced Server), automatically installs network load balancing. As previously mentioned, Windows 2000 Server doesn't support NLB. When you install Application Center 2000, though, it adds the NLB drivers to the server. Make sure when you install Application Center 2000, it appears in the Network Properties dialog box. If you don't have the driver installed, it won't work. If you need to check the driver, follow this path: Click Start | Settings | Control Panel | Network and Dial-up Connections. Select an adapter and right-click it. Select Properties | Install Button, and then highlight Service. Click Add, and select NLB or network load balancing. This is seen in the next illustration.

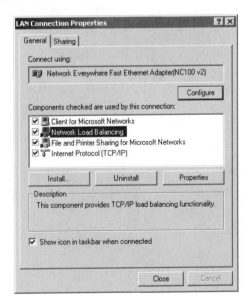

- Make sure your server is *not* running as a domain controller. If you're running a domain controller, then the installation program won't let you continue as per the installation requirements.

- One of the most important things to plan before you install Application Center 2000 (and one of the biggest failures of installation) is keeping the same directory and drive structure between all cluster nodes. Because replication is a large part of the Application Center 2000 cluster, the drive structures where the program and system files reside must be identical. If not, then you'll have a failed installation because the first node in the cluster will run a check to make sure this requirement was met. They can be integrated later with some work but, for ease of installation and configuration, make sure you pay close attention to this bullet or it could consistently hang you up when at installation.

- Another main point to mention is the NICs you use must be compliant with the Hardware Compatibility List (HCL) or the installation could hang you up. Of course, you want to make sure all your hardware is compliant with the HCL. Don't take shortcuts in this area; it isn't worth the headaches.

- Plan your IP addresses accordingly (as you've done with every other installation thus far). Make sure you have the appropriate interfaces configured with valid and static IP addresses. Don't use DHCP.

- When using Application Center 2000 Network Load Balancing, you must use two NICs.

- You need to have two IP addresses per node and the cluster controller will be responsible for the VIP (Virtual IP Address) for the entire cluster so you will need one more IP address for the VIP. In other words, if you have a two-node Application Center 2000 cluster, you need two IP addresses per node, which equals four, and a single IP Address to denote the VIP, so a total of five is needed.

Other Load-Balancing Options

Other load-balancing options, as mentioned previously, are also available in Application Center 2000. Application Center 2000 enables you to use CLB). With CLB, requests for COM+ components are load balanced across all the CLB members. Third-party hardware/software load balancing is also supported, as you saw in Chapter 1. Third-party load balancing can be accomplished with a separate device that forwards traffic to each node member. Cluster types with Application Center have support for three basic types:

- General/web cluster
- COM+ application cluster
- COM+ routing cluster

General/Web Cluster   A *General/Web cluster* is a name given to describe any standard cluster that uses a grouping of servers to process client requests or web-based requests (see Figure 4-2). These clusters can include, but are not limited to:

- Internet web servers
- Staging servers (used to deploy content to the rest of the cluster)

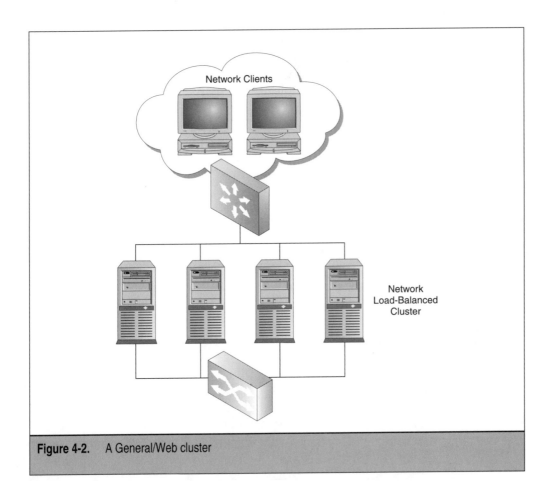

Figure 4-2.   A General/Web cluster

- COM+ load-balanced routing servers
- COM+ component servers
- One member stand-alone servers

The General/Web cluster is the cluster type you'll use most often.

COM+ Application Cluster   Another viable cluster option is to set up a COM+ application cluster. The *COM+ application cluster* is a cluster of servers that will manage a grouping of COM+ components. When you build this type of cluster, you need to take into consideration that you'll want each COM+ component in the set of components to be load balanced placed on every single node in the cluster. Application Center 2000 enables you to manage this. Look at Figure 4-3 to see an example of a COM+ application cluster.

COM+ Routing Cluster   Another cluster type you can employ is the rarely used option of creating a COM+ routing cluster. The *COM+ routing cluster* enables you to create a routing solution where COM+-based Win32 applications are used and routed via this cluster. Look at Figure 4-4 to see an example of a COM+ routing cluster.

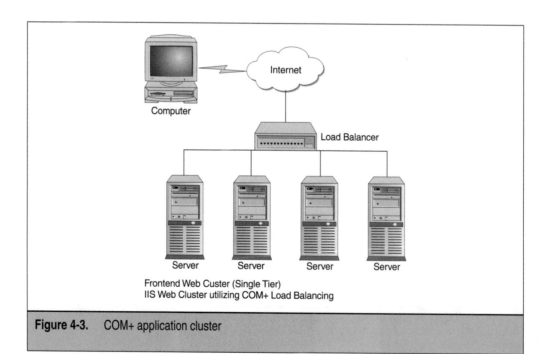

Figure 4-3.   COM+ application cluster

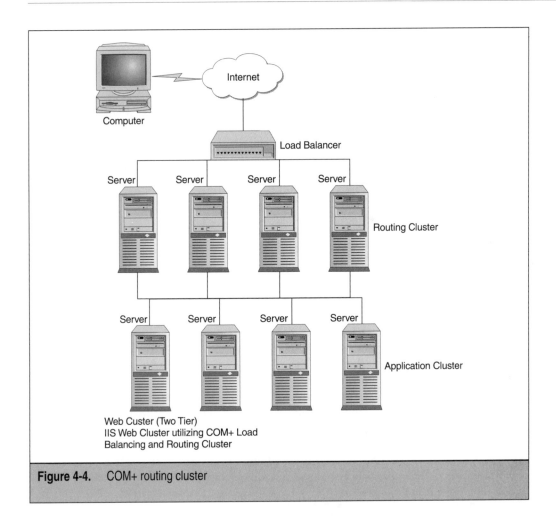

Figure 4-4.   COM+ routing cluster

PREPARATION AND INSTALLATION

As previously discussed in great detail, you must plan, design, and test before setting up these types of solutions, such as Application Center 2000. In my experience, I've learned many tricks and tips by thoroughly testing before implementation. Without the proper lab work in advance, and without creating a decent pilot, failure is more likely to occur. Now that you're this far in the book, you should feel comfortable with the methodology we're using and be able to think about all the pitfalls you might encounter.

Before we start the install, you should know what type of cluster you want to install. You have the three choices of

- **General/Web cluster**   The cluster hosts Web sites and local COM+ applications, or will be used for staging applications, monitoring or synchronization. This cluster supports application deployment and Component Load Balancing (CLB).

- **COM+ application cluster**   The cluster hosts only COM+ applications that can be referenced by other Web sites or Windows-based applications.

- **COM+ routing cluster**   The cluster routes requests to a COM+ application cluster.

If you look at the dialog box closely, it also briefly explains the different types you'll want to select. In this chapter, we install and create a General/Web cluster.

Planning the Deployment of Application Center 2000 in n-tier Environments

When designing and planning your Application Center rollout, you need to plan what you want as far as designing scaling out versus scaling up. *Scaling up* means to build up the one box you're using for everything, such as adding hard disk space, memory, better CPUs, and so forth. With *scaling out,* you add more machines to the equation. Scaling out would add two or three more machines for load balancing or clustering. Scaling up is used more for mainframe types of situations where everything resides on one machine. The scaling-out method would be seen in a client/server situation where you could add more servers for scalability. Regardless of what you decide, always design for scalability in general. AC2K allows room to scale up and out, especially when you can add nodes to the cluster transparently. You never have to take the cluster down to add or remove a node from the cluster. Reliability must be addressed in the design for your systems, especially a web environment. You need to make sure your users can always access the web servers and sites. The machines must always be accessible, so they need to be reliable. AC2K provides reliability with many tools to check the status of your clusters and nodes. Be sure that if you plan to use AC2K, you lay out the entire design within Visio 2000 or some other type of diagramming tool. Also, make certain the entire deployment is thoroughly thought out and designed appropriately.

The installation process of Application Center 2000 is quite simple. First, set the network properties on your cluster nodes. For this example, we'll use a two-node cluster. Open the network properties of the server that will be the first node you install Application Center 2000 onto and configure its IP addressing. You can use the same IP addressing we used for the last two chapters. Your public network can be 192.168.1.0 /24 and your private Heartbeat network can carry the 10.0.0.0 /24 subnet. Again, as long as you know how to do this, it doesn't matter what IP addressing classes you pick—just make sure it's applicable to your current environment. Once you configure the nodes with their respective IP addresses, you can start the installation process of Application Center 2000.

An Attended Installation

Put the CD-ROM in and you'll autorun the Installation Wizard. When you put the AC2K installation disk in, you're prompted with a dialog box with the following options. If you can't get autorun to work, browse to the CD-ROM, and run setup.hta.

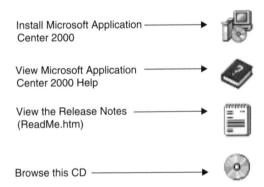

Install Microsoft Application
Center 2000

View Microsoft Application
Center 2000 Help

View the Release Notes
(ReadMe.htm)

Browse this CD

When you select to install Application Center 2000, you're prompted with a second dialog box, with the following steps.

1. Install Microsoft Windows 2000 Service Pack 1

2. Install Microsoft Windows 2000 Post-Service pack 1 fixes

3. Install Microsoft Application Center 2000

This dialog box requests you add the requisite software patches before continuing with the install. Also, slot yourself a considerable amount of time to do this install because it'll take a while to get all the service packs and hot fixes installed.

Once you install Windows 2000 Service Pack 1, all the post-Service Pack hot fixes, and/or Service Pack 2, you can continue with the installation of Application Center 2000. Remember, nearly everything you get from the dialog box, as shown in the previous illustration, comes directly from the CD-ROM from which you're installing. However, you'll want to go online to Windows Update and check for any more updates to install. At the end of this chapter, I outlined some of the new updates to Application Center 2000 that you might want to review, as well as Installing Windows 2000 Service Pack 2.

Once you satisfy all the preinstallation update requirements, click the Install Microsoft Application Center 2000 link, which launches the actual installation process. Agree to the licensing agreement, and then choose Custom for an installation option. You'll be prompted to install all components on to the Windows 2000 Server you're working on currently.

Again, make sure you have enough room on your disk, especially if you're installing on top of live production systems. Once you're done, click Next, and you'll be finished with the basic installation.

Unattended Installation Options

With an *unattended installation,* you can install Application Center 2000 either via the command line or by batch file. Table 4-3 shows you all the options available at your disposal when contemplating an unattended installation. In the table, you can see an option for AC logging, *ac.exe,* which is a command line utility that enables you the functionality of performing the unattended installation. In Chapter 2 and 3, we looked at command-line options like wlbs.exe and nlb.exe. This tool—ac.exe—is the same type of tool.

If you want to see the exact msiexec command, use any of the following samples:

Default installation	msiexec /i "path" /q /lv* filename.log
No AC Logging	msiexec /i "path"/q /lv* filename.log ADDLOCAL=Server,Client
With AC Logging	msiexec /i "path"/q /lv* filename/log ADDLOCAL = Server,Client,ACLogging
Server only	msiexec /i "path"/q /lv* filename.log ADDLOCAL=Server
Administrative Client only	msiexec /i "path" /q /lv* filename.log ADDLOCAL=Client
Sample monitors	msiexec /i "path" /q /lv* filename.log ADDLOCAL=SampleHealthMonMonitors
Specifying the PID	msiexec /i "root\Microsoft Application Center 2000.msi" /q PIDKEY=pid_key

Default Installation	This option installs the Administrative client if you haven't installed the hot fixes first. Server, Administrative client, Application Center Events, and Performance Logging are installed (this is a default configuration). All features are available with this installation.
No AC Logging	The full server and Administrative client are installed. The full server and Administrative client features are available, but specific logging features aren't available.
With AC Logging	The full server and Administrative client are installed. The full server and Administrative client features are available with all logging features.
Server only	Only the full server—not the Administrative client, Application Center Events, and Performance Logging—is installed. Server Only: No AC Logging is included by default. To exclude No AC Logging for Server only, use No AC Logging.
Administrative Client only	Only the Administrative client—not the full server, Application Center Events, and Performance Logging—is installed. Use this installation for remote administration. The computer on which this option is installed can't become a cluster member. An Administrative Client only installation must include With AC Logging.
Sample monitors	Several Microsoft Health Monitor 2.1 rules for Microsoft SQL Server and other monitoring tasks are installed.

Table 4-3. Unattended Installation Options

Troubleshoot Installation Problems   In any installation, you're bound to have problems. This one, with Application Center 2000, is no different. If you followed all the preplanning, you shouldn't have too many issues, but if you do have problems, make sure you jot them down to research later. What I've done in the past is to set up the pilot of the production system in the lab and purposely run installation after installation until I find a failure. When you install to production systems, you want to make sure you're ready for anything.

BASIC CONFIGURATION OF APPLICATION CENTER 2000

Now you have Application Center 2000 installed and you want to start using it. You need to begin the configuration process, so you can use your new management tools. The first thing you need to do is create a new cluster. In this section, we create a new cluster, analyze what the cluster controller does, and learn how to add nodes to the cluster.

Creating a New Cluster

Your first task when configuring Application Center 2000 is to create a cluster. First, open the Application Center 2000 MMC by going to the Administrative Tools folder (in the Control Panel) and select the Application Center 2000 Console. When you open it, you see the option to create a new cluster in the right-hand side contents pane. Click it to begin the creation process.

1. When you click the Create a new cluster link (see the next illustration), you'll have the option to create or join a cluster. Because this is a new cluster, you'll want to create a new cluster.

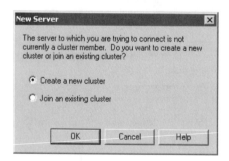

2. Next, you'll be welcomed with the wizard (as seen in the following illustration) that will guide you through the rest of the process of creating a new cluster.

3. When you click Next, you see the following illustration, which is the wizard scanning your machine to see if you have the basic prerequisites for network load balancing. If your NLB information is questionable, you'll be asked about it.

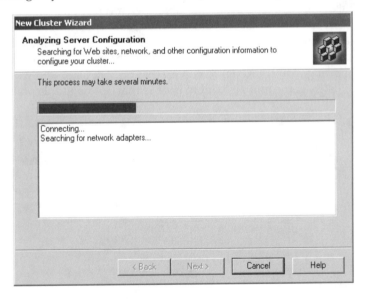

4. You won't see the next illustration unless you purposely configured NLB options on the server before trying to create a new cluster. In this figure, you're

asked about an existing configuration. You can either keep the settings or let Application Center 2000 reconfigure them for you, as recommended.

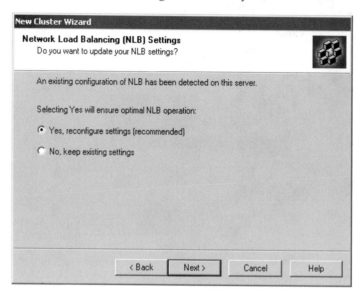

5. Click Next, and you'll be prompted about what type of load balancing you want to use, as shown next. Because we're creating a load-balanced cluster that will use NLB to balance the incoming client requests, select the NLB option, and then click Next. If you were going to use a hardware device to perform the load balancing, you could opt to choose that option. Or, if you want to create a stager cluster, you could also opt to choose that option at this point.

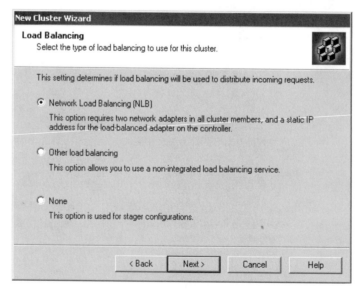

6. Once you click Next, you'll be naming the cluster, which you can do in the following illustration. I named it AC2K (for Application Center 2000) Cluster, but you can name it whatever you want. Pick something meaningful. You can also add a description if you like.

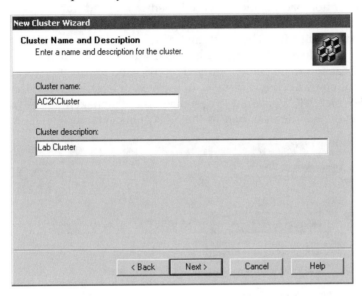

7. After clicking Next, you have to select a cluster type, as discussed earlier in the chapter. The options are as follows:

- **General/Web cluster** The cluster hosts Web sites and local COM+ applications, or will be used for staging applications, monitoring or synchronization. This cluster supports application deployment and Component Load Balancing (CLB).

- **COM+ application cluster** The cluster hosts only COM+ applications that can be referenced by other Web sites or Windows-based applications.

- **COM+ routing cluster** The cluster routes requests to a COM+ application cluster.

For this exercise, select to create a General/Web cluster, which will host a simple web site.

8. When installing the cluster, you're asked to select specific bindings from your NIC cards to be used either for load balancing or for management, which incorporates heartbeat traffic. *Heartbeat traffic* is the signaling and the management link used for the heartbeat: replication, synchronization, and any other nonload-balancing- based client-requested traffic. The reasoning behind this design is that the management traffic would inhibit valid request-based traffic. Therefore, all traffic not for management functions is strictly for load balancing, which makes the cluster much more efficient. Heartbeat and management traffic is considered *private traffic*. The NLB traffic could be considered *public traffic*. In the next illustration, you'll be asked to select which NIC you want to designate as the management network and which you want to designate as the NLB public adapter.

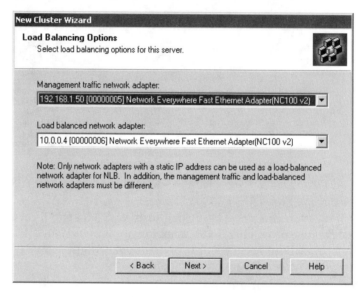

9. When you click Next, you'll be asked about monitoring. In the next illustration, you'll have to set up monitoring notifications if you want to be notified of problems. We look at this in more detail in Chapter 8 but, for now, you can set up your e-mail address, as well as the e-mail server name.

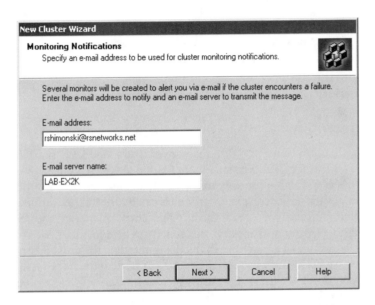

10. Click Next, and you'll complete the new Cluster Wizard. You'll have to wait for the cluster to analyze your settings options and create the cluster, which can take up to five minutes. The following illustration shows the completion of the New Cluster Wizard.

In this section, we looked at creating a new Application Center 2000 Cluster. We must add a second server to the cluster to make it a two-node cluster, but let's quickly look at the server, which has just become your cluster controller. You need to know how to work with the cluster controller and understand what its function is in the cluster before performing any additional cluster configuration.

The Cluster Controller

When using Application Center 2000 to manage clusters, one server is always referred to as the cluster controller. The *cluster controller* is the server in charge of the rest of the cluster nodes. It's responsible for keeping the entire cluster operating properly and with the current content. The cluster controller is normally the first node in the cluster, the one server from which you create the cluster. You can change the server node cluster controller assignment to another node later on but, for now, let's look at what it does. Every cluster needs a machine that's designated as the cluster controller. The controller can be easily found by right-clicking each node within the cluster, and going to All tasks. If you don't see the option to Designate as Controller, then you're looking at the cluster controller. The cluster controller is usually the first machine to join the cluster and it's the place where you'll manage the entire cluster because it enables you the most functionality for administering the cluster. If the server currently acting as the cluster controller fails or needs to be taken offline for maintenance, you can designate any other online member of the cluster to take on its duties. You can put your applications on the cluster controller. The cluster controller coordinates with the other computers of the cluster to synchronize and replicate the applications and content among the cluster.

Synchronization Fundamentals

Application Center 2000 can manage cluster synchronization and deployment. The beauty of Application Center 2000 is it uses a single image to represent all the required content for a cluster deployment. This makes synchronization and deployment of applications easy. You have three types of synchronization modes for the entire cluster:
Automatic Synchronization mode:

- *Automatic Synchronization* is the process of automatic updates of the IIS metabase or any content deployed on the cluster controller to all nodes within the cluster.

- When changes are made on the cluster controller, the changes are automatically pushed out.

Periodic Synchronization mode:

- *Periodic Synchronization* is the process of updating all nodes, regardless of whether the content has changed.

- The default is 60 minutes, but this can be configured.

- The impact of synchronization can affect the cluster controller, so a good design step is not to set this interval too short.

Manual Synchronization mode:

- *Manual Synchronization* is the manual synchronization of whatever you select to be synched up.

- You can do manual synchronization in two ways: with the AC command, or by right-clicking the nodes and selecting to synchronize cluster.

- You can also select applications to be synchronized. Figure 4-5 shows the synchronization of applications.

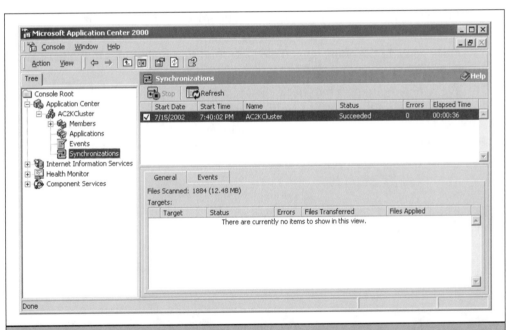

Figure 4-5.   Synchronizations of applications

Adding a New Member to an Application Center 2000 Cluster

To create the most basic cluster, you need to open the Application Center MMC, which is found in the Administrative Tools folder within the Start menu.

To add the node, do the following steps:

1. Create a brand new cluster by clicking the hyperlink within the MMC under the Application Center Basics heading. When you first open the Application Center 2000 MMC, it's in the Contents pane. Select Existing Cluster.

2. This prompts you to add one server to the management console. Remember, it's critical that you adhere to the minimal installation requirements outlined earlier in the chapter or you'll be unable to join this second node to the cluster.

3. Follow the prompts and add the server you want to make a two-node cluster. Note, I won't rehash the same screenshots and details as adding the first node. You'll be able to follow along easily. I do want to go over some of the more important details of possible failure and why, though.

4. In the following screens, add the node and select the NICs (just like the first node).

5. Once you add the node, open the console and find both nodes in the left-hand navigation pane of the MMC.

6. We're only building a two-node cluster, but you can continue this process up to 32 nodes if you want to add that many.

7. You've now successfully added a node to your cluster. You can reopen the Application Center 2000 console to see your servers up and running, and listed under one cluster group.

POSTDESIGN TIPS AND TROUBLESHOOTING

In this section, we look at field-proven issues, solutions, and troubleshooting steps for failures and problems with Application Center 2000 deployment, installation, and basic configuration.

Memory Check

Check your memory use! Your server, although set for minimum requirements, needs to be checked when you finish installing Application Center 2000. Use Task Manager, as shown in the following illustration, to check your server's memory use. In the last column, you can see that with Application Center 2000 replication, the console, IIS running (inetinfo), and all the other services you need to run on your server, your server's memory will be used quickly. The heightened speed of the servers comes from caching most of the important services (like inetinfo) in memory.

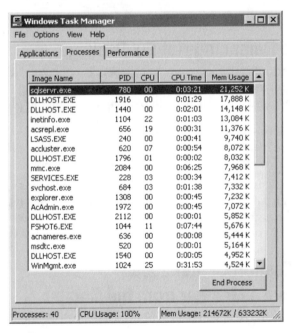

Changing Node Names

Be careful about changing your node names. Instances might exist where you need to change the name of a cluster node, whether because of company changes or another reason. If you change the name, you could experience loss of the cluster node and the error message shown in the following illustration. The cluster node name I changed wouldn't let me add it back into the cluster, so be aware that this happens at times. The way to fix this is by changing the name back to what it was (this is why you need to document everything), and then reopen the cluster, and the name will be there.

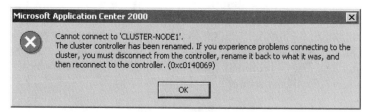

The Network Load Balancing Hot Fix Package

The NLB Hot Fix Package is a fairly new hot fix package that you'll need to apply to keep your server updated. You can find this on the Microsoft.com downloads section of the web site. The NLB Hot Fix is used to resolve the following problems:

- The NLB Windows Management Instrumentation (WMI) provider is known to have a severe memory leak in a process called WinMgmt. This leak, 50MB of memory in 17 hours, can cripple your server for memory.

- Another problem the hot fix can correct is modifying a node's load weight setting in the configuration for NLB, which will *end* all existing client connections to that node through the VIP (virtual IP address). If you don't want this to happen and cut off all your client connections, then apply this hot fix.

Uninstalling Application Center 2000 Doesn't Remove a Member from the Cluster

Another problem I often see is when a client uninstalls Application Center 2000 to remove a server from the cluster group. In other words, the client wants to remove a node from the group and uninstalls Application Center 2000 to do it. This doesn't work well and isn't recommended. Often, the client removes the server this way, only to open the MMC again and see the server is still located within the group. (I did this in the lab when I was first learning how to use Application Center 2000.) This is a common error.

Another problem is when the client makes this mistake, and then tries to re-add the node to the cluster, it won't work because it's already there! To remove a server from a cluster group properly, open the MMC and expand the console down to select the node you want to remove. Right-click all tasks and remove the node from the cluster. Note, if this is the cluster controller, you won't be able to remove it from the cluster until all other cluster nodes have been removed, leaving the cluster controller as the last member of the cluster. When all other nodes are removed first, you'll have a command listed to disband the cluster. If you made the mistake of not removing the node and uninstalling Application Center 2000, then you can run the Application Center 2000 administration tool so you can connect to the cluster again and remove it properly. This generates an error, but you can safely ignore it, continuing to remove the cluster properly. This is a well-known issue, so it might be included in a future service pack for Application Center 2000.

CONCLUSION

In this chapter, you learned the fundamentals of Application Center 2000, its basic installation and configuration, how to plan for it, and why to use it. We also get heavily involved with learning how to use Health Monitor to monitor nodes and clusters for optimization.

CHAPTER 5

Designing a Clustered Solution with Windows SQL Server 2000 Enterprise Edition

In this chapter, you build, from scratch, a Windows Cluster solution using Windows Server 2003 and SQL Server. At press time, Microsoft's newest version of SQL Server, codenamed "Longhorn," is too far out to be in beta, so we'll build a clustered solution with Windows Server 2003 and Microsoft SQL Server 2000. We'll look at all the planning you need to do, the actual installation, and then the configuration of the two-node cluster. After this, you can see many of the things that could go wrong with your new SQL database cluster, as well as some advanced troubleshooting issues.

PREDESIGN PLANNING

As with everything else covered in this book so far, taking the time to plan and design your solution properly is the key to success. You simply can't wing it. Every chapter has stressed the importance of preplanning and design work, which is equally important in this chapter. In this section, you install SQL Server 2000 Enterprise Edition (required for clustering) on to a two-node failover cluster using Windows Server 2003. In Chapter 1, you learned the importance of implementing a clustered solution. In the chapters that followed, you also saw how to implement clustered and load-balanced solutions to achieve high availability. Now, you learn how to build a backend database tier into your Highly Available solution. Failover clustering in SQL Server 2000 is built on top of the Clustering Service within either Windows 2000 or Windows Server 2003 servers. You want to have a cluster because, generally, SQL Server is where your company's data is stored in the form of one or more databases. You can see a typical SQL Cluster topology in Figure 5-1.

Not to have access to this data could prove crippling if your company depends on it. The Cluster Service allows a controlled form of access to a shared disk where your databases can reside. In time of failure, the other node can provide access to this shared storage. The same form of reliability (covered in Chapter 2) also goes for designing a RAID solution on the shared storage for redundancy and reliability. You must take everything into consideration before you install SQL Server on to your cluster because without reading and planning, you might make a few mistakes that could cost you time or be damaging to the preexisting cluster. Let's look at, and find out why, and then learn what the proper steps are for planning.

SQL Server Component Planning

When designing and planning a SQL Server cluster solution, you must understand what you're working with to plan for it properly. You need to address many items of importance before installing and you must perform an unbelievable amount of preparation work first to achieve SQL cluster success.

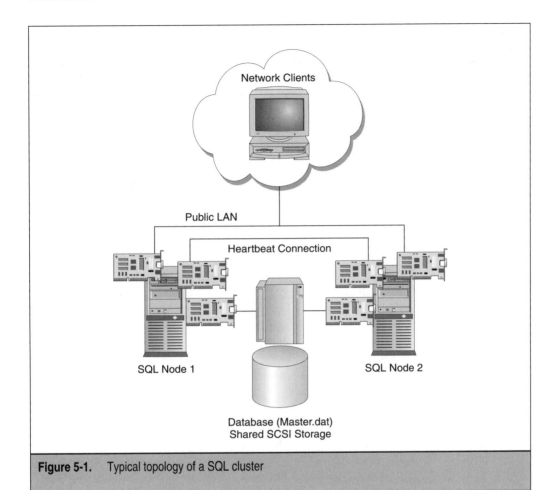

Figure 5-1. Typical topology of a SQL cluster

First, you should know that SQL Server 2000, when clustered, is placed on top of a preexisting cluster solution. This means you first need to read either Chapter 2 or Chapter 3 before you begin this chapter. SQL Server 2000 is built on top of an existing cluster and is a cluster-aware application. The SQL Server 2000 becomes a Virtual Server on top of the existing cluster solution.

SQL Server Virtual Server Name

The SQL Server Virtual name is the name of the SQL Server you'll reference. This could be confusing because you'll be naming your cluster nodes and you might think you're naming them to be the actual SQL Server, but this isn't the case. As you reference a single name for SQL Server shared between two or more nodes, it must be unique to the cluster. This is called the *Virtual Name,* which is what all applications and clients will use to refer to the SQL Server instance you created. The cluster nodes will only be referenced by their Virtual Names, not by their individual names.

SQL Server Virtual Server IP Addressing

You have one single IP address the clients need to access between two or more clustered nodes. This is why planning accordingly beforehand is important, so you don't have a problem during implementation. To reach the SQL Server instance, you need a Virtual Server IP address.

SQL Server Virtual Server Administrator Account

You need either a preexisting or a new account to serve as the Virtual Server Administrator account. You can, however, use an Administrator Account (or a preexisting account), but remember what you learned earlier: in a test lab environment, this is okay, but when in production, you might want to create a separate service account for this purpose alone. The reason is, eventually, you'll have to change a password, or delete or disable the account. When this happens, chaos will consume your SQL implementation because it could cease to function for you. The new account you create (or the preexisting one you use) can serve as the SQL Server service account. The account must be a domain administrator, so when you create it, make sure this is a group you select and add to the account.

Shared Components of a Clustered SQL Server

As just highlighted, you have two or more nodes clustered with a Virtual SQL Server instance, and an IP address and an account they also share. Now, let's look at some of the other components that must be shared between instances of SQL Server when it's clustered. The following components in Table 5-1 are the underlying shared components.

Remember, while planning your SQL Server cluster, you must understand your limitation on exactly what you can create. For instance, when you install SQL Server as a clustered resource (Virtual Server), then you have one default instance and up to 15 named instances. When discussing instances, you also must look at what kind of failover support to plan for when clustering SQL Server. You have the option of having single instance or multiple instance failover. *Single instance clusters* replace what you know as an Active/Passive arrangement. *Multiple instance clusters* replace what you know as an Active/Active arrangement.

Single Instance Cluster   When designing a single instance cluster, remember, a single instance cluster has one active instance of SQL Server owned by a single node only.

Full-Text Search	Each instance gets its own clustered full-text search resource. This search relies on the underlying Microsoft Search service. This service is shared by all instances.
Microsoft Distributed Transaction Coordinator (MSDTC)	Only one MSDTC resource exists per cluster.
Microsoft Message Queuing (MSMQ)	All applications using MSMQ have the same limitation as with MSDTC. All instances share a single resource.

Table 5-1.   SQL Server Shared Components

Any other nodes in the cluster are in a wait state. This is the same as saying an Active/ Passive cluster has one node operational to accept client requests, while the other stands idle waiting, but not accepting client requests.

Multiple Instance Cluster   When building multiple instance clusters, you can build up to four nodes. When you do, you can also have support for up to 16 instances. You'll want to design for having no more than four instances, though, to keep the ratio one to one . . . or four nodes, four instances. When you design each virtual node, you also want to ensure you have one shared disk resource per virtual node. You can keep physical disks all in one single hardware-based array, but you'll want to verify that your design allows your logical names to be unique for each instance.

You'll understand more of the terminology as you continue reading this section, so when the time comes to run the setup, your design will be sound and you'll understand what's being asked of you.

SQL Server Cluster Model

SQL Server 2000 has support for the *shared nothing cluster model*, where each node manages its own resources and provides nonsharing data services. You can set up failover with SQL Server 2000 by configuring one of two models: Active/Active and Active/Passive.

Active/Active (Multiple Instance)

When using the Active-to-Active configuration, each node in the SQL Cluster has an instance of SQL Server, which is managed by the Cluster Service. Each instance is responsible for its own data set. When a failover does occur, the node that's still available takes over for the failed node. Each node keeps a separate master database, as seen in Figure 5-2 and the following illustration.

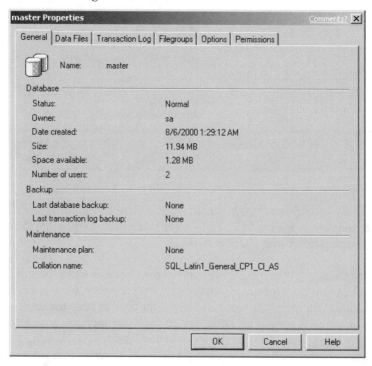

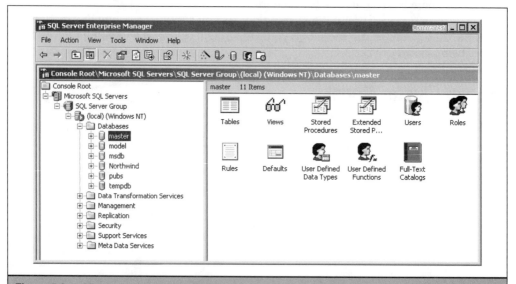

Figure 5-2. Viewing the master database

One good reason to go with an Active/Active solution is if you want to partition your database. Because nodes in an Active/Active cluster each have their own instance of SQL Server, this design is better for partitioned databases. Partitioning offers the advantage of load distribution and redundancy, but requires more effort to bring online and is, therefore, harder to configure.

Active/Passive (Single Instance)

With Active/Passive, instead of multiple instances, the cluster runs only one single instance of SQL Server and is managed via the Cluster Service. When a client makes a request, only one node can answer at a time. When that node fails, the other node takes over for it during failover. When using this configuration, the two nodes share a master database. In this chapter, we'll configure a simple Active/Passive two-node cluster.

Everything covered here is only to give you an idea on how to lay out your plan for SQL Server clustering. Most of this terminology is an add-on to Chapters 1, 2, and 3. You should understand the general concepts of clustering, load balancing, and high availability, and you should know the terminology used to explain the same basic concepts when designing a SQL cluster. Let's look at some cost issues.

Planning for Failover-Based Pricing

Be careful when you design a solution with SQL Server and clustering. This is because you might get hit with some heavy pricing for the components and software you need. Always visit **Microsoft.com** for the latest pricing or contact a reseller but, when you license SQL Server, you can do so through paying per processor. Also, specific costs are related to your design. If you plan to go with Active/Passive failover, you could have a price break waiting for you. When you license the SQL product via processor, you can bend the rules when configuring Active/Passive failover. What's nice is the Passive computer doesn't require a processor or a server license. Active/Active configurations require licensing both servers because you're using both servers simultaneously.

Another good way to plan your server rollout (and cost analysis) is to plan for more capacity than you think you might use. To be cheap on disk space when designing a database cluster is a mistake. Trying to get by with the bare minimum in the beginning isn't cost-effective. You end up spending much more money adding more hard drive space than it would have cost to build in extra capacity at the beginning. As a good rule of thumb, you should try to plan for two or three years down the road and determine what you expect to need. If you run low on space, this could cause you bad performance, and then your Highly Available solution will no longer be as highly available as you want.

SQL Server 2000 Minimum Requirements

When designing a Windows 2000 or Windows Server 2003 cluster with SQL Server 2000, you must take into account the added requirements you'll need. Now, more than ever, the requirements will either spell success or disaster for you. I can guarantee if you skimp on requirements for a SQL Server implementation, you'll be unhappy. First, let's look at Table 5-2, so you can learn the minimum requirements. After that, we'll review sound design advice for your implementation.

If you've never run SQL Server before, you'll be amazed at how much memory it requires. You can easily see that the sqlservr process runs high in memory. The following illustration shows memory usage up to 20,372K under no stress.

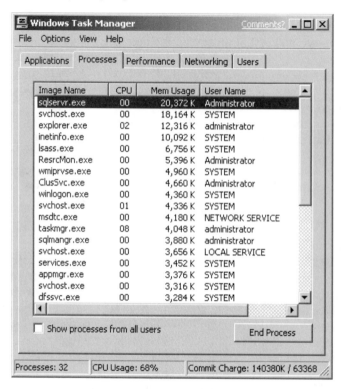

Processor	Intel Pentium or Compatible CPU 166 MHz or Higher
Operating Systems	SQL Server 2000 Enterprise Edition runs on Microsoft Windows 2000 Server and Windows 2000 Advanced Server (and Datacenter Server), as well as being tested to function on the Windows Server 2003 line of servers. Remember, to cluster your server, you need to run Windows 2000 Advanced Server or higher (Server 2003) and you must use SQL's Enterprise Edition to use the Clustering Functionality.
Memory	Enterprise Edition: 64MB RAM; 128MB or above *highly* recommended. Also, take into consideration the actual operating system (OS) on which you're installing SQL. That server also has its own requirements, as discussed in Chapter 2 and 3.
Hard Disk	Enterprise Edition requires 95–270MB free hard-disk space for the server, but how much disk space you need depends on how many add-ons you select. Always overshoot the requirements for disk space when applicable.
Other	CD-ROM, video, and both Windows and application-based service packs.

Table 5-2.   SQL Server Minimum Requirements

When planning your SQL Server cluster, you need to follow the guidelines of the minimum requirements, but exceed them as much as possible. You also need to take into account what else you might be running on this server. I have the SQL Enterprise Manager, the Cluster Administrator, and a few other utilities open at the same time, and I already have my server running at 145MB of used memory. Any good SQL Server implementation should be running anywhere from 512MB of RAM all the way up to a gigabyte of RAM, if possible. Let's look at some more detailed high-level planning for your SQL Server implementation.

Planning Tips for SQL Server 2000 Failover Cluster Servers

In this section, I want to create several lists for you to follow when you plan the scaling of your nodes in respect to SQL cluster planning.

- Make sure you know what the workload of your nodes will be. Although you might not know what this is, you can test for it in the lab. Benchmarking performance of your applications when running on the server can give you an idea of what's expected.

- Project your possible workload in the future, if possible. Do you foresee a gradual rise in workload or will this be stagnant with little growth? Do you see a sharp rise in growth? Planning now saves time later.

- You can also use the server's System Monitor found in the Performance MMC, within the Administrative Tools folder in the Control Panel. We discuss this tool in Chapter 8, but this is what you can use in your lab to get an idea about hardware resources for your server.

- Make sure you plan for your nodes to be configured with the same hardware resources or make the failover node more powerful. Never create a node you will "failover" to another node that has fewer resources than the original node. This can cause degradation of performance to a server during the failover.

- Visit the SQL Server web site to review for any last minute hot fixes and service packs that need to be applied for functionality and safety reasons at **http:// www.microsoft.com/sql**.

- You can also visit the HCL for hardware resources that are compliant with SQL Clustering. You can visit the site at **http://www.microsoft.com/hcl**.

Placement of SQL Server in the N-Tier Architecture

Design considerations for SQL Server within an N-tier architecture are important to follow. As you move closer to rolling out this solution into your Enterprise Server, you need to pay close attention to where you'll place the clusters in respect to the rest of the servers in your infrastructure. Figure 5-3 shows the main components of an N-tier architecture and where SQL Server will reside in a two-node cluster.

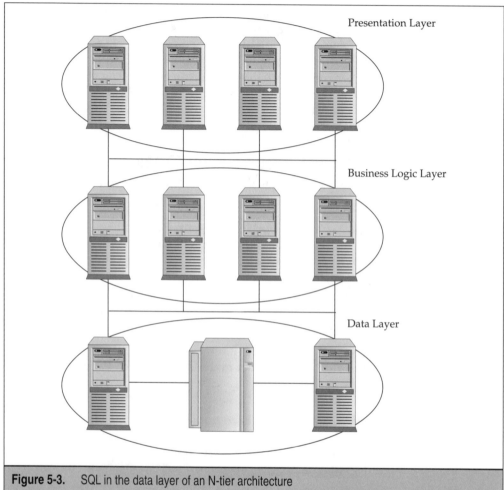

Figure 5-3.   SQL in the data layer of an N-tier architecture

Remember, this is only a guideline. You needn't follow this architecture layout to the letter. Just make sure you know where you want to put this cluster and how to position it best for your company's benefit.

Virtual Server

When you install SQL Server, you won't install it normally as you might have in the past. In this chapter, you'll install the server as a Virtual Server. When you prepare your server nodes for a SQL Server cluster, be familiar with the Cluster Administrator and what's found within it. When you install SQL Server, the Cluster Administrator will become an element within that console. When you install SQL Server, it brings up an option to install as a Virtual Server, as seen in the next illustration.

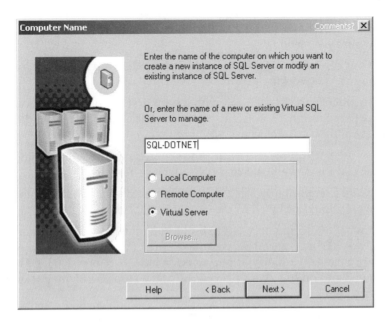

Each cluster group within the Cluster Administrator can contain, at most, one Virtual SQL Server. A Virtual Server will also be configured with its own IP address separate from that of the cluster. This way, the clustered resource is unique and separate from the clustered nodes that grant you access to it. When you plan your SQL Cluster, you need to have an IP address separate from all other hosts on the network to use for only that instance of SQL Server. The following is a layout of IP addresses you might want to consider.

- Public LAN Default Gateway: 192.168.1.1 /24
- Public LAN SQL Node 1: 192.168.1.2 /24
- Public LAN SQL Node 2: 192.168.1.3 /24
- SQL Server Virtual Server IP: 192.168.1.30 /24

Remember, though, this is only a guideline and you can (and should now be able to) select which IP addresses you need to configure for your network and cluster solutions. Now, let's review a checklist you'll want to follow for preparing for the SQL Server cluster solution.

Preinstallation Checklist

The following is a detailed check list of points to complete before you install SQL Server on your nodes to create a SQL Cluster.

1. Read the beginning of this chapter and make sure you have all your minimum requirements squared away based on hardware.

2. Make sure you have all the installation media, CD-ROMs, and any other form of software you need.

3. Plan your IP addressing scheme and allocate what you need from a spreadsheet, database, or networking group.

4. Plan to practice the installation with a pilot first. If you want to go straight to production, though, thoroughly plan your back-out plan and make sure you have it handy if failure occurs.

5. Make a full backup copy of your production data. Then, if anything fails, you can rebuild the servers and reapply the data afterward.

6. Hardware Compatibility List (HCL)-based hardware should be used and the hardware should be listed in the cluster category.

7. Select what platform you want to build your cluster on. If you're using Windows 2000 Advanced Server, make sure you go through Chapter 2 and prepare a cluster properly. If you select Windows Server 2003, go back through Chapter 3 and build a cluster properly. Make sure all service packs and hot fixes are applied.

8. Your Cluster Service nodes need to be logged into a domain. The domain must be readily available for the cluster service accounts to log into the domain or the service will fail.

9. Your Cluster Service account must also be active and available to log into the domain.

   Now that you have your cluster platform available, you need to start working toward SQL-specific configurations.

10. Disable NetBIOS for all private network Heartbeat NIC cards before you start the SQL Server setup program.

11. Check all the server event and error logs to make sure you don't mistake old problems for new ones. You can make copies of all the old logs, so when you go through your installation and configuration, you can go right into the new logs and quickly see problems that are the result of the installation and configuration of SQL Server on your cluster.

12. You must configure MSDTC to run on a cluster, which you learn about in the following section.

Installing and Configuring MSDTC

Microsoft Distributed Transaction Coordinator (MSDTC) is required by SQL Server 2000 in a cluster for distributed queries, replication functionality, and two-phase commit transactions. In a distributed environment, you must run transactions across multiple systems at all times. Much of this is important to maintain the integrity and consistency of the data on each system. MSDTC provides for complete transaction management in a distributed environment. MSDTC coordinates transactions that span multiple databases and message queues. If the MSDTC service is stopped or disabled, then these transactions won't happen.

After you install Microsoft Windows 2000 Advanced Server and/or Windows Server 2003, and then configure your cluster, you must run the Comclust.exe program on all nodes to configure MSDTC. Then MSDTC can run in Cluster mode. In this section, you learn all the configuration steps you need to know and set up before installing SQL Server as a Virtual Server.

By default, when MSDTC installs, it configures itself to the cluster group and sets its log on the quorum disk. This is fine but, because MSDTC will work from node to clustered node, you should configure MSDTC in a cluster as a resource. When working with SQL Server clustering and MSDTC, you might want to take a few things into consideration. For instance, if you're clustering SQL Server, then only one instance of MSDTC is needed. You can configure MSDTC as a resource in the cluster group, which we'll do momentarily. Also, you'll want to (per Microsoft's guidelines and recommendations) install the MSDTC resource in a group other than the main cluster group. You can simply create a new cluster group (as explained in Chapters 2 and 3) and create the instance there. Although this is a design recommendation, it isn't totally necessary. Microsoft recommends that if you have it set up in the cluster group, then you should leave it as is. If the cluster isn't yet in a production-based role, then the recommendation is that SQL Server be unclustered and you follow the following steps in this section to move the MSDTC resource to a group other than the original cluster group.

To configure MSDTC manually, do the following:

1. On your first cluster node, open Cluster Administrator, and create a new cluster group.

2. Select that group, and right-click it. Go to New | Resource.

3. Once you select Resource, a new dialog box opens, as seen in the following illustration.

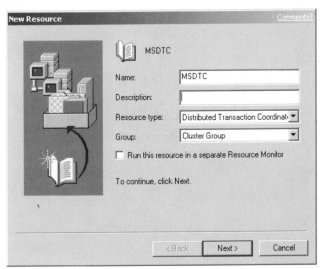

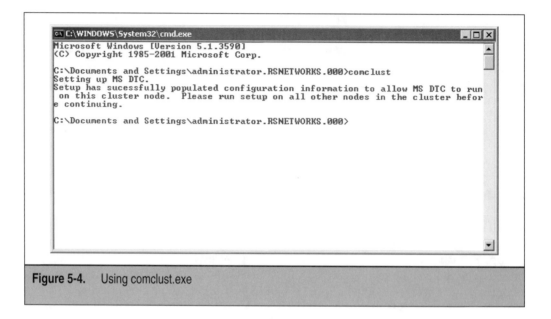

Figure 5-4. Using comclust.exe

4. Create the new resource by entering the name of the resource (MSDTC) and which group you want to install it into. Select the resource type, which is also MSDTC.

5. Click Next, and then finish creating the resource. Close Cluster Administrator to finalize the process of making a new resource.

Using comclust.exe

You can manually (and quickly) install the MSDTC service in the cluster by going to your cluster nodes and, at each, open a command prompt:

- At a command prompt, type **comclust**, and then press ENTER, as seen in Figure 5-4.

INSTALLATION AND CONFIGURATION OF SQL SERVER IN A CLUSTERED SOLUTION

In this section, we look at the actual installation of SQL 2000 into a clustered solution. SQL 2000 is *cluster aware,* which means it can easily be installed to a clustered solution if it's enabled on the servers on which you want to install.

1. To install SQL Server into a cluster, you need to insert the SQL Server 2000 Enterprise CD-ROM into the server node on which you want to install. Once inserted, you see the splash screen, as shown in the following illustration. After the Install Wizard opens, click the SQL Server 2000 Components option, and then click the Install Database Server option.

2. Next, enter the name of the computer on which you want to create a new instance of SQL Server. In Figure 5-5, the problem is the Virtual Server option is grayed out.

3. In Figure 5-6, the Virtual Server option isn't grayed out. The difference (and what I'm trying to show you) is the SQL Server 2000 Enterprise Edition software package is cluster aware. In other words, in Figure 5-5, I installed SQL Server on a server that wasn't part of a cluster. It wasn't a cluster node. In Figure 5-6, I installed SQL Server on to a cluster node, which immediately gave me the option to create a Virtual Server.

4. Once you select the Virtual Server option, click Next. In the following illustration, you get the option to enter your name and company. Although entering your company isn't necessary, fill in your name and company if desired, and then click Next.

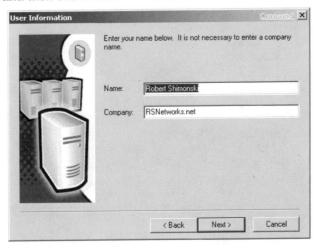

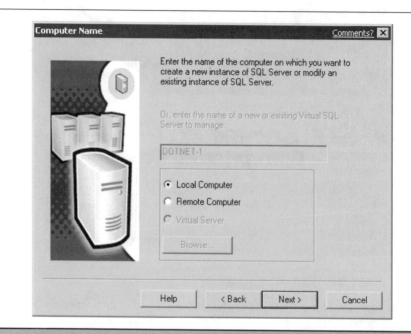

Figure 5-5. No Virtual Server option

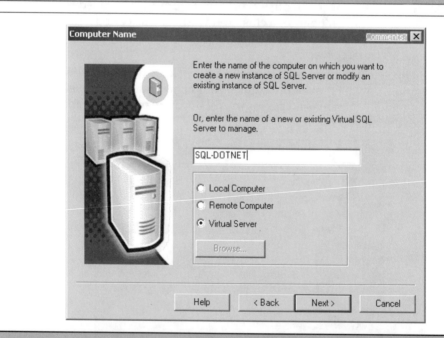

Figure 5-6. Virtual Server option available

5. You then see the License Agreement and must click Yes to agree with it. Remember what was mentioned earlier in the beginning of the chapter about per-processor licensing. Make sure you plan all this out properly. Otherwise, you'll be paying for much more than you think later on when it might be impossible for you to disband this cluster because your company's data may be highly dependent on it.

6. Click Yes to the agreement (as seen in the following illustration). This will finalize the process and continue the installation. Once you agree, you'll be given your first configuration option for the cluster. In Figure 5-7, you can configure a failover cluster.

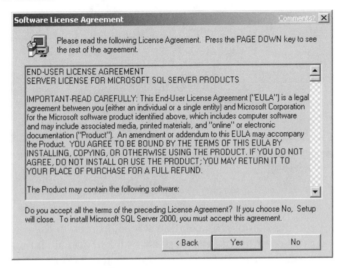

7. In Figure 5-7, you need to configure the SQL Server (Virtual Server) IP address mentioned earlier in the chapter. This is the IP address that will be assigned to the instance of SQL Server in the cluster. It has nothing to do with any NIC installed or the Cluster VIP itself. This IP address is solely for the SQL Virtual Server. Make sure you configure the network it's going to use (I selected the LAN interface instead of Heartbeat) and click the Add button to add it. Click Next when you complete these steps. Then, select the disk you want to install to and click Next. Make sure you don't install SQL Server to the quorum because the recommendation is you install to a separate disk on the server. If you do, then you can install it, but you'll also be warned, as shown in the following illustration.

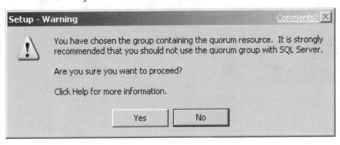

Failover Clustering Comments? ✕

Enter virtual server information.

Virtual server name : SQL-DOTNET

IP address: 192 . 168 . 1 . 30

Subnet: 255 . 255 . 255 . 0

Network to Use: LAN ▼

Add   Remove

IPAddress	Subnet	Network

Help   < Back   Next >   Cancel

Figure 5-7. Configuring failover

8. Next, move to the Remote Information screen, as seen in the next illustration, where you must enter the username, password, and domain information of a user who will be a valid administrator for your clustered nodes. Then, click Next.

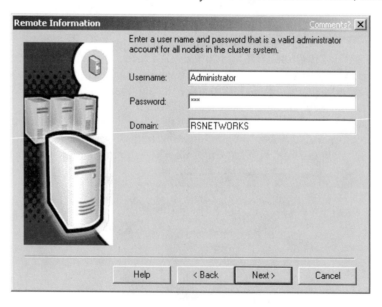

Remote Information Comments? ✕

Enter a user name and password that is a valid administrator account for all nodes in the cluster system.

Username: Administrator

Password: ×××

Domain: RSNETWORKS

Help   < Back   Next >   Cancel

9. You can skip the default installation and uncheck the box to let you install a named instance of SQL Server on this node, as shown in the following illustration. Enter a new instance name (I called it SQLLAB), and then click Next.

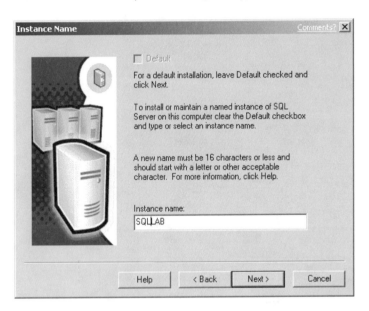

10. Now, you can enter the setup type, as seen in Figure 5-8. You have the options to install *Typical,* which gives you the most common options; *Minimum,* which gives you a scaled-down version of SQL Server (not recommended because you should be able to have enough hard disk space to install the whole product if needed); or *Custom,* where you can choose among any and all options available to you during install.

11. In this scenario, let's choose Typical. You might have a problem setting up the Resource to the Program Files folder, as shown in Figure 5-8. This is because the Cluster Service won't let you install the program files on the actual quorum. You could get an error and, if you do, simply change the path of the drive to a drive that isn't the actual quorum drive. Be aware, as discussed in Chapter 2, you should have a few separate disks set up for this installation already.

12. In the following illustration, you can set up the Services Accounts for SQL Server. Here, you can specify the Domain User account you want to use for each service. Because this is a simple setup,

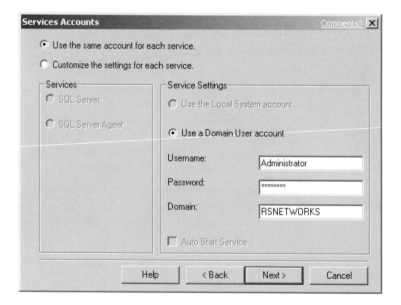

Figure 5-8. Setup type

I chose to have the same account used for each service—this is the administrator account.

13. Once you enter your account, click Next, and then you supply an Authentication mode. Enter a strong password for the SA account. It has been (and will continue to be) the hacker's choice for exploitation, so when you enter your password, make sure you secure it, and don't use anything susceptible to an attack or easily guessed. A blank password is *not* recommended. Windows Authentication is the better choice, but I selected the mixed mode to give you more insight on the SA account. You can see the SA login in the next illustration.

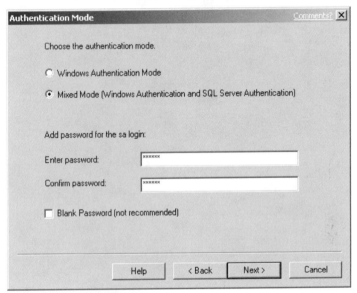

14. Once you enter your password, click Next. The following illustration shows verification of the files to be copied to your hard disk.

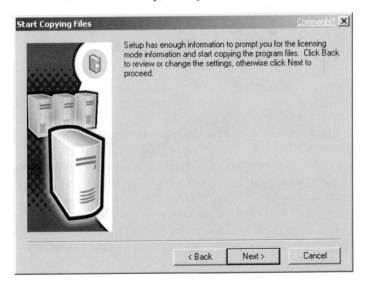

15. Next, select your Licensing mode as seen in the next illustration. Here, I selected to use the processor license for two processors. Again, this might be costly, so go online (or call a reseller) and get this information before you start your design. You can plan your pricing scheme by visiting **http://microsoft.com/sql/howtobuy/ production.asp**.

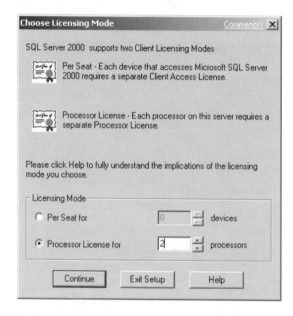

16. Once you click Continue, you begin your installation. As you can see in Figure 5-9, the screen cuts over to installation on your nodes and, in some cases, you could have to wait up to five minutes for installation to complete.

17. Once you complete installation, you can see your SQL Server success by opening the Cluster Administrator, as shown in Figure 5-10, and view the new SQL instances. Again, this is a matter of preference, but it's a good idea to install each instance into its own group.

Again, this server is used for a pilot therefore, in a live scenario, you want to create a separate cluster group (like I created in the test group) so your SQL Instance won't be part of your main cluster group. If you need to move items to a new group (if you made a mistake on where you wanted them placed), see "Moving Resources" later in this chapter.

Your final steps should be to examine all Event Viewer logs thoroughly for possible problems and document what you find. Now you have a clean installation of SQL Server on a node. You want to preserve this state in a baseline so, if you start working on the node and you have a problem, you'll know the last task you worked on might have created the problem, instead of a faulty installation. Let's look at some troubleshooting concepts, just in case your installation didn't go smoothly.

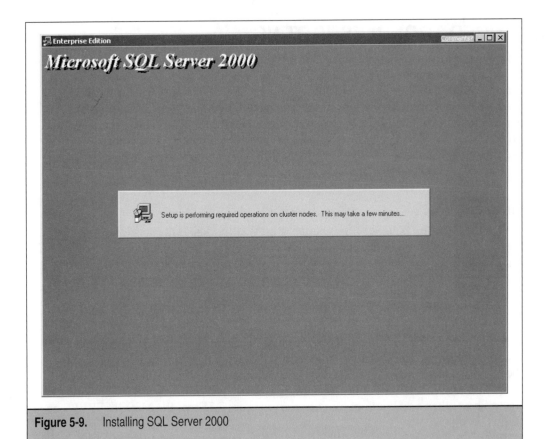

Figure 5-9. Installing SQL Server 2000

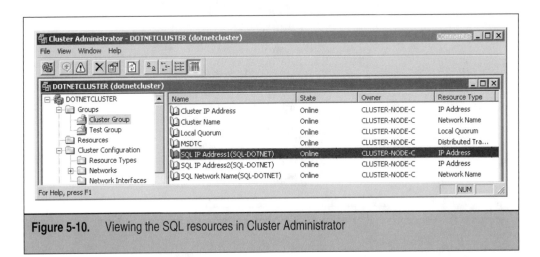

Figure 5-10. Viewing the SQL resources in Cluster Administrator

ADVANCED TROUBLESHOOTING

You'll find the mechanics of setting up a SQL Cluster are quite easy, but they can also be highly problematic. As a network or systems engineer, your responsibility is to quickly (and accurately) find and solve the problems at hand, as well as try to keep them from happening in the first place. The installation and configuration of SQL Server clusters are the hardest (and most nerve-racking) to deal with. You have to understand that SQL Server is a database server, which means your company's data is on that group of servers. This isn't something you should take lightly because the degree of risk is elevated.

Running Services

First, check that the SQL Service is running on your nodes. If the service doesn't run, then you won't have a SQL Server at all. Remember, you're clustering the database. If you don't have a SQL Server service running, you won't have access to the database. In Figure 5-11, you can see immediately if your service is running or not. In Figure 5-11, you can see the SQL Server Service Manager.

The SQL Server Service Manager is configured, by default, to be placed in your Startup folder in your Start Menu Programs folder, so it launches as soon as your server boots up. If it isn't there, then you can launch it via the SQL Server Program group found in the Start Menu's Program Files folder. Once you launch it, you can see the big green arrow next to the server, which means it's running. Also, you might see the scaled-down version of this icon sitting in your system tray (on the right side of the taskbar) when you boot up. You can see in Figure 5-11 that the MSSQLSERVER on

Figure 5-11. Service Manager

Cluster-node-C is running, which is also a good indicator. If any of these indicators are showing negative (like a big red stop icon), then you can try to start the service right here in the Service Manager.

Event Viewer Errors

You might not have many problems, but when you do have an issue, you'll probably get your biggest clues from the Event Viewer. To get to the Event Viewer, go to the Computer Management Console located in the Administrative Tools folder within the Control Panel. Within the console, you'll find the Event Viewer with the Application, Security, and System Logs. These are set up by default. The more services you install to your nodes (DNS, Active Directory), the more logs you will have, but these are your default logs. When you open the logs, search for any recent SQL Server activity, as shown in the following illustration.

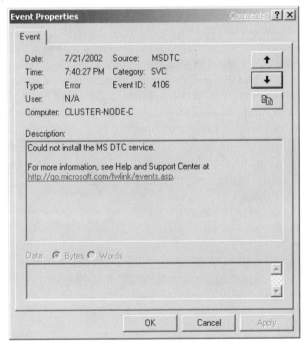

Although, at times, they could be hard to read (and understand), you can get clues as to what's going on from such recorded events. Here, you see a problem exists with the MSDTC Service. This one was rather easy, but not informative. The Event Viewer is hit or miss, but it's silly to bypass it because it might help in some way.

Other Error Messages

Other error messages could come directly from the Cluster Administrator. Here, you can look at three error messages I was able to generate by deleting a few key DLL files and making some incorrect configuration changes. (Don't do this unless you have a lab server or a backup!)

In the next illustration, you can see the Cluster Administrator isn't allowing me to use the SQL Server Resource.

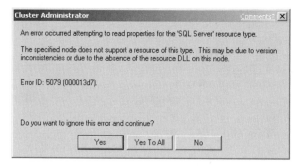

Further investigation leads me to the following illustration, where I can see that all the SQL Server resources created during installation have been successfully damaged from my system modifications. This isn't to show you how to wreck a server node. Instead, I want to show you how your server is going to react to possible problems you could have. Here, you might have to reinstall the SQL Server resource if you don't have a valid backup.

Once I can finally open the Cluster Administrator, I see my Cluster Group is also showing me a problem exists. In Figure 5-12, Cluster Administrator flags the Group

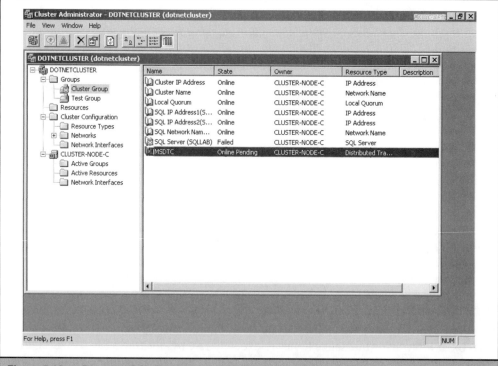

Figure 5-12. Damaged SQL Server resource in Cluster Administrator

(with a big red *X*) as well as the actual resource that could be damaged. Here, the SQLLAB resource we made during the installation has been damaged.

Again, I don't expect you to mimic this (unless you really want to!), but I want you to see how the Server node will tell you there's a problem. Let's look at more obscure problems and fixes.

IP Addressing Problems

IP addressing problems are common. Many times, during an installation, the IP addressing supplied (or applied) is wrong. When this happens, you have only one choice: you have to change the IP addressing. When you attempt to bring your SQL Server virtual instance online, you could have a cluster failure or you might not see an error, but have TCP/IP communication problems. If this happens, you could have an issue. This issue might exist because you went into the properties of the SQL IP address and changed information needed by the resource. The following illustration shows SQL IP parameters.

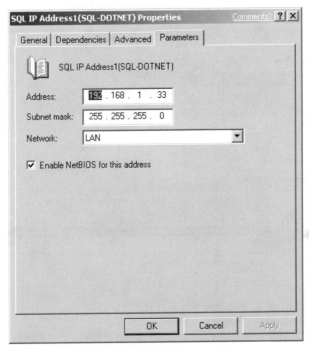

Client connections over TCP/IP fail and you change the TCP/IP addressing to the correct numbering scheme. Now, you have error messages coming up in your error logs. If this is the case, you might have a problem with your Virtual SQL Server not successfully binding to port 1433. Here is the possible error:

```
SuperSocket Info: Bind failed on TCP port 1433
```

Again, this is what you could get as an error if you change the Virtual SQL Server IP address with the Cluster Administrator tool. If you must change the IP address of the SQL Server Virtual Server, then you must follow specific steps to accomplish it. Let's see how to fix this problem.

First, look at the logs where you can find the SQL Server listening ports:

- Open the SQL Server Enterprise Manager.

- Once opened, drill down to the Management folder, as seen in Figure 5-13.

- In the Management folder, you'll find the SQL Server logs and archives.

- Find the message about SQL Server listening on specific ports.

NOTE When looking for the source, know that SPID stands for Service Process ID.

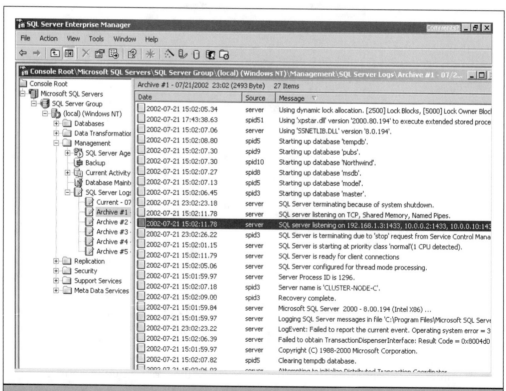

Figure 5-13. SQL Server logs and archive

Restart the SQL Server installation as previously outlined. Start the install, and remember to select and use the SQL Server 2000 Setup program Advanced\Maintain Virtual Server for Failover Clustering option. To use this Advanced\Maintain Virtual Server for Failover Clustering option, follow these steps:

1. Insert the SQL Server 2000 Enterprise Edition CD-ROM and let it start to install.
2. Click Install Database Server.
3. In the Welcome screen, click Next.
4. You can select the name of the Virtual Server you want to modify.
5. Type the name of the Virtual Server you want to modify (as seen in the following illustration), and then click Next.

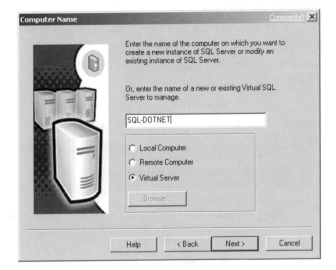

6. Click the Advanced Options tab, and then click Next.
7. Select Maintain a Virtual Server for Failover Clustering, and then click Next.
8. The Failover Clustering dialog box is now open.
9. You can add an IP address for additional networks, remove and replace an existing IP Address, or remove IP addresses that are no longer needed.
10. Replace the IP address and click Add | Next.
11. Click Next once again, unless you want to modify more options.
12. Verify all preexisting information by clicking Next.
13. Click Finish to complete the changes.

Now, your IP addressing changes are complete. Reopen the Cluster Administrator and verify by viewing the properties of the IP address resource.

Changing Service Accounts on a SQL Virtual Server

Other changes you might have to make (and that could damage your SQL installation) might be to the Service Account. In SQL Server 2000, you must follow necessary steps to change the service startup accounts for a clustered SQL Server. If this account (which you configured during installation) is changed or altered in any way, then you could have problems. To fix it, you need to do a few things. First, the account must be a domain account. The account you use must act as part of the operating system, logon as a service, and replace a process-level token. Without these polices in place, the account won't work (this is covered in Chapter 2 the section, "Cluster Service Account Advanced Configfuration"). The service account for the Cluster Service must also have the right to log in to SQL Server. The service account for SQL Server also must be an administrator in the cluster. To fix this, you can do the following:

1. Open the SQL Server Enterprise Manager console by going to Start | Programs | Microsoft SQL Server | Enterprise Manager.

2. Open the console and expand down to the actual Server object under the SQL Server Group.

3. Right-click the Server object and select Properties.

4. Once you click Properties, you see the following dialog box.

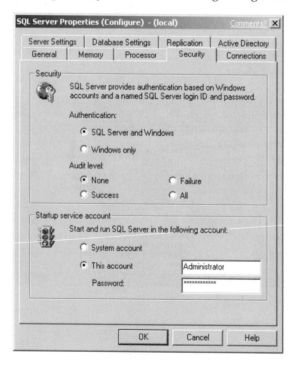

5. Click the Security Tab and, on the bottom of the dialog box, you can see the option to change the Startup Service Account.

You can also run the SQL Server 2000 setup in the Administrative\Maintenance mode again, but this way is much easier.

Changing a Clustered SQL Server Network Name

Although you have a way within the Cluster Administrator to rename instances, you'll find that doing so could create some massive problems—for instance, the possible denial of service to the resource. Because this is so easy to change (and damage), you need to know how to change the SQL Server Network Name correctly and how to fix it if it's damaged. You should know the correct way to rename a clustered SQL Server 2000 Virtual Server is simply to uninstall and reinstall SQL Server 2000 with the new Virtual Server name. That's it! I know this might seem like a hassle, but more of a hassle could come your way if you do this another way.

Make sure that before you go through with the uninstall and reinstall process that you have recently backed up your databases. You don't want to lose your data. If you have a problem getting things back online, then you have a protected copy of your data.

Moving Resources

Earlier, I purposely made the mistake of placing the SQL Resource in the Main Cluster Group. Now, we'll look at how to move the SQL Resource if you make a mistake and have to move resources from one group to another. This is how you do it without having problems:

1. Open the Cluster Administrator in the Administrative Tools folder.

2. Open the Groups folder and select the Group with the resources you want to move.

3. Right-click the resource you want to move and select the Change Group option.

4. You can specify which group you want to move to.

5. In the next illustration, verify you want to move the resources.

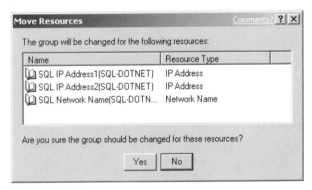

6. Clicking Yes moves the resources to the new group you specify.

7. In Figure 5-14, you can see the resources are now in the new group you moved them to.

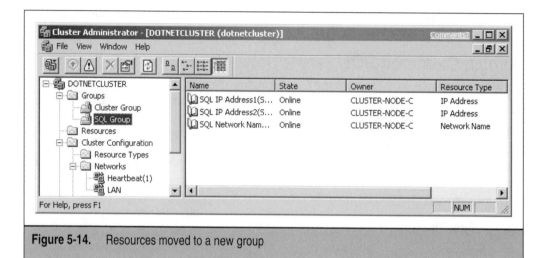

Figure 5-14. Resources moved to a new group

Network Failure

At times, you might experience a large network outage or a disconnection from the network. When this happens, it's up to you to use your troubleshooting skills to verify what the problem is. In Figure 5-15, you can see your first clue is in the Cluster Administrator. First, the Cluster Groups go offline and appear to have massive errors. Your true indicator is that the LAN connection has failed somehow and is showing up as down within the console.

When you see this, you can start checking your local network connection first and work your way outward to the cable, switch, or hub port. Once you verify the problems, you might want to refresh the console (View | Refresh) to see if your server still reports a problem.

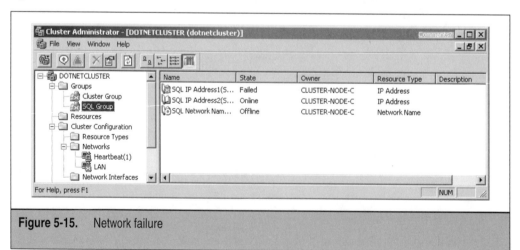

Figure 5-15. Network failure

Sqlstpx.log	Log for the SQL Server setup, where *x* is the number of the setup attempts. You'll find multiple instances of this file if you have multiple setups.
Sqlclstr.log	Log for the clustered SQL Server used for troubleshooting the SQL Server.
Cluster.log	The main cluster log file for troubleshooting cluster-related issues.
Sqlstp.log	The log from the user interface part of setup used for troubleshooting possible issues related to set up.

Table 5-3.   SQL Server Cluster Log Files

Log Files

When you're in a total jam, you can always look at the log files on the server. Listed here are the basic log files that can help you in your troubleshooting. You can generally find the logs under the winnt\cluster directory, but you can simply find them by running a search on your server's drives for the *.log file. When you find them, single out a few that are dedicated to cluster-based operations and SQL Server. These are the files seen in the following Table 5-3.

CONCLUSION

In this chapter, you learned the fundamentals of clustering SQL Server 2000 Enterprise Edition. When planning your SQL Server 2000 Enterprise Edition Cluster deployment, you have much to take into consideration. This chapter's intent was to start you from the beginning and take you to the end, so you can successfully plan, design, purchase, install, configure, and troubleshoot a two-node failover cluster on either Windows 2000 Advanced Server or Windows Server 2003. Although every scenario or problem can't be covered or planned for, you should have enough tools not only to get you started, but also enable you to start, finish, and do some advanced troubleshooting on a SQL Cluster.

For further reading, log on to **http://www.sql-server-performance.com**. This site is a good resource for tweaking your installation after it's up and running. To learn more about SQL Server fundamentals, read *SQL Server 2000 A Beginner's Guide,* by Dusan Petrovic (ISBN: 007212587X).

In the next chapter, we take a wide look at clustering and load balancing many different solutions, so hold on! We've only begun to design some great solutions.

CHAPTER 6

Designing a Highly Available Solution with Windows Services

In this chapter, the main focus is to take a good look at the Windows Services you can cluster and load balance. In other words, up until now, you've seen massive amounts of highly available designs, installations, and configuration of operating systems (OSs) and BackOffice/ Server 2003 servers. In this chapter, you learn about Clustering Services on an already established cluster, such as clustering Dynamic Host Configuration Protocol (DHCP). *DHCP* is a service that enables you the freedom of not having to manage static IP assignments on your network hosts. You see how to make this available and the chapter ends with some high-level troubleshooting tips. This chapter should seem like a breather to you from all the high-end designs we went through in Chapters 2 through 5. Also, make sure you've read Chapters 1 through 5 because, if you haven't, you won't have the core knowledge needed to perform the tasks in this chapter. Let's look at Windows Services.

HIGHLY AVAILABLE WINDOWS SERVICES

Up to now, we've discussed the importance of high availability. In today's nonstop world, you need to make sure your network and systems services are highly available to your user population. This should include IP addresses, so connectivity to the network is always guaranteed, and WINS services to make sure the level of broadcast traffic is kept to a minimum. In this section of the chapter, the focus is on the DHCP service and how to make it highly available for your company or business.

Highly Available DHCP Services

DHCP is a service that, when installed and configured correctly, will take a massive administration burden off any network administrator or engineer. DHCP works with the assignment of IP addresses on your network. In other words, when you want your network clients to communicate with any device on the network, they need to speak the same protocol and be assigned with a unique logical address. This address (called an *IP address*) allows for this. The problem associated with this assignment process is this: unless you have something to do it for you, you must go to each device and manually assign it an address. Problem two is, as I just mentioned, that each address must be unique. So, how do you manage network hosts based on assignment of an IP address and keep them unique? With a DHCP server, that's how.

With DHCP, the service allows for any client on the network (when configured to do so) to request an IP address from any DHCP server you have configured. This server "leases" the address to the client and makes a record of it, so it won't assign it to any other host. Now you never have to keep a spreadsheet of who has what address and, even better, you needn't worry about duplicate addressing being an error on your part. Now you can have a nice console to manage all your hosts, see who has what address, and even configure the DHCP scope (a range of IP addresses) to include the network segment's default gateway, WINS and DNS server addresses, and a ton of other configuration settings much more easily than before. Now that you have a basic understanding of the DHCP server service, you need to understand why you need to make it highly available. The DHCP service is what keeps your network running. If you lose the DHCP server, then when the clients try to renew their leases on current IP addresses, they won't be able to and will either have no IP address at all or revert to an APIPA address if they're Windows 98/2000 or later hosts.

Automatic Private IP Addressing (APIPA) is a feature of the Windows 98, Windows 2000, XP OSs, and Me that allows for the clients to self-configure an IP address and a subnet mask when a DHCP server isn't available. Microsoft has reserved an IP address range for this functionality alone. The IP address range is 169.254.0.1 through 169.254.255.254 and sets a default class B subnet mask of 255.255.0.0. The client will use this address until the DHCP server comes back online. This is helpful in small networks that aren't routed but, for your global enterprise, having this functionality is frustratingly painful if your DHCP server crashes. You can use the following link to disable APIPA or to learn more about it: **http://support.microsoft. com/ default.aspx?scid=KB;ENUS;Q220874%20for%20ME/98/2K**.

To stop the problems that can occur with a DHCP server failure, you can make it highly available, which we show in the next section.

Configuring DHCP for High Availability

Now that you're familiar with the fundamentals of DHCP and why it should be included in your high-availability design, let's begin the steps on how to configure it. First, you need to review Chapter 2 and Chapter 3, where you learned how to cluster Microsoft Windows 2000 Advanced Server and Windows Server 2003. You need to work with an already clustered solution, so if you need to rebuild it, now is the time. If not, then you can apply this configuration later after you've read through it.

Following these steps enables you to install Windows 2000's DHCP service:

1. First, you must have a running Windows 2000 Advanced Server. When you're booted up, open the Control Panel. Go to Start | Settings | Control Panel and select the Add/Remove Programs Control Panel applet.

2. Once you open the applet, select the Add/Remove Windows Components button. When you click it, you open a dialog box that enables you to install the DHCP Service, as seen in the following illustration. Add the DHCP Service if it isn't already installed. You might need the Windows 2000 Advanced Server CD-ROM if you don't have the i386 directory on your server.

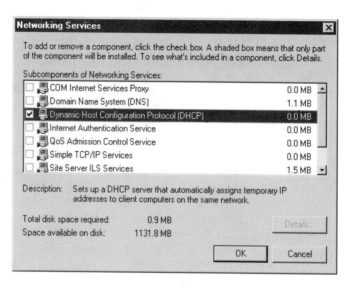

3. Now that you have the service installed on one server, you'll want to prepare for the clustering process. To make DHCP highly available, add a second server. Before you do this, though, make sure you only install the services. Don't configure the scopes at this time. (As previously mentioned, the scope is the group of IPs the server doles out.) Scopes will be configured after both servers have DHCP installed and the services running.

4. You can open the DHCP console, as shown in Figure 6-1, to see the basic installation and configuration of the DHCP service. Here, you can see the DHCP Service is installed, but not ready to dole out addresses yet.

5. Bring up the second node and also install the DHCP service on it. Make sure you don't create a scope.

   Now, you have two servers, both running DHCP, which you want to cluster. Let's configure the cluster resource.

6. Authorize the DHCP server by going to the DHCP console in the Administrative Tools folder in the Control Panel. Open the DCHP console and click the DHCP Server in the console, right-click it, and then select Authorize. If you don't have this option yet, you can also manage these servers through the Manage Authorized Servers dialog box found by right-clicking the console root node.

7. Open the Manage Authorized Servers dialog box, as seen in the following illustration. Select the server to authorize (you can press refresh to see if they show up) or choose Authorize to select which servers you want to authorize. Make sure you authorize the DHCP Server if you're running in an Active Directory environment, so it can respond to client requests.

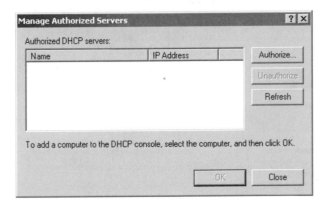

8. Now you're ready to configure DHCP as a resource in the cluster. To do this, open the Cluster Administrator tool, as shown in Figure 6-2. Once opened, you can go to the File menu and choose to configure a new application. Once selected, open the Cluster Application Wizard.

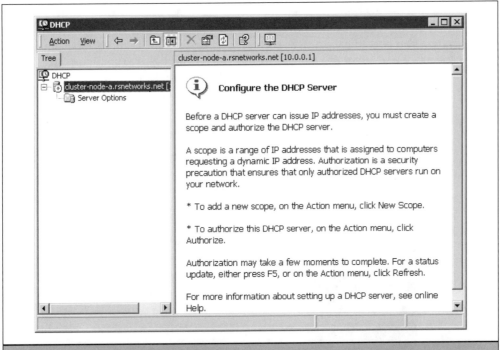

Figure 6-1.   Viewing the DHCP Server console

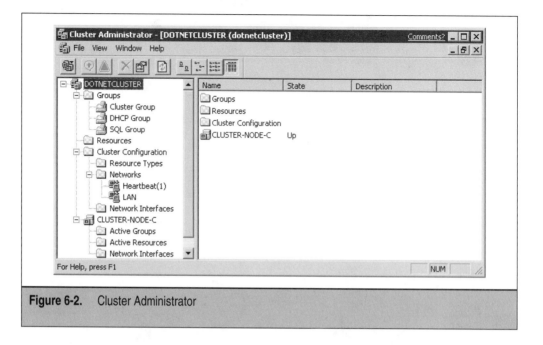

Figure 6-2. Cluster Administrator

9. When you open the wizard, as seen in the following illustration, you begin the process of creating a DHCP cluster. The wizard helps to configure an application to run in a cluster. This wizard takes you through all the steps you need to follow to create or select a Virtual Server and prepare an application to be clustered.

Next, as seen in Figure 6-3, you can create a Virtual Server. Again, to reiterate what was learned in past chapters, a Virtual Server is what the client will access

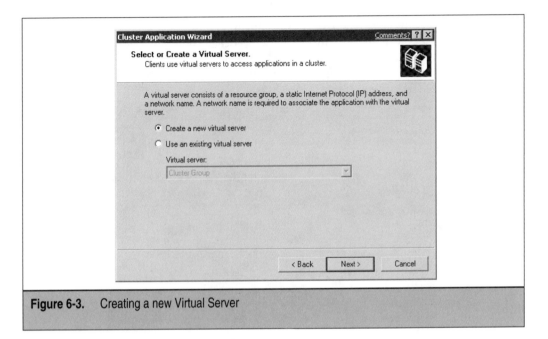

Figure 6-3.   Creating a new Virtual Server

to get to the applications on the cluster. Two nodes exist and what they share between them is a name and an IP address, which the client will access to get to the resources hosted on both nodes.

10. In Figure 6-3, you have the option to create a new server or you can use one that's already created. Select which one you want, and then click Next.

11. In the next illustration, you can create a new resource group for your Virtual Server. Because I already made one prior to launching the wizard, I'm selecting it here. You can also create a new one if you want to.

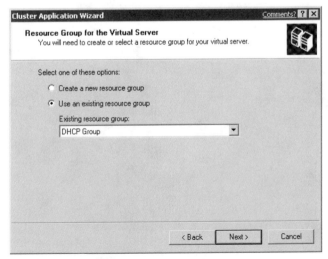

12. After selecting your resource group, give it a name for the Virtual Server, as seen in the following illustration. Do this so you can have a meaningful name that represents a role within the cluster. I kept it simple, but you can make the name as elaborate as you need to keep it distinguished from the rest of the resources. Then, click Next.

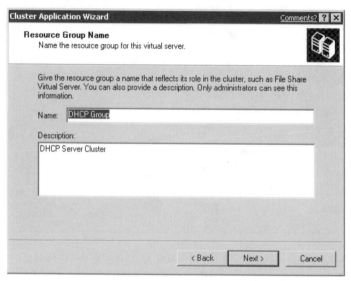

13. Now that you have your new Virtual Server and resource group set up, you need to configure an IP address to associate the resource with the cluster and the clients. In the following illustration, you can configure the IP address and the network name. You need to supply a unique IP address that the clients will access to get to the resource, which is the DHCP service. In this example, I supplied an IP address and a network name the clients will need to use to access this resource.

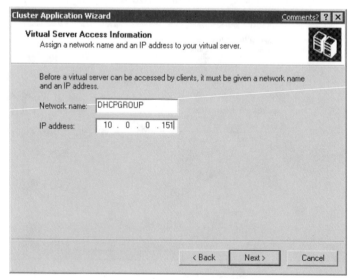

14. After clicking Next, you have to select some advanced Virtual Server properties, as seen in the following illustration. You can configure quite a few things here. First, understand that up to now, you've provided what's needed for the resource to function, but you can configure a few more things now instead of later. Select Resource Group Properties and click the Advanced Properties button.

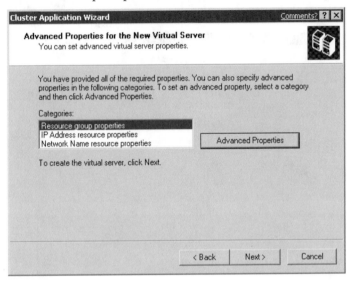

15. In the next illustration, check over the failover and failback options. You learned about both services in the first few chapters of the book. If you want to configure these options, do so now. Also, remember, all these are optional and you can configure them later. They're only here for ease of use.

16. In the next section of Advanced Properties configuration you'll configure IP address parameters further than what you already designated earlier in the wizard. This is shown in the next illustration. The Parameters tab is important for the success of your DHCP resource. In this tab, you'll find the IP address you already assigned the Virtual Server but, more important, you can see what network it wants to use.

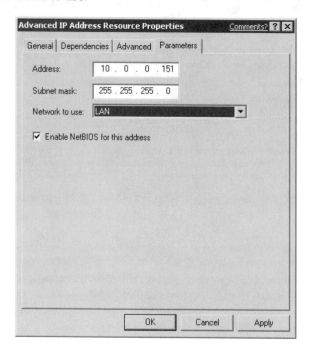

17. Understand that when you use the Cluster Service, you always have two individual network cards connected to two completely different networks. If you configure the resource on the wrong network, then clients won't be able to reach it. In this tab, you can configure on which network the resource is located. In this example, I configured the LAN network instead of the Heartbeat network. By default, when I looked at it the first time, it was set for the wrong network, so that would have impeded communications. You must configure this properly for the cluster to work! Visibly verify that your connections are properly marked and connected for communications to take place. You can click Apply when you've set it the way you want it.

18. The last resource you can configure is the Advanced Network Name Resource Properties, as seen in the next illustration. In this dialog box, you can configure the network name if needed. This has already been done, though, so you have no need to change it.

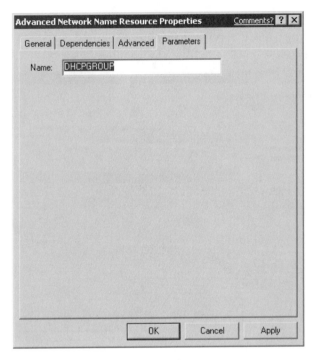

19. Next, configure the manager of the resource. In this part of the wizard, you can create a cluster resource to manage the actual application you're clustering. Here, you'll answer Yes and create a resource for the application, as shown in the illustration.

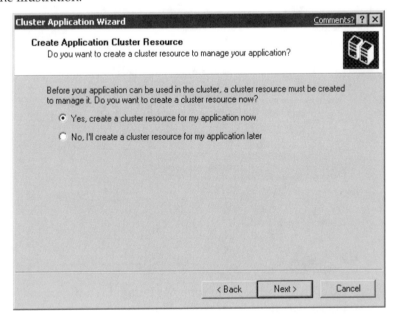

20. After clicking Next, the following illustration shows you how to set up the resource type. DHCP Service comes preconfigured, so you needn't worry about it. Simply drop down the menu and select the DHCP Service option.

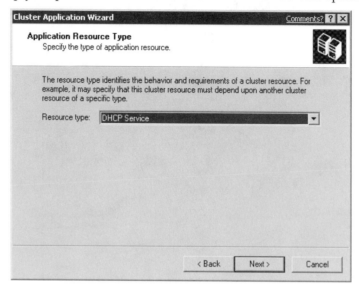

21. Click Next again. You'll need to specify a name for this specific resource. I selected the DHCPGROUP but, again, you can select whatever seems logical in your own environment. After you configure what you need in the following illustration, click Next to create the resource.

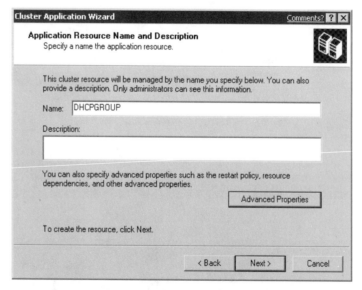

22. You can also click the Advanced Properties button to configure the Restart policy and other dependencies if you need to do so. Click Advanced Properties.

In the next illustration, you can see the options available, such as the Restart or Do not restart options, within the Resource Group. The restart policy allows the group to restart itself after a certain threshold passes.

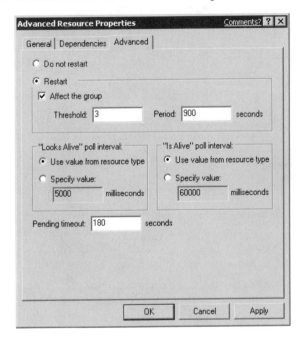

23. If you need to configure Dependencies, then you can also work through that configuration here. Click the Dependencies tab and choose Modify. Then, double-click a physical disk resource, an IP address resource, and a network name resource, so you can add them. Click OK to have them all added.

    In Figure 6-4, I removed one resource, so you can see what happens if you don't meet the requirements, such as having a name, an IP address, or a shared storage device.

24. In the next illustration, you generate an error if any of the resources are missing that need to be applied, such as an IP address or shared storage devices. Make sure you have your cluster configured properly or you won't be able to finish the configuration. I always add or create problems in the test environment to help solve problems that could arise during the configuration of the production environment.

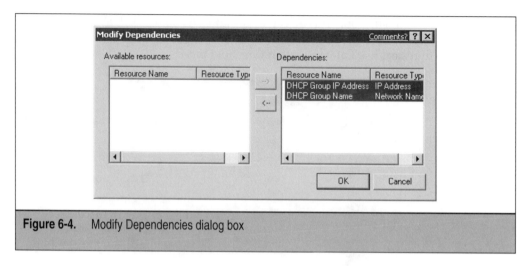

Figure 6-4. Modify Dependencies dialog box

25. This is the time to cluster your DHCP service. Once you click Next, the wizard prompts you for the location of the DHCP database files. Select the dependent disk that was left out of Figure 6-4. Close the wizard and you'll have to bring the group online. You can right-click it, and then select Bring Online.

26. That's it! Now you only need to configure your scopes and you're finished. Open the DHCP console and right-click the server on which you want to set up the scope.

Congratulations! You've built your first resource into the clustered server solution. Now, you should feel comfortable knowing your DHCP service is highly available. You can always test the solution, if needed, by powering down one server and seeing if the other server takes over. If so, then you're all set. If not, you need to do some troubleshooting to see why this didn't work. Some of the most common causes of failure are misconfiguration, so go back through Chapters 1 through 3 if you're having an issue with your cluster. Now, let's look at our next resource: the Windows Internet Naming Service.

Highly Available WINS

Just like DHCP, Windows Internet Naming Service (WINS) is a service used on the server to make life easier for you and your network. *WINS* is a core part of the Windows 2000 and Server 2003 operating systems. Although you can do away with this service in a pure Windows 2000 and above network, it still comes standard with all servers' OSs you purchase. WINS is responsible for managing the NetBIOS name to IP address association on your network in a database, so you can cut down on the amount of NetBIOS broadcasts that occur on your network. The NetBIOS protocol, when configured on any workstation, generally broadcasts its name by default, causing massive amounts of broadcast traffic, depending on the size of your network. All other services like the Master Browser service, for example, which helps maintain the browse list in My Network Places, is also made better by the use of the WINS service. When it's used correctly, WINS is a network bandwidth saver. Now that you understand what WINS can do for you and your network, you should also be able to make it highly available. Let's see how.

Configuring WINS for High Availability

After reading so much of this book, it's no wonder you probably want to cluster and load balance everything you see! Although this is a great idea for reliability and disaster-recovery scenarios, it does cost more and it adds complication to the design, which you'll see when you create a Highly Available WINS solution. Before we get into the complexity of maintaining it, let's look at setting it up. In this example, I cut out some of the excessive screenshots you'll see as being redundant from the DHCP configuration exercise. You can follow most of the same steps, except where inapplicable. I'll let you know the differences in configuration and steps. First, the same rules apply when it comes to working on building a highly available service. You need the cluster in place already, so make sure you have a Microsoft Windows 2000 Advanced Server or Windows Server 2003 running and functional. You might want to review Chapters 2 and 3 to make sure you have it configured properly. Let's look at the install.

1. First, make sure you have a viable cluster up and running. This is important. Don't install WINS yet to any server.

2. Next, add WINS (as the WINS service) to your cluster nodes.

3. To add the WINS service to your servers, go to Start | Settings | Control Panel | Add/Remove Programs | Add/Remove Windows Components.

4. Once you select this button, open the Components dialog box, and move to the Networking Services category. Don't select anything yet, though, because we have more configurations to make here.

5. Click Networking Service | Details button.

6. Clicking the Details button enables you to drill down into the Networking Service, as seen in the following illustration where I checked WINS for installation, and then press the OK button.

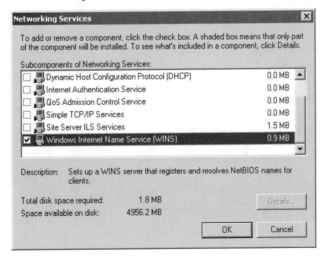

7. Once you finish, you'll begin the install of the service. As you did with DHCP, follow the prompts and install the service.

8. You can now install the WINS service on the other node in the cluster.

9. Now that you've finished installing WINS on each node, you'll want to adjust your IP addressing configuration.

   You need to adjust your TCP/IP configuration so the server points to the Virtual IP address (VIP) for WINS. To accomplish this, continue the steps.

10. Right-click My Network Places | Properties.

11. Right-click Network Connection | Properties.

12. Click TCP/IP and select it. Once it's selected, click the Properties button.

13. Click Advanced | click the WINS tab.

14. Enter the VIP address to be used for WINS. You can see this in Figure 6-5. Now your clustered nodes will register their records with WINS successfully.

15. Once you finish installing WINS on each node and have configured the proper IP addresses, you must create a clustered resource for them both to be a part of. The hardest thing to remember about clustering is you must make two entities appear as one and this is where the creation of the clustered resource comes in to play.

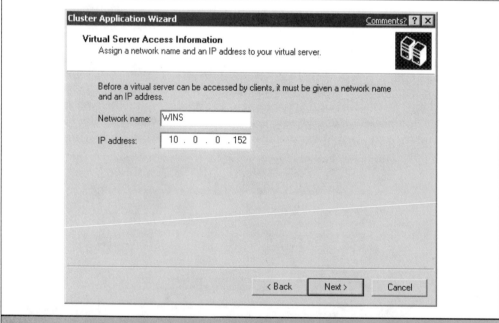

Figure 6-5. Creating a clustered WINS resource

16. Also, remember, you need three dependencies: shared storage, a shared network name, and a shared IP address, as shown in Figure 6-5.

    As you did with DHCP, you can create this resource with the Configure Application Wizard. This is always the quickest and easiest way for you to create a resource. The wizard walks you through each step.

17. Start the Cluster Administrator tool by going to Start | Programs | Administrative Tools | Cluster Administrator.

18. You need to connect to the cluster you want to configure.

19. In Cluster Administrator, go to the Configure Application option in the File menu.

20. Run the Cluster Application Wizard.

21. Once you run the wizard, as seen in the following illustration, you continue through the same steps as you did when we clustered the DHCP service.

22. After the wizard greets you, click Next, so you can either create a new Virtual Server or configure an existing Virtual Server. I recommend you create a new one for this exercise.

23. After you follow the prompts to create the Virtual Server, you can then create an application resource on the Create Application Cluster Resource page, as seen in the next illustration.

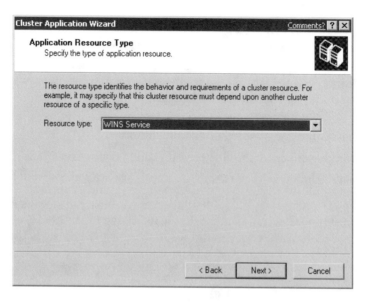

24. Click the resource type named WINS Service, and then click Next.

25. Create a name and description for the new WINS resource.

26. Select the Advanced Properties, so you can add a physical disk resource, an IP address resource, and a network name resource. Remember, again, this is basically the same process you used to configure DHCP earlier.

27. Add your new resources as dependencies and follow the rest of the wizard through its defaults to finish creating your new Cluster Application.

28. Note, the wizard eventually prompts you for the location of the WINS database files and this is important. You must make sure that the WINS database files are placed on the disk in the group. If you don't, it will fail. Take care not to change this to a disk that isn't in the group you just configured.

    The default location is initially for the dependent disk, so you shouldn't have to configure anything.

29. That's it! Follow the rest of the wizard prompts to the end and select your defaults. You have now created a new WINS resource.

This new resource is a little more difficult to care for, so let's continue this discussion on WINS. To finish the WINS cluster resource you just created, make sure it shows up in the Cluster Administrator and is in an online state. If it is in an offline state, then you can right-click it, and then click Bring Online. Test your group by making sure the cluster resource has been properly clustered. Do this by right-clicking the group and selecting Move Group. If your group moves, then you can rest assured the basics of clustering the WINS resource have been done properly. Now, you should feel comfortable knowing your WINS service is highly available, so let's look at more advanced features of clustering your resources.

Highly Available Databases

In this section, we look at some of the details that revolve around clustering a service and how it affects the systems you're working with. Because WINS shares a database that's populated with NetBIOS and IP address–based records, you must make that database accessible to both clustered nodes. Then, when items are deleted or changed, both nodes have the same information to hand out to requesting clients. The following are some additional details to remember when sharing a database in a cluster:

- The database files must be configured properly to support sharing between the cluster nodes. For this to happen, you need to make sure that when you configure WINS on a node, your Winstmp.mdb and Wins.mdb files need to be considered. Make sure they're installed on the clustered storage device, so they can share it.

- On a set of clustered nodes, the WINS database and its related files reside on a cluster storage device in the path specified for the WINS resource, as seen in Figure 6-6 and also here:

    %SystemRoot%\System32\WINS

Figure 6-6. Viewing the WINS database files on a local drive

- When you back up the WINS directory, you need to know some of the items it creates. When the backup is done, a subfolder under the WINS folder called Wins_bak is created, as well as a subfolder under that named New, which will contain copies of the Wins.mdb file, the Wins.pat file, and a copy of the jet database log file. The jet database log files will be numbered: JXXXXXX.log. All these files are important and, if necessary, will be used to restore the WINS database.

- Finally, make sure you don't change any permissions on the directory! Don't change the default settings for the NTFS file system permissions on your %SystemRoot%\System32\WINS folder or you might lose access to it from your accounts and it could cause errors to arise.

Now that you know where the database resides and what pieces are attached to its overall functionality, let's back up the database so, if the data is lost or damaged, you have a way to recover your information quickly.

Backing Up and Restoring WINS on a Cluster

Backing up a WINS database on a Windows-based cluster is important. In this section, you learn how to back up this (and any) database, so you can be ready for such a disaster if it strikes.

If you were running a traditional WINS server that wasn't clustered at all—just installed and managed as a stand-alone server—then you could back up the WINS database directly from the WINS MMC console. You can do this by going to the WINS MMC located at Start | Settings | Control Panel | Administrative Tools | WINS. Once you open the MMC, you can back up the WINS database by going to the Back Up Database command in the Action menu, as seen in the next illustration.

This isn't available here because the database is clustered and can't be backed up. This creates a problem, so you need a valid workaround. You have to find a way to back up the database in case of a possible disaster. Here's how you can restore a system in case a clustered solution fails.

Make sure you completely understand the last two sections. You must have an established and functional cluster solution to install the WINS service on to and you must have a shared drive resource where the \Winnt\System32\Wins folder will reside. This way, the shared disk is where all your files are, and is the one place you can back up the entire shared database. Next, you should know what your game plan is going to be to back up the database because the option to do so isn't available. If it isn't available, then you have only one alternative: back up the shared resource with a backup program. Now, you can use any program for your shared storage backup but, because most people will have Ntbackup available, we'll look at that option.

1. When you want to start the backup, your first task is to take the WINS resource offline. Go into the Cluster Administrator, right-click the resource, and then select to take it offline.

2. Once offline, you can run the Ntbackup utility. To run it, go to Start | Run, enter **Ntbackup** in the blank run box, and enter **Ntbackup** on the Open field. Press OK and you open Ntbackup.

3. Once you open the Ntbackup utility, a wizard or the welcome screen greets you. If you get the wizard, click the option to select Advanced mode and you'll go to the welcome screen. If you went directly to the welcome screen, you need to click the Backup tab, as seen in Figure 6-7.

   In Figure 6-7, you can see WINS folder was selected in the left-hand navigation pane of the Ntbackup utility.

4. The right-hand pane is the individual file within that WINS directory. Select the WINS directory. By default, you also select all the files within it.

   If you're using the Ntbackup utility for this purpose, you might have issues with the Windows Scheduler. Using the scheduler could become increasingly difficult because you might not know, at any given time, which of your clustered nodes will own the required resource group. Cluster.exe, discussed in Chapter 2, can be incorporated into batch files to automate what you need to make happen. The batch file can also be used to incorporate Ntbackup batch jobs. You need to know how to make a basic batch file to automate what you need done. The batch file you can write will be able to move the group to the right node, so you can take the node offline to back up the database. Once you finish, you can also use the batch file to bring the node back up online when you finish, and then move the group back to the other node if you want. Refer to Chapter 2 to learn about the command-line features to perform this step.

5. Next, open the WINS MMC again and we'll learn another way to back up the database, which I find much easier than the previous way. Here, you can have the database backed up on shutdown.

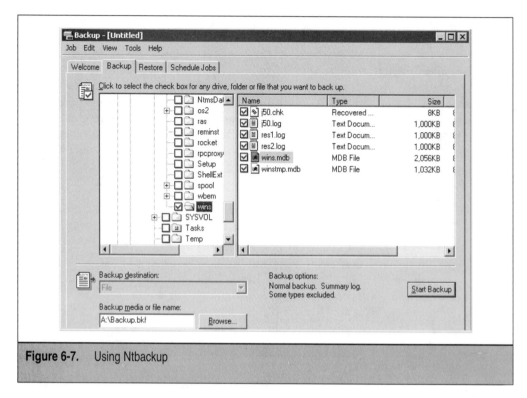

Figure 6-7. Using Ntbackup

6. Open WINS MMC and right-click the WINS server | Properties | General tab. Click to select the Back up database during server shutdown check box, as seen in the next illustration.

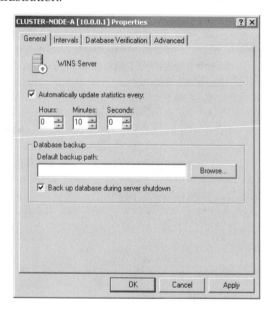

This backs up the WINS database each time a shutdown occurs. The only downside to this is having the shutdown. This is also less flexible than the other method, but it's much easier to manage and is recommended because of its ease of use.

Don't use this as a way to test a production cluster. You'd want this set for when your servers have problems and have to be rebooted. This isn't something you'd want to use on a server if you don't have to because better methods are available for a higher price. This is simply another solution you can use if you want to use the tools you already have available.

CONCLUSION

What you learned in this chapter can be applied to nearly any service. Now that you know how to do the two hardest ones, you should have no problem going through and clustering the gambit of what Windows 2000 and Server 2003 servers will let you cluster.

Let's recap what you've learned up to now. In this chapter, you learned how to apply some of Microsoft's networking infrastructure services, such as WINS and DHCP, to the high-availability model. Services like DHCP always must be available to service your network clients. If they aren't available, you could lose service on your network. Applying Highly Available solutions like the ones you've read about in this chapter might save you some headaches in the future.

CHAPTER 7

Building Advanced Highly Available Load-Balanced Configurations

In this chapter, you learn how to take your knowledge of load balancing and apply it to building load-balanced solutions facing the Internet. In this chapter, you continue to build your knowledge from all the previous chapters in the book and focus on advanced NLB concepts to apply with Windows Server 2003, which includes theory, design, and security. Once you understand what this product does, we'll build a load-balanced cluster with it. The chapter ends with troubleshooting tips and things to remember when rolling out a high-availability solution. We're nearing the end of the book and this is the last chapter in which we build an actual cluster. By now, I hope you've built enough clusters so you can design one for yourself or your organization. Let's begin by looking at some advanced network load balancing (NLB) predesign planning.

PREDESIGN PLANNING

In this section, we look at some of the advanced features of using NLB. NLB was covered in Chapter 3, where you learned how to set up a load-balanced solution with Windows Server 2003.

First, let's do a small review, and then build the more advanced features.

NLB Advanced Design and Troubleshooting

In this section, we'll explore some design tips and tricks to build on your current NLB knowledge, and design a Highly Available NLB solution for your network. This first discussion centers on NLB traffic considerations and planning. Then you learn about design tips for installing and mixing node types.

NLB Traffic Planning

While using NLB, you want to ensure your data isn't bottlenecking anywhere because, as we've mentioned previously, it's critical for you to optimize every part of a Highly Available solution for it to work as advertised. You want it to operate faster, if anything else. You also want to make sure the Highly Available solution is scalable and redundant, but you definitely want to be certain your bandwidth needs are considered first.

In the following diagram, I'll highlight a possible network load-balanced solution and explain each section of the diagram for planning bandwidth considerations. In Figure 7-1, I planned a simple NLB Highly Available solution for a provider of web services. This is a web portal that requires nothing more than a secure web site. In other words, keep it simple, we aren't selling anything. All I need is a reliable web site that's always up and running (like a listing of information) and it must be secure from the Internet. You also want to ensure no one will be penetrating your company's network from the Internet. Remember, the design itself isn't what we're focusing on now. Our real focus is on the actual network design in relation to traffic design. Let's look at each section in depth.

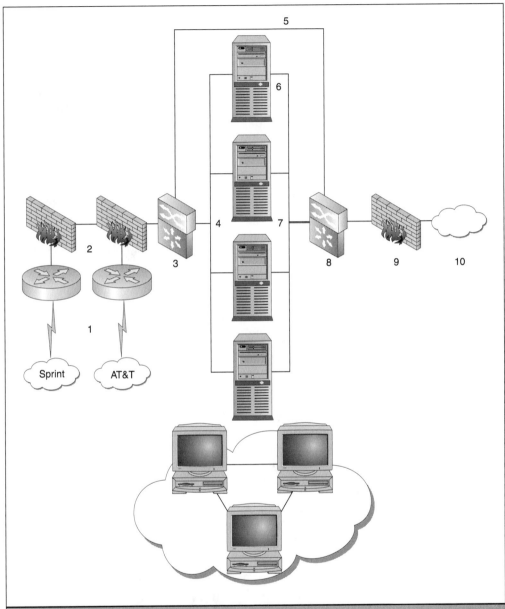

Figure 7-1.　Sample diagram of a possible network load-balanced solution

In Figure 7-1, I numbered sections of the diagram I want you to pay attention to when planning bandwidth and trying to optimize your investment.

1. In the first section of the diagram, I flagged the Internet-based routers for you to review. You need to do an analysis on what kind of traffic could come to your new web site. Let's say this is some kind of informational site, such as Maps of New York, and you know you're going to get hundreds of hits every hour, with peak traffic during holiday months. You don't want to undercut yourself, so plan your bandwidth wisely. I recommend starting with at least a full T1 (1.544MB) line, so you can reprovision it and downgrade it, if necessary. Reprovisioning lines, although it's a hassle, isn't a difficult task. I also recommend you get two lines and have them connect to two different points of presence (POP). You needn't get two ISPs or Telcos to do this either. You can get Sprint and AT&T or you can ask AT&T to give you two different POPs. This adds redundancy within the Telco itself because if it has problems, you have a second chance at life! Next, you want to have the best router hardware you can get. Although I like all flavors of hardware, I am definitely a Cisco advocate. I suggest a 2600 series Cisco Router or above. You can use older 2500s, but I advise you don't because most of them have Ethernet ports, not Fast Ethernet Ports. You're locking yourself into 10 Mbps and half-duplex, instead of 100 Mbps and full-duplex communication, which eliminates CSMA/CD and collisions on the wire. Finally, make sure you have enough memory in your routers and that your cabling has been tested and verified.

2. In the second section, you want to pay attention to your firewalls. Now, I am also a fan of many firewall vendors and brands so I won't sit here and tell you which ones you should purchase, but making a highly available and load-balanced solution out of the firewalls should also be on your list for this solution. I suggest making sure that whichever one you pick (Checkpoint, Symantec, Cisco, Nokia), it is scalable, and if possible, redundant. Since we already started talking about Cisco, I will continue with them. In this diagram, you can visualize that we have two Cisco PIX firewalls (I am using Version 515 here). I have two, and between them I have a failover cable for redundancy in case one of them fails. I will also make sure that they are running at 100 Mbps and full-duplex on each Fast Ethernet Port. Make sure that the connection (100 Mbps full-duplex to the Switch) is located on section 3.

3. In the third section, you have your first switch connection. Again, you can use whatever you want, but I will continue with Cisco. I have a Cisco 4006 series switch with Layer-3 functionality. In other words, it's a switch and a router combined. Each port of this connection is configured at 100 Mbps and full-duplex and that CPU and memory utilization is very low. Also, the switch I chose is a little overkill for the solution, but I have another plan for this company to implement ecommerce and a new DMZ, so I am planning for scalability! I am also using

this switch because it is the lowest grade Layer-3 switch in its class with the port density I need for future growth. The 4000 and the newer 4500's are the smallest enterprise switches I would use.

4. In the fourth section, I am highlighting the front-end connections to the NLB cluster nodes. This would be the connection to the NIC cards that have a Virtual IP address enabled. Figure 7-2 shows the IP address view of Figure 7-1. The Virtual IP address is 12.1.3.10 and this front-end network must be at 100 Mbps full-duplex if possible. This is where most of your traffic will be on the Cluster. Make sure the NIC cards on your NLB hosts are optimized with the best possible drivers, the best possible cards and set at 100 Mbps full-duplex hardcoded to eliminate auto-negotiation problems. Auto-negotiation is what a port on a switch or a NIC card does to adjust to the line speed present. In other words, if you have a network Switch with 10/100-Mbps ports and NICs that will work at that speed, auto-negotiation will make a best effort to adjust to speed that both are willing to operate and communicate on. Every port that auto-negotiates must advertise the modes in which it is able and willing to operate, and most likely, if you have up-to-date gear, you will find that it will negotiate to the higher speed like 100 Mbps.

5. In the fifth section, make sure your uplink from your front-end switch to your back-end switch is also optimized at 100/full. Be careful to avoid switch flooding, as covered in Chapters 2 and 3. You don't want your back-end network flooded with heartbeat traffic, so you might want to use a hub and an uplink to the switch to save money or set up a separate VLAN. Either way, make sure your main traffic paths are optimized as much as possible.

6. In the sixth section, make sure your back-end NIC cards are set at 100 Mbps and full-duplex. The only time this changes is if you want to eliminate switch flooding and if you use a hub. If this is the case, leave the NIC to autonegotiate the speeds you want.

7. In the seventh section, make sure your heartbeat traffic over your private network is optimized. This isn't the most crucial point of the cluster, so make it the best you can, using at least 10 Mbps and half-duplex, although setting this to 100 Mbps and full-duplex is definitely the better solution.

8. In the eighth section, this is your back-end network switch. I have another Cisco 4006 with Layer-3 capabilities for routing between the different subnets. I have this connected to my front-end network switch and my back-end network firewall. All connections are optimized at 100 Mbps full-duplex.

9. In the ninth section, you must put a back-end firewall into a network of this kind. Because you're connecting to the public Internet, make sure you have, at the least, the most minimal form of protection you can get. In this case, you can see an uplink between the servers from switch to switch could be

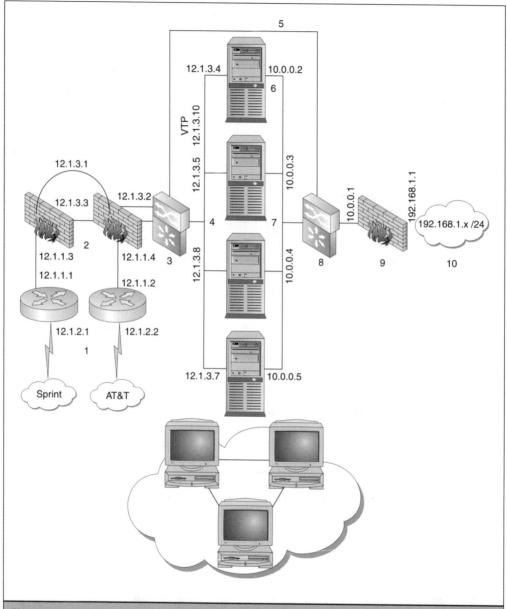

Figure 7-2. TCP/IP view of the NLB solution

exploited. With the back-end firewall, you protect yourself completely. Make sure this firewall is also running at 100/full. You can also add in a second one if you felt it was needed for reliability. Because this won't stop your customers from getting to the web site, which the failure of the first front-end firewalls could have caused, you might not want to invest the money into a second firewall.

10. In the tenth section, your firewall connects to your private network. I assume another Cisco switch is there to connect to, so make sure whatever you use is configured at 100/full.

That's it! You just planned out traffic management for your NLB cluster. If you didn't do this and you had bandwidth problems, it could take you a long time to determine what happened. If this is the case, then you could possibly add a lot of time overall to your design and implementation. It's best to plan this out early and make it happen to eliminate any possibility of a bandwidth problem in the first place. I've been asked if the heartbeat packets use up a lot of bandwidth. They take up nothing. To prove my point, I put a protocol analyzer on the hub the heartbeat traffic was traversing and it didn't pick up anything on a heavily used NLB cluster. Because the heartbeat packets take up less than 1,500 bytes (a standard Ethernet frame is 1,514), and are transmitted one per second, then 10–100 Mbps per second is more than enough to meet the maximum NLB cluster size of 32 nodes. Another thing to plan for when dealing with NLB planning and bandwidth considerations is that you don't need a separate back-end network for heartbeat traffic. Dividing as much of the traffic as possible when you can is always beneficial. Also nice is to have a back-end heartbeat-based network for security and management reasons, so your best bet is to implement it into your Highly Available solution. You never know when you'll be totally inundated with traffic. NLB also produces flooding in network traffic, so now you can eliminate the need for a hub on the back end, but this is only applicable with Windows Server 2003. Windows Server 2003 introduces a new feature called Internet Group Management Protocol (IGMP) support and here are its details:

- IGMP support helps limit the flooding to only those ports on the switch with NLB nodes connected to them.

- IGMP support can satisfy the need for the NLB algorithm by making certain that traffic meant for the cluster is received, while it makes sure non-NLB machines don't see traffic intended only for the NLB cluster.

- IGMP support can only be enabled when NLB is configured in Multicast mode and not in Unicast mode. In the next section, I quickly explain the benefits of using Unicast mode instead of Multicast mode. Use Unicast mode when you can, as covered in Chapter 2.

- If you want to bypass this entire configuration altogether, use a Virtual LAN (VLAN) and put all the ports for the heartbeat traffic within that VLAN. A VLAN is a grouping of ports configured in a single broadcast domain. If you want one VLAN to talk to another VLAN, you can route between them even if the IP addresses are on different logical segments. In Figure 7-3, you can see I took three switch ports and configured them as VLAN 10 in the switch. This uses the 10.0.10.0 network and nodes 10.0.10.2 through 10.0.10.4 belong to it. I did the same thing for VLAN 20 for the 10.0.20.0 network (this is a general idea on how you can configure Unicast mode and VLANs for NLB).

This wraps up the discussion on bandwidth planning for a NLB cluster. Remember, the more you plan for it in the beginning of the implementation, the better it will be when you roll it out. Having poor bandwidth or bottlenecks can make your Highly Available network saturated with traffic.

Multicast and Unicast Modes of Operation

Another question I hear all the time about advanced NLB topics is "What exactly is the difference between Unicast and Multicast mode?" You can look at what I'm talking about by going to Start | Settings | Control Panel | Network Connections and looking at a LAN connection. Once you open the connection, go to the NLB driver, highlight it,

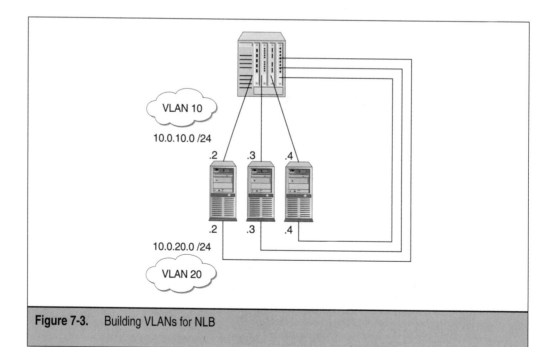

Figure 7-3.   Building VLANs for NLB

and then select Properties. The NLB Properties dialogue appears, as shown in the following illustration.

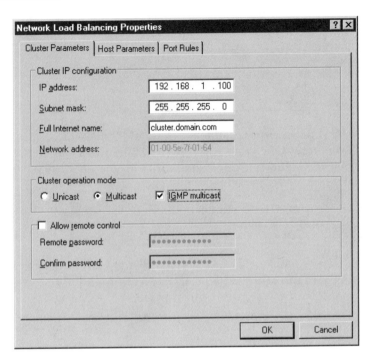

Once you open the setting, you'll notice options for a Cluster Operation mode set. You can have the following:

- Unicast
- Multicast
- Multicast with IGMP support

You should also be aware that you can only configure these options a certain way. For example, if you look at the next illustration, I selected unicast, and then tried to put a check in the Multicast box IGMP, but this isn't an option. You need to select multicast (the radio button), and then select IGMP Multicast.

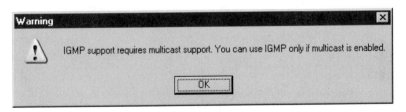

In the following illustration, you'll also get a warning if you do it the right way. Implications exist when using multicast support. We examine these issues momentarily.

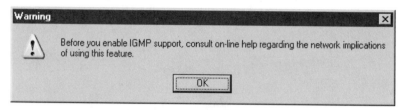

Before we go any deeper, you need to understand IGMP, which is an Internet layer (or a network layer on the OSI model) protocol that provides a way for an Internet computer to report its multicast group membership to adjacent devices.

NOTE   You can find more basic information about IGMP at **http://www.cisco.com/univercd/cc/td/ doc/product/software/ios120/120newft/120limit/120s/120s15/12s_igmp.htm**.

Now that you have some background on IGMP and know where to find these settings, let's return to the original point, which was highlighting the difference between unicast and multicast for designing purposes on your Highly Available NLB cluster. The question many technicians and engineers will ask is which one should they use and, more important, why? Configuring NLB isn't difficult, but concepts like these can be annoying to configure unless you know what you're configuring and why! You should know that Unicast mode is set by default. You'll always use Unicast mode unless you change it. Unicast mode allows NLB to reassign and change the MAC address. In the following list, your workstations will be assigned the same MAC address. In Multicast mode, this isn't done. Instead, you have NLB control using a multicast address assigned to the adapter, instead think about if you plan to implement one technology over the other. Again, this is all your own preference as to how you might want it configured:

- Unicast mode enables you to work with your routers and switches without advanced configuration on these devices.

- A problem with Unicast mode is that all hosts in the cluster have the same IP and MAC addresses; the nodes themselves can't communicate with each other on the front-end network.

- Using Multicast mode removes the unicast problem of having the same IP and MAC addresses because use of this mode adds a multicast address to the NLB cluster.

- A problem with Multicast mode is the ARP reply sent out by a NLB cluster node, in response to an ARP request, maps the cluster's unicast IP address to its multicast MAC address. This is a major problem because a Cisco router won't allow such a mapping! Because of this problem, a Network Engineer must add a static ARP entry to the router, which maps the NLB cluster IP to the MAC address of the node.

Multicast mode adds more administrative overhead to your roll out. Your best solution is to look at the information provided here and implement what best fits your environment. This sums up our discussion on NLB mode selection to help you create an advanced Highly Available NLB solution.

Mixing NLB Nodes

Another advanced topic we need to discuss is mixing types of NLB nodes. You might think that to use NLB, you need to have only Windows 2000 Advanced Servers or only Windows Server 2003. The question here would be: "If I could mix nodes of any OS into the same cluster, then what are my options?" In the following lists, the OSs to consider include

- Windows NT 4.0 (Enterprise Edition)
- Windows 2000 Advanced Server
- Windows Server 2003 (Enterprise Edition)

From the previous list, first consider why you're even going to mix them in the first place. A scenario for mixing is this: you already have a Windows 2000 Advanced Server NLB cluster and you're testing a new technology like Server 2003. You might also have to rent or lease new servers in peak periods where you could want to "scale out" your web farm NLB cluster to deal with increased traffic. In this case, you don't want to worry about what OS you choose. Eventually, Windows 2000 could be end of life (EOL) and you might have to use dissimilar systems, so you aren't forced to upgrade your whole solution just to add some nodes.

Now that you have a reason why you might want to mix, let's look at your options.

- You can mix Windows NT 4.0, Windows 2000, and Windows Server 2003 as long as they support WLBS or NLB.
- A commonality of NLB and WLBS is the heartbeat packets they can share between them, no matter what the platform. The heartbeat packets from NLB in Windows are backward-compatible with WLBS.
- At press time, you can't use a mixed environment and benefit from the features of Windows Server 2003 like Virtual Cluster, IGMP, bidirectional affinity, and so on.

The most important thing to remember is that if you mix, you lose some newer functionality. You can mix the technologies, as long as you plan for keeping your cluster using older technology and don't plan to use any newer features. I suggest only mixing newer solutions, such as Windows 2000, with the older one. If you want to plan an entire new solution with Windows Servers 2003, then you might not want to mix older solutions like Windows 2000 because, even though this will work, you might have configured some newer features that Windows 2000 won't support. This is simply a design recommendation.

More NLB Best Practices

In this section, are some tips and tricks to improve the performance and manageability of your NLB cluster.

- TCP/IP is the only protocol you can use, as evident in the next illustration. Also, you can disable or remove any other protocols bound to your network connections. Based on the illustration, you can see I have only what I need to use.

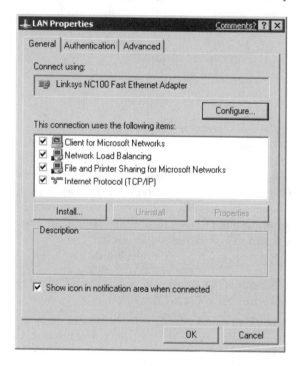

- Next, look at using logging from within nlbmgr.exe. As you learned in Chapter 3, you can use the NLB Manager to configure and administer your load-balanced nodes. You can also use NLB to configure logging for the nodes. In the next illustration, you can see where you set the log settings. To get to this dialog box, select the NLBMGR utility | Options | Log Settings.

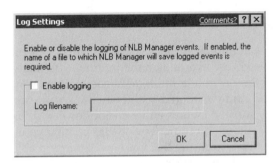

- Once you open this dialog box, select Enable logging and add a log file name into the Log filename field, as shown next. Click OK.

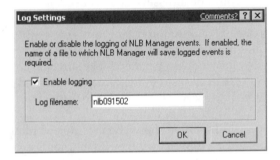

- Configuring the NLB Manager to log each NLB Manager event can prove useful in troubleshooting scenarios.

- Your last tip is to decide how you want to configure NLB, which can be configured either through the Driver properties within your network connections list or by using NLBMGR. Use NLB Manager to configure NLB clusters. Using both NLB Manager and Network Connections together to change NLB properties brings about problems in the cluster. You take a chance by doing it this way. Stick to NLBMGR to configure NLB clusters. In my testing phase, I found that manipulating IP addresses using both tools (even though I was doing it correctly) always caused a duplicate IP address-warning problem. Once I stuck to using only one tool, I had little or no problems.

- NLB manager (NLBMGR) can configure only Server 2003 NLB clusters. You can manage clusters that contain Server 2003 Enterprise and Windows 2000 Advanced, or NT 4.0 (Enterprise Edition) servers, but NLBMGR can only manage them, not configure them.

With this collection of tips, you should have a nice head start in testing and running an advanced load-balanced solution.

NLB Security Design

In this section, you look at implementing security on your NLB solution. Because, for the most part, NLB clusters are exposed on the Internet, you might want to consider the following areas of this section to implement some security in your cluster. You aren't immune to attack. And you're in denial if you think your site won't be attacked or probed at least once by someone who's either curious or malicious in nature. The more important your site, the more you could find attacks coming your way. Part of creating a Highly Available solution is to ensure that you have security enabled wherever possible since a security breach can bring your network solution to its knees. Again, although this book focuses on high availability with Windows solutions, it's also a book on how to create overall Highly Available solutions. Not mentioning things like redundancy, scalability, and security would be a disservice because a lack of attention to any of these areas could cause your Highly Available solution not to be available at all!

Physical security is one of the most important forms of security. You can implement all the logical filtering and intrusion detection in the world, but if someone has physical access to the server console, then it doesn't matter. Make sure you have the server consoles locked and secured. You may even want to implement a lock-and-key solution on the rack the server might sit in. If the server is in a closet, lock the door. Implement a security camera, if possible.

Your next security-practical solution should be the implementation of a firewall and intrusion detection system (IDS), especially if the NLB cluster is exposed to the Internet.

While looking at Figure 7-4, let's see what we're interested in securing and why.

You can see that your NLB cluster is exposed to an Internet connection, which is what you want because you're clustering a web site. However, you need to make sure no one is hacking or attacking your site, or trying to penetrate the internal network behind your NLB cluster. What you need to consider is implementing some security.

You can see that the Internet connection (probably given to your enterprise via an ISP or Telco) terminates at the smart jack (demarcation point) and you're now responsible from the demarcation point to your customer premises equipment (CPE). Please note, this might only hold true if you asked to manage your own equipment because, in some instances, the ISP might manage the implementation all the way to the firewall or router.

Look at the line drawn through the demarcation point—you need to consider security from this point to the NLB cluster. Each point is vulnerable all the way to the cluster, and if any point is exploited, you might have an issue on your hands. Let's look at each point of security you need to address.

- First, lock down the Internet accessible router. You can add access control lists to the router and make sure you're using static routes, not a routing protocol. A routing protocol could learn too much and, if penetrated, it might give out too much information about your Internet network.

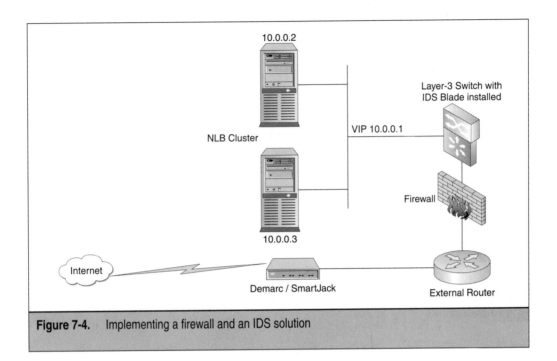

10.0.0.2

Layer-3 Switch with
IDS Blade installed

NLB Cluster

VIP 10.0.0.1

Firewall

10.0.0.3

Internet

Demarc / SmartJack

External Router

Figure 7-4.   Implementing a firewall and an IDS solution

- Always install a firewall! You can't fully rely on it for overall security protection, but not to have one is ridiculous. Make sure you place it between the external and internal router on your network.

- The switch I installed here is Layer 3–capable, so it's acting as both the internal router to the network and a high-speed switch. You can now install intrusion detection blades directly to the switch, which means you can have a solution that enables you to set up VLANs, high-speed switching, Layer-3 routing, and, now, IDS.

- IDS will (if properly maintained and updated with new signatures) look for certain activity on the network and check this against a signature database it carries. If a match occurs, then an alert is sent to an administrator or logged. This is how you can proactively monitor your network segment for penetration.

You can do much more with the internals of all these devices, but this should give you a general idea and an overall security mindset to apply to any NLB solution you design and implement. Let's look at some more network security issues directly related to NLB.

NLB Security and Possible Penetration

Another issue you could find problematic is a lack of security on your back-end network. We've spent a lot of time describing all the security measures you might want to address coming from the Internet, but a well-known fact is this: many attacks originate from the inside of the company by malicious employees. Let's look at a few scenarios you should be aware of.

A malicious hacker can exploit heartbeat packets sent via the back-end network by adding his/her own personally crafted packets to disrupt NLB operations. NLB heartbeat messages use a unique Ethertype 0x886F (part of the actual frame), which helps to add to the security posture, but is hard to stop if a rogue server is operating on the network segment. Rogue NLB servers could send heartbeat packets that disrupt cluster operations. The best way to protect against both these threats is to implement VLANs with assigned ports to the servers you're load balancing. This way, if you add five ports to VLAN 20, then no one can simply add a server to the NLB cluster by plugging it in to the switch.

BUILDING A HIGHLY AVAILABLE SERVER 2003 NLB SOLUTION

In this section, you build a Server 2003 NLB cluster using some of the basics you learned in Chapter 3 and adding a few advanced topics.

Building a Load-Balanced Cluster with Server 2003

In this section, you work off the cluster solution you built in Chapter 3 and get into more advanced details. In Chapter 3, you built a load-balanced cluster with Windows Server 2003. The next steps you take build from that previous installation and configuration. I repeat a few of the main concepts from Chapter 3 but, if you haven't read Chapter 3, I suggest you do so before continuing. Let's begin.

1. You need to have at least two servers to configure a load-balanced solution. Although you can scale out much more than two, you need at least two. Let's look at configuring a two-node NLB cluster. First, you must have two Server 2003 servers ready to be load balanced.

2. You can't have Windows Clustering Service installed. You can see if it's installed by going to the Services console in the Administrative Tools folder. Open the Services' MMC and look for it as Cluster Service. If you try to use NLB without removing the Cluster Service, you'll be given a warning by the system, as shown in the following illustration.

3. Next, you need to design an IP addressing scheme. To keep this simple, use the following:

   Cluster Address: 192.168.1.150

   Cluster Node (1)

   Public NIC: 192.168.1.25

   Heartbeat: 10.0.0.25

   Cluster Node (2)

   Public NIC: 192.168.1.26

   Heartbeat: 10.0.0.26

   Again, I arbitrarily picked these numbers. You can use whatever works for your organization, but make sure you abide by the rules of networking when you design a load-balanced infrastructure.

   Remember, when configuring a cluster, you must have at least one VIP. In this scenario, it is 192.168.1.150.

4. Next, after you have the servers ready and the IP addresses configured, you need to install the NLB drivers. Once you do, you can install the NLB driver on your NIC. You only need to do this on one connection—even if you have two NICs—because it installs the driver by default on both.

5. As you can see from the next illustration, installing NLB is simple. Be aware, though, that if you don't configure it through NLBMGR, you could run into issues later. Install it here, but preferably configure it in the NLB Manager.

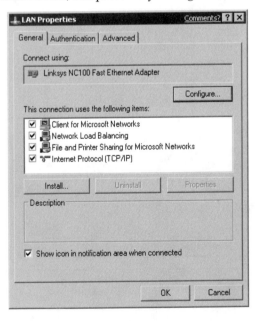

6. Once you have both nodes configured with the NLB drivers, you can move to the next step, which is to configure the nodes in the NLB Manager console. Open the NLBMGR console by going to Start | Run and type **nlbmgr.exe**. Press ENTER and you'll open the console. NLB Manager is a new feature in Windows Server 2003. By using the NLB Manager (nlbmgr.exe), you can easily perform the most common NLB cluster control and configuration options from within an easy-to-use GUI. You can see the NLB Manager in Figure 7-5.

Perform the following tasks in the NLB Manager:

- Connect to existing clusters
- Create new clusters
- Delete clusters
- Add hosts to a cluster
- View the properties for a cluster
- Issue the Query, Start, Stop, Drainstop, Suspend, and Resume commands to a cluster
- Delete a host from a cluster
- View the properties for a host

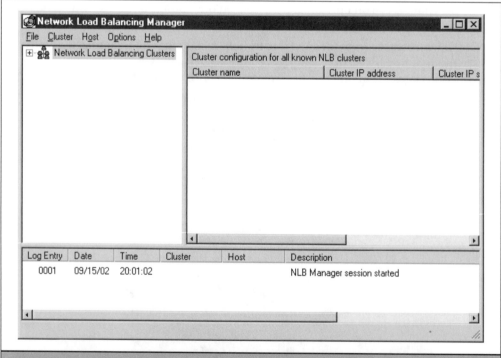

Figure 7-5. The NLB Manager

- Issue the Query, Start, Stop, Drainstop, Suspend, and Resume commands to a host
- Specify the credentials to use when connecting to a host
- Specify logging to occur

7. Right-click the NLB clusters icon, as seen in the left-hand side pane in Figure 7-5, and select one of two choices: Create a Cluster or Join a Cluster.

8. If you choose to join a cluster, then you get the Connect dialog box, shown in the next illustration. Here, you enter a node within the cluster, so you can get to the main cluster to administer.

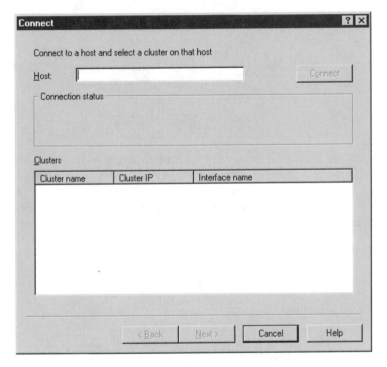

9. If you want to get to an already preexisting cluster, you need to enter one of the node addresses (that's part of the cluster) into the Host field. Enter an IP address of a node and you're shown the Clusters section of the dialog box indicating what clusters are available to administer.

10. Once an interface appears, as seen in the following illustration, click Next to connect to the cluster shown. In the Connection Status area of the dialog box, you can see if the cluster can connect and the status of that connection. Make sure you select a NIC that corresponds to the Virtual IP address. 192.168.1.25 is on the same subnet as my VIP, which is 192.168.1.150, so once I connect to this node, the entire cluster will appear.

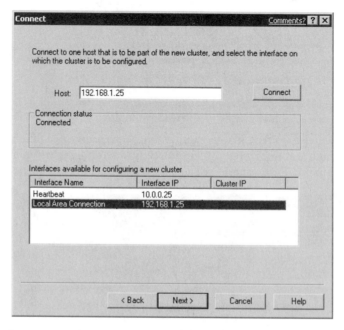

11. If you choose to make a cluster, the Cluster Parameters dialog box appears, as shown in the following illustration. This is where you create a brand new NLB cluster. You want to assign that new Cluster IP you designed earlier. You can enter the new cluster here, as well as the subnet mask, the Internet domain name, and the modes mentioned earlier.

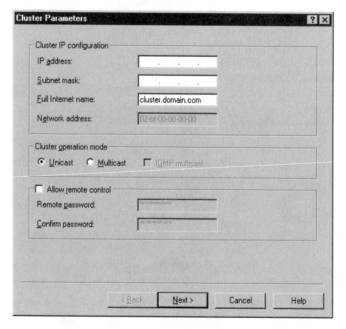

12. As mentioned in Chapter 3 in the section, "Allow Remote Control", you don't want to enable this unless it's absolutely necessary. This is a security risk unless you know it's enabled and you have strong passwords on it. I suggest leaving this unchecked unless you need it.

13. Next, decide whether you want to join an already existing NLB cluster or make a new one. For this chapter, we discuss making a new one.

14. To add the first node, return to the previous illustration and set a new IP address for the cluster. Use the number we assigned for the VIP.

15. You can then add one node at a time. In the next illustration, I set the first node into the cluster with an IP address of 192.168.1.25. Notice I have the priority set as 1. This priority is the unique host identifier.

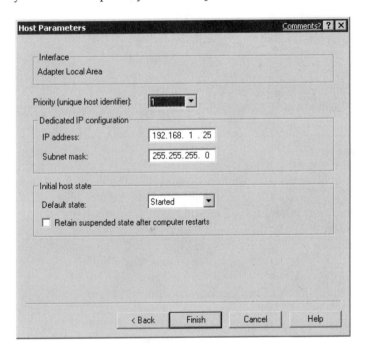

16. Let's look at how you can add a second host to your NLB cluster using the NLB Manager. Right-click the cluster node in the NLBMGR console and select to add a new host. Once you do, you can enter the IP address and connect it to the NLB cluster. To configure the node further, set the IP address and subnet mask, but more importantly, notice the Priority, as shown in the following illustration. This is set as two for the unique host identifier (Chapter 3 discussed host identifiers).

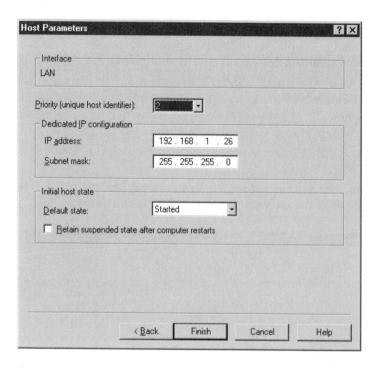

Now, that you've added your nodes to the cluster, let's look at the NLB Manager and some of the problems you might encounter. Remember, if you want to continue to add nodes, then you can do the same thing. Right-click the cluster and add a node. You can also add another cluster. Doing this will create more than one cluster for you to manage in the same console.

In Figure 7-6, you can see your two nodes are configured and ready to go. I have a problem, though. You can see in the figure that, within my cluster, I have a node with an hourglass, which means it's in the process of connecting to the cluster. Notice in the right-hand side pane that NLB isn't bound and that's the problem. The status of your nodes can give you a good hint on what your nodes are doing. You can also look at the log entry in the bottom pane of the NLB Manager for a detailed listing of problems you might encounter as well as those of successful transitions.

Now look at Figure 7-7. I intentionally made this considerably worse to show you what this console will flag. Remember, we also enabled logging earlier in the chapter. In Figure 7-7, I changed the IP addresses and enabled the cluster service. You're given explicit details on what the problem is and how to troubleshoot it.

As mentioned before, the Cluster Service started and this threw everything off. All I had to do was look in the bottom pane of the NLB Manager, and then click the error I wanted to investigate. As I opened it, I could see one of my critical errors came from the cluster node that had the cluster service enabled, as shown in the following illustration.

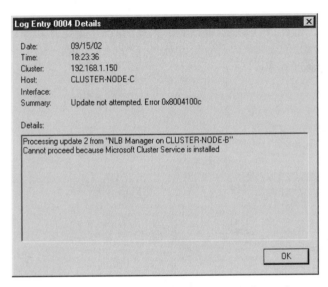

In Figure 7-8, you'll notice there's a problem with one of my cluster nodes. In this one, the status on the right-hand side pane shows the host is unreachable. This is a problem because I blocked ICMP, which is the protocol ping uses. The reason this isn't good is because NLBMGR uses ICMP to contact the nodes.

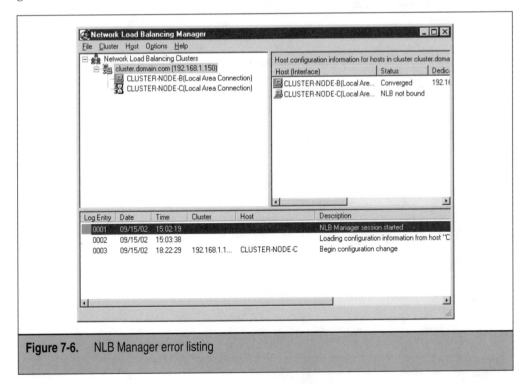

Figure 7-6. NLB Manager error listing

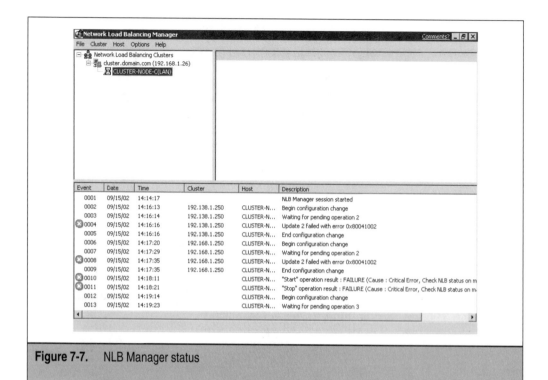

Figure 7-7. NLB Manager status

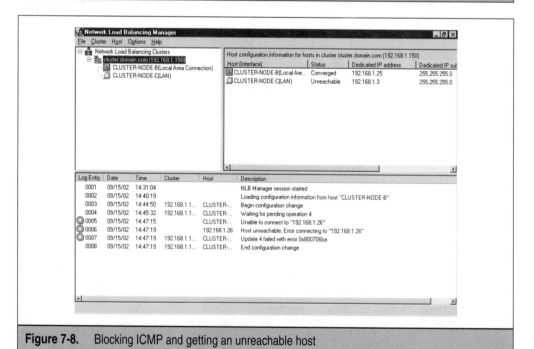

Figure 7-8. Blocking ICMP and getting an unreachable host

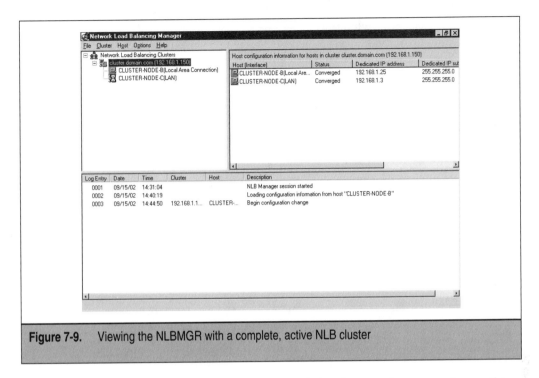

Figure 7-9. Viewing the NLBMGR with a complete, active NLB cluster

Finally, I set up everything correctly. Notice it's in converged status and everything is working well, as shown in Figure 7-9. That's it! You built a NLB cluster and tested it thoroughly.

CONCLUSION

In this chapter, you learned the advanced topics of creating Highly Available solutions with Windows Server 2003. You built on the concepts learned in Chapters 1 and 3 to build load-balanced solutions. In this chapter, you took this a step further and learned the process of proper design and configuration, not only of the NLB cluster, but also regarding security and high availability. These are important concepts you need to master before you roll out a Windows Server 2003 clustered solution.

You finalized the last cluster to be built within this book. Before moving on, I want to stress a few points.

- Design, Design, Design! It's the most important part. You don't want a solution that loses money for your company.

- Test! You need to do a great deal of research and planning to implement a Highly Available solution, especially if you take it out to the Internet where you need to consider security, routing, switching, and many other advanced infrastructure solutions. All this must be taken into account, so you can make the right decisions and not implement the wrong technology.

- Be selective about what you want to roll out whether it's a failover type of cluster or a load-balanced cluster. Although they share the same name, they are completely different in form (you can review this by rereading Chapters 1 through 3).

In the next, and final, chapter, you learn the details about all the testing and monitoring that goes into Highly Available solutions, including how to monitor your clusters, baseline them, and test them for proper use.

CHAPTER 8

High Availability, Baselining, Performance Monitoring, and Disaster Recovery Planning

In this chapter, you learn what you need to do after the cluster is operational. In the first chapter, I explained the basic concepts of high availability, including definitions of each high-availability component. In the chapters following Chapter 1, we reviewed many solutions using Windows 2000, Windows Server 2003 solutions, and how to integrate them successfully into your environment. This chapter covers advanced planning procedures, Disaster Recovery Planning, and monitoring the solution you now have available. This chapter will open your eyes to the ongoing maintenance you need to do long after you finish this book. After you read this chapter, you'll be able to do advanced planning for high availability, implement a Disaster Recovery Plan and a performance monitor, as well as baseline your servers and monitor your cluster nodes for problematic issues.

PLANNING FOR HIGH AVAILABILITY

Taking the time to plan and design is the key to your success, and it's not only the design, but also the study efforts you put in. I always joke with my administrators and tell them they're doctors of technology. I say, "When you become a doctor, you're expected to be a professional and maintain that professionalism by educational growth through constant learning and updating of your skills." Many IT staff technicians think their job is 9 to 5, with no studying done after hours. I have one word for them: Wrong! You need to treat your profession as if you're a highly trained surgeon except, instead of working on human life, you're working on technology. And that's how planning for High Availability solutions needs to be addressed. You can't simply wing it, and you can't guess at it. You must be precise—otherwise, your investment goes down the drain. This holds true for any profession but, from the rush of people into this field from the early '90s, you'd be surprised at the lack of knowledge out there from people making decisions such as high-availability planning. Make no mistake, if you don't plan it out, you could be adding more problems into your network! Let's continue with what you need to achieve.

Planning Your Downtime

You need to achieve as close to 100 percent uptime as possible. You know a 100 percent uptime isn't realistic, though, and it can never be guaranteed. Breakdowns occur because of disk crashes, power or UPS failure, application problems resulting in system crashes, or any other hardware or software malfunction. So, the next best thing is 99.999 percent, which is reasonable with today's technology. You can also define in a Service Level Agreement (SLA) what 99.999 percent means to both parties. If you promised 99.999 percent uptime to someone for a single year, that translates to a downtime ratio of about five to ten minutes. I would strive for a larger number, one that's more realistic to scheduled outages and possible disaster-recovery testing performed by your staff. Go for 99.9 percent uptime, which allots for about nine to ten hours of downtime per year. This is more practical and feasible to obtain. Whether providing or receiving such a service, both sides should test planned outages to see if delivery schedules can be met.

You can figure this formula by taking the amount of hours in a day (24) and multiplying it by the number of days in the year (365). This equals 8,760 hours in a year. Use the following equation:

percent of uptime per year = (8,760 – number of total hours down per year) / 8,760

If you schedule eight hours of downtime per month for maintenance and outages (96 hours total), then you can say the percentage of uptime per year is 8,760 minus 96 divided by 8,760. You can see you'd wind up with about 98.9 percent uptime for your systems. This should be an easy way for you to provide an accurate accounting of your downtime.

Remember, you must account for downtime accurately when you plan for high availability. Downtime can be planned or, worse, unexpected. Sources of unexpected downtime include the following:

- Disk crash or failure
- Power or UPS failure
- Application problems resulting in system crashes
- Any other hardware or software malfunction

Building the Highly Available Solutions' Plan

Let's look at the plan to use a Highly Available design in your organization and review the many questions you need to ask before implementing it live. Remember, if the server is down, people can't work, and millions of dollars can be lost within hours. The following is a list of what could happen in sequence:

1. A company uses a server to access an application that accepts orders and does transactions.

2. The application, when it runs, serves not only the sales staff, but also three other companies who do business-to-business (B2B) transactions. The estimate is, within one hour's time, the peak money made exceeded 2.5 million dollars.

3. The server crashes and you don't have a Highly Availability solution in place. This means no failover, redundancy, or load balancing exists at all. It simply fails.

4. It takes you (the systems engineer) 5 minutes to be paged, but about 15 minutes to get onsite. You then take 40 minutes to troubleshoot and resolve the problem.

5. The company's server is brought back online and connections are reestablished. Everything appears functional again. The problem was simple this time—a simple application glitch that caused a service to stop and, once restarted, everything was okay.

Now, the problem with this whole scenario is this: although it was a true disaster, it was also a simple one. The systems engineer happened to be nearby and was able to diagnose the problem quite quickly. Even better, the problem was a simple fix. This easy problem still took the companies' shared application down for at least one hour and, if this had been a peak-time period, over 2 million dollars could have been lost.

Don't believe me? Well, this does happen and this is what prompts people to buy a book like this. They want to become aware, so the possibility of 2 million in sales evaporating never occurs again. Worse still, the companies you connect to, and your own clientele, start to lose faith in your ability to serve them. This could also cost you revenue and the possibility of acquiring new clients moving forward. People talk and the uneducated could take this small glitch as a major problem with your company's people, instead of the technology. Let's look at this scenario again, except with a Highly Available solution in place:

1. A company uses a Server to access an application that accepts orders and does transactions.

2. The application, when it runs, serves not only the sales staff, but also three other companies who do business-to-business (B2B) transactions. The estimate is, within one hour's time, the peak money made exceeded 2.5 million dollars.

3. The server crashes, but you do have a Highly Available solution in place. (Note, at this point, it doesn't matter what the solution is. What matters is that you added redundancy into the service.)

4. Server and application are redundant, so when a glitch takes place, the redundancy spares the application from failing.

5. Customers are unaffected. Business resumes as normal. Nothing is lost and no downtime is accumulated.

6. The one hour you saved your business in downtime just paid for the entire Highly Available solution you implemented.

One aspect we haven't touched on in this book is people. We discussed the technological details in previous chapters but, now, let's look at how you can position human resources to help with Highly Available solutions.

Human Resources and Highly Available Solutions

Human Resources (people) need to be trained and work onsite to deal with a disaster. They also need to know how to work under fire. As a former United States Marine, I know about the "fog of war," where you find yourself tired, disoriented, and probably unfocused on the job. These characteristics don't help your response time with management.

In any organization, especially with a system as complex as one that's highly available, you need the right people to run it.

Managing Your Services

In this section, you see all the factors to consider while designing a Highly Available solution. The following is a list of the main services to remember:

- **Service Management** is the management of the true components of Highly Available solutions: the people, the process in place, and the technology needed to create the solution. Keeping this balance to have a truly viable solution is important. Service Management includes the design and deployment phases.

- **Change Management** is crucial to the ongoing success of the solution during the production phase. This type of management is used to monitor and log changes on the system.

- **Problem Management** addresses the process for Help Desks and Server monitoring.

- **Security Management** is tasked to prevent unauthorized penetrations of the system.

- **Performance Management** is discussed in greater detail in this chapter. This type of management addresses the overall performance of the service, availability, and reliability.

Other main services also exist, but the most important ones are highlighted here. Service management is crucial to the development of your Highly Available solution. You must cater to your customer's demands for uptime. If you promise it, you better deliver it.

Highly Available System Assessment Ideas

The following is a list of items for you to use during the postproduction planning phase. Make sure you covered all your bases with this list:

- Now that you have your solution configured, document it! A lack of documentation will surely spell disaster for you. Documentation isn't difficult to do, it's simply tedious, but all that work will pay off in the end if you need it.

- Train your staff. Make sure your staff has access to a test lab, books to read, and advanced training classes. Go to free seminars to learn more about high availability. If you can ignore the sales pitch, they're quite informative.

- Test your staff with incident response drills and disaster scenarios. Written procedures are important, but live drills are even better to see how your staff responds. Remember, if you have a failure on a system, it could failover to another system, but you must quickly resolve the problem on the first system that failed. You could have the same issue on the other nodes in your cluster, and if that's the case, you're living on borrowed time. Set up a scenario and test it.

- Assess your current business climate, so you know what's expected of your systems at all times. Plan for future capacity especially as you add new applications, and as hardware and traffic increase.

- Revisit your overall business goals and objectives. Make sure what you intend to do with your high-availability solution is being provided. If you want faster access to the systems, is it, in fact, faster? When you have a problem, is the failover seamless? Are customers affected? You don't want to implement a Highly Available solution and have performance that gets worse. This won't look good for you!

- Do a data-flow analysis on the connections the high availability uses. You'd be surprised how much truouble damaged NICs, the wrong drivers, excessive protocols, bottlenecks, mismatched port speeds, and duplex, to name a few problems, can cause the system. I've made significant differences in networks by simply running an analysis on the data flow on the wire and, through this analysis, have made great speed differences. A good example could be if you had old ISA-based NIC cards that only ran at 10 Mbps. If you plugged your system into a port that uses 100 Mbps, then you will only run at 10, because that's as fast as the NIC will go. What would happen if the switch port was set to 100 Mbps and not to autonegotiate? This would create a problem because the NIC wouldn't communicate on the network because of a mismatch in speeds. Issues like this are common on networks and could quite possibly be the reason for poor or no data flow on your network.

- Monitor the services you consider essential to operation and make sure they're always up and operational. Never assume a system will run flawlessly unless a change is implemented . . . at times, systems choke up on themselves, either by a hung thread or process. You can use network-monitoring tools like Tivoli, NetIQ, or Argent's software solutions to monitor such services.

- Assess your total cost of ownership (TCO) and see if it was all worth it. In other words, at the beginning of this book, you learned how Highly Availability solutions would save money for your business. So, did Highly Availability solutions save your business money? Do the final cost analysis to check if you made the right decision. The best way to determine TCO is to go online and use a TCO calculator program that shows you TCO based on your own unique business model. Because, for the most part, all business models will be different, the best way to determine TCO is to run the calculator and figure TCO based on your own personal answers to the calculator's questions. Here's an example of a specific one, but many more are available to use online at **http://www .oracle.com/ip/std_infrastructure/cc/index .html?tcocalculator .html**.

This should give you a good running start on advanced planning for high availability, and it gives you many things to check and think about, especially when you're done with your implementation.

Testing a High-Availability System

Now that you have the planning and design fundamentals down, let's discuss the process of testing your high-availability systems. You need to assure the test is run for a long enough time, so you can get a solid sampling of how the system operates normally without stress (or activity) and how it runs with activity. Then, run a test long enough to obtain a solid baseline, so you know how your systems operate on a daily basis. Use that for a comparison during times of activity.

DISASTER RECOVERY PLANNING

In this section, we discuss Disaster Recovery Planning. In the first chapter of the book, disasters were covered. You learned what disasters could do to you and your organization if they weren't prevented. A disaster is an unavoidable catastrophe that occurs unexpectedly. Recovery is going from disaster to full production again. So what constitutes a disaster? Here are a few disasters you could experience.

- Hackers, exploits, and security breaches
- System failure, disk failure, and so forth
- Power failure
- Fire accidents
- Storm accidents
- Water accidents, flooding
- Earthquake accidents
- Terrorist attacks
- Crime and vandalism
- Extreme weather, such as cold, heat, dryness, and humidity
- Loss of staff that operated or maintained such systems

As you can see, a disaster can stem from nearly anything! In this section, you learn what it could take for you to recover from a disaster by using a Disaster Recovery Plan (DRP).

Building the Disaster Recovery Plan

If you think about it, having high availability in any solution is just like having a built-in Disaster Recovery Plan! If you have a two-node cluster and one fails, the disaster is the failing of a node and the recovery is the failover to the other node. This is a form of disaster recovery. Disaster struck and you recovered because you were prepared. To make this process more formalized and presentable to management, you'll want to build this into a documented plan, but the mechanics of being redundant and failsafe are the fundamentals of the plan itself.

Acceptable Downtime Rules

To start your DRP, you must first assess your business and its running solution. Here are some initial thoughts. What is an acceptable amount of downtime?

I ask this question frequently and I always get a blank stare. I say this because, many times, businesses think that by implementing a DRP, they immediately evade disaster. Sorry, that's not how it works. You have different levels of disaster recovery that dictate how much you can recover and how quickly. When detailing downtime, management needs to talk to customers and other users of services to consider how much of a hit business can take during a downtime and still survive. Here's an example:

> You're the owner of an ecommerce site that sells widgets online. If you sell widgets 24 hours a day to international and domestic markets, then you're generating revenue 24 hours a day from your web sites. You would want this load balanced and redundant. If your site was down for more than 30 minutes, you could have your buyers go to some other widget seller and they might never return. And this is after only one failure! You could lose business that quickly without a DRP and solution in place, so your amount of acceptable downtime is little to none, if possible.

Another example is an application server that resides on your company's intranet. If you have engineers who can only access the server during working hours, then you have an acceptable downtime of little-to-none during working hours. All maintenance must be completed in off-work hours. You can use this same scenario and say, if the engineers only lost access to the company's documents and drawings for three hours at a time without losing money, then your acceptable downtime is three hours. If acceptable downtime is high, then your cost is low and vice versa.

Disaster Recovery and Management

You need to have your management buy into the DRP. I've seen too many management teams toss DRPs out the window because of costs. But disasters can always strike, so it behooves management to take ownership of an effective DRP. Senior management must understand and support the business impacts and risks associated with a complete system failure. If you're a public company, you might even be held liable, to a certain degree, if negligence can be proved. This is a serious matter when data is involved. Management needs to understand the risks with and without implementing a high-availability solution, as well as how to fund the DRP.

Identifying Possible Disaster Impact

Now, let's discuss what impact-based questions you can ask to help guide your business to a highly available and disaster-free environment.

- How much of the company's material resources would be lost?

This question is important to assess. While it isn't one of the biggest reasons for having a high-availability solution, it's an important one, nonetheless. If you lose material-based resources because of disaster, it could be costly to business. Think of what might happen if you had a Windows 2000 cluster with SAP/R3 running on it and controlling all the resources for your company. In other words, SAP/R3 is an Enterprise Resource Planning (ERP) application that helps you manage your company's material goods. If you had a disaster on your system and all the data was lost, you would risk losing all the shipping information, perhaps your material database, or even worse, inventory. All these items are critical to business and without them you might be unable to run your business. Because of this alone, it's critical for you to assess the possible loss of your material resources data.

- What are the total costs invoiced with the disaster?

This is the number one issue based on why you need to make an assessment. You can take the total costs' number and use it in a scenario to justify the cost of what you plan to put into the high-availability solution. I use this number (which I get from analysis and statistics) to explain the TCO of the high-availability solution. An example of total costs is every cost incurred from start to finish of any disaster that takes place. In other words, if the hard disk fails on a server and it didn't failover, then the time it took to replace that drive (lost business), the cost of the employee who has to take time out of the work week to fix this disaster, and the costs of the hardware and software that might be needed are an example of total costs.

- What costs and human resources are required for rebuilding?

If you experience a disaster that's outside the scope or realm of what your organization is staffed to deal with, then outside help or consulting services might be in your future. If this is the case, you need to factor this price/cost into the entire high-availability solution and DRP.

- How long will it take to recover if a disaster strikes?

You know what they say: time is money. Assess how long it could take to get your company back online after a disaster and how long until it's fully recovered. You need to address the fact that if you're down due to a disaster, then the longer it takes to bring your systems back online, the more money your business could potentially lose.

- What is the impact on the end users?

End users are your workers. They're the fuel for the engine. If they aren't working, then little-to-nothing will get done. This is important if you value the term "productivity" in your organization. If disaster strikes, depending on the impact of the disaster (and possible lack of a DRP), you might find your workforce is sitting around or hanging out at the water cooler.

- What is the impact on the suppliers and business partners?

Having a disaster can disrupt your relations with your business partners who might rely on your services. Nothing is worse than losing business yourself and taking your partners down with you. This is considered highly unacceptable and needs to be factored into your overall DRP.

- What is the affect on your share price and confidence from consumers?

If you're a publicly held company, your stockholders could lose capital from your disasters and pull money out from your stock. This isn't good and it can only hurt the business image, as well as the revenue stream.

- What is the impact on the overall organization?

This is the sum of all the previous questions. If you think about it, having a disaster and having all the previous questions answered negatively might force your company out of business. Always ask questions of this type if you're debating whether you should have a DRP.

Systems, Network, and Applications Priority Levels

Now that you have a good reason to have a DRP, you need to start fleshing it out a bit more. Regarding your systems, network, and applications, you need to create a system that classifies them on a chart, for example, a three-layer chart using an Excel spreadsheet. This ensures resources, money, and effort all get channeled to the system, network, or application that's deemed most important. Usually mainframes, e-mail, routers, and switches turn up as number one on my list of mission-critical components, but this is for you and your analysis to decide. Let's look at my levels:

- *Mission critical* or *high priority* is deemed anything you can't live without. The damage or disruption to these systems would cause the most impact on your business. An example is if your systems were completely inoperable.

- *Important* or *medium priority* would dictate any system that, if disrupted, would cause a moderate, but still viable, problem to you and your network systems. An example is if a problem came up (like a disk drive error), which, if neglected, could potentially cause a business interruption for you.

- *Minor* or *low priority* is any outage you have that's easily restored, brought back online, or corrected with little damage or disruption. This is still a disruption, but it doesn't impact your systems or your business. An example is if a system has a problem with its monitor.

Resiliency of Services

When working with Highly Available solutions, you need to add resiliency to your plan. Cisco, as well as other network vendors, defines *network resiliency* as "the ability to recover from any network failure or issue, whether it is related to a disaster, link, hardware, design, or network services." Resiliency should provide you, the implementer of such technologies, with a comfort level that if you have a failure, you could survive it with Highly Available solutions. You need to plan for resiliency by checking the following areas of your network:

- Make sure your WAN links are redundant. You can implement secondary-frame connections or point-to-point links, or dial backup lines with ISDN.

- Make sure your routing protocols are dynamic if you want them to learn other paths in case of disaster. Static paths won't necessarily do this for you.

- Make sure you have multiple networks or Telco carriers. If one carrier has an issue, you can fall back on the other one. MCI WorldCom is a perfect example of this.

- Make sure you have hardware resiliency in every form—hard disks, routers, firewalls, cabling, you name it.

- Make sure you have power redundancy in the form of UPS or backup generators.

- Make sure you have network services resiliency, such as DHCP, and so forth in case of failure.

This isn't a definitive list because it all depends on what you have at your location, but make sure you make your own list, based on what your network has and uses.

Delivering a Disaster Recovery Plan

Now you have a plan on paper! So, what's next? Be sure the plan is full of details and is well documented. Make certain your staff studies it. Schedule a class for everyone to learn about the plan and include a verbal test on the DRP as part of the class.

SYSTEM MONITORING AND BASELINING

Server monitoring and baselining should be the next position you take with high availability. You must know what your systems are doing at all times and, even more important, what they do on a normal basis. If your systems normally run at 35 percent CPU utilization and you see a jump to 55 percent, then you know you have a problem. If you baseline your systems at 100MB of RAM on a normal basis, then when it jumps to 160MB, this could be a clue that you have a memory leak or another kind of problem. Ask the following questions about systems monitoring:

- How many times have you used the performance monitoring tools that have come with the software and hardware you purchased?
- How many times have you monitored to see if it was needed?
- How many times do you baseline?

I know, the answers to these questions will be different from reader to reader, but I suspect the majority of readers will give the following answers:

- I rarely ever use the performance-monitoring tool on the systems I purchase.
- I always upgrade systems based on their performance via complaints and guesswork, but never use performance-monitoring tools to ascertain the real data needed to make such a decision.
- I usually tell my superiors that the systems are running fine based on my daily management of them (hence, a baseline) but, because I don't do performance monitoring, I'm not sure.

If everyone told the truth, you might see these answers appear from many administrators worldwide. I don't blame you either if you weren't completely honest. As IT budgets scale back and the workforce gets tighter, who has the time to baseline the systems?

In all honesty, if you make the time, it'll be worth it. I have all my systems at work baselined. I know when a system is sick immediately. I can tell because the numbers are off. If you get a good baseline, this can make your life easier when you're asked inevitable questions such as the following:

- Is the network acting up today? It seems a bit slow.

- Is the server having a problem? I can't seem to access directories quickly today.

- Is the system down? I'm freezing up over here.

Okay—a show of hands. How many times have you heard this? "Too many" is a good answer. I can, however, remove all blame from the server immediately because, after a quick health check of the system (against my preestablished baseline), I can see if something is affecting the server, router, or switch rather quickly.

Why Monitor and Baseline?

The main reason for monitoring is to troubleshoot. You never want to assume a system is the culprit unless you troubleshoot it. In a system outage, you'd be surprised how hard finding the problem is in an entire infrastructure.

You also need to monitor your systems to make sure they're operating in a healthy fashion so, if needed, you can scale it up or out to increase performance.

- Disk I/O is a big problem

- Reducing CPU usage is a challenge

- Reducing memory usage is a challenge

- Reducing the network traffic to and from the server is a challenge

These are reasons you monitor and baseline. You want to optimize these categories. A baseline is simple to get, but tedious and time-consuming. You need to monitor the server by selecting either the few items I previously listed or choosing from hundreds of other counters available, and then documenting what the settings are at certain times of the day. Do this at least over a four-week period of time. You also need to take peak periods throughout the day, the month, and the year into consideration. Here's an example of each:

- Each day, server performance takes a hit as the entire network user population begins to log on and access files between 8:30 A.M. and 9:00 A.M. every morning.

- Each month, a month-end inventory check occurs where all the documents on a file server are constantly accessed by more people than normal.

- Each year at Christmas time, the load on the web servers triples because of heightened amounts of hits and buying activity.

This is what I mean by taking peak periods into account. Your baseline should include documentation for these peak periods and they should be taken into account when you do monitoring. Now that you have a baseline, let's look back to Windows Server 2003. This is the time to learn how to do some performance monitoring, so you can check your systems carefully to know they're running optimally as high-availability solutions.

Using Performance Monitor on Your Servers

In this section, you use the Performance Console that comes as a standard tool in Windows 2000 and Window Server 2003. You set up your servers, so you can monitor them to get your baseline or any other statistics you might need. The following are a few items of interest to remember as you work through this section:

- For those of you who used NT 4.0, you no longer need to run perfmon from the command prompt with –y and –n switches. You can still run perfmon from the command prompt to open the console.

- The Performance Console monitors all statistics. You can find it in the Administrative Tools folder within the Control Panel, as seen in Figure 8-1.

- Closer study of Figure 8-1 shows you this isn't called the Performance Monitor. Instead, it's called the System Monitor and it's located within the Performance Console.

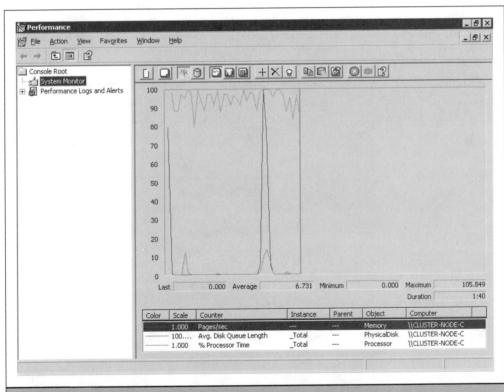

Figure 8-1.   Viewing the Performance Console

System Monitor graphically displays statistics for the set of parameters you selected for display. You can do this by selecting counters. Counters are almost unlimited as well. You learn how to configure them shortly but, for now, note the selected counters at the bottom of the console. The System Monitor uses these counters, and creates a graph and logs for you. These are unlimited because whenever you install something on the server, such as DNS, WINS, DHCP, RRAS, or anything else these programs add counters to the System Monitor for you. This gives you a massive detailed view into the systems you run. It also adds counters when you add other platforms to the server, such as BizTalk Server 2000 and Exchange Server 2000.

System Monitor also creates a nice graph for you to follow that increases each time, based on a set interval. Again, before you do an exercise to learn how to set all this up, you're stepping through the functionality of monitoring performance with the System Monitor.

In Figure 8-2, I set one counter to look at CPU processor time only. This is the default view when you first open the System Monitor, but it can be changed. Note the toolbar located within the right-hand side pane of the System Monitor. On the top of the graph, is a long toolbar with plenty of options for you to choose from.

In Figure 8-3, you can see I selected the View Histogram option, as seen by the bars displayed. This gives you a cleaner view, compared to a graph view, into the System Monitor in case you must add multiple counters, as I did in Figure 8-3.

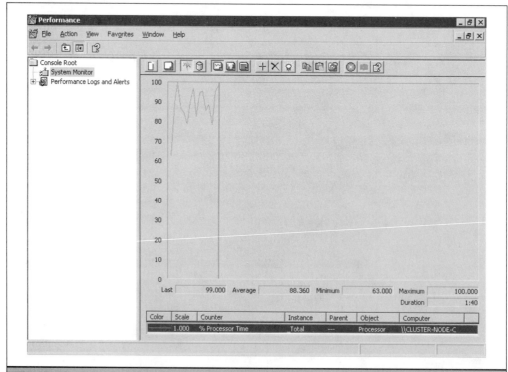

Figure 8-2. Adjusting the graph on the System Monitor

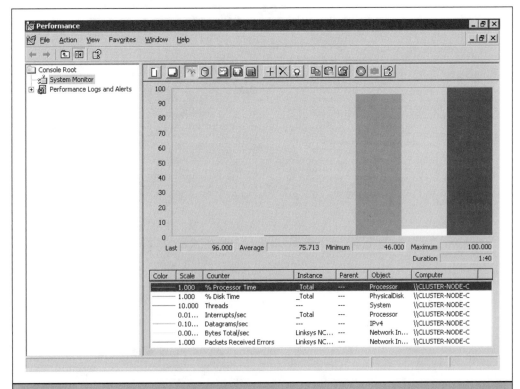

Figure 8-3. Viewing the histogram in the System Monitor

The View Report option, as shown in Figure 8-4, is another way to view the same information. This view cuts everything but raw data text out of the chart.

Now that you can access the monitor and have a general understanding of what you're seeing, let's get into Configuration mode. The next section provides the mechanics for you to build your own performance monitoring range.

Configuring the Performance Console

You can do some customization directly on the System Monitor. Before we add counters, let's look at the basic configuration of the monitor itself. In Figure 8-5, you can find the System Monitor Properties dialog box. Unfortunately, getting to this dialog box is only through the toolbar, so you need to look at the toolbar mentioned in the last section. Select the Properties icon, which is fourth from the last on the right. Click this icon, and you open the Properties Sheet.

Once opened, you can see General, Source, Data, Graph, and Appearance tabs. Although you can configure many things within these tabs, let's focus on the most important items for configuring high availability. We don't want to get too deep into configuring System Monitor.

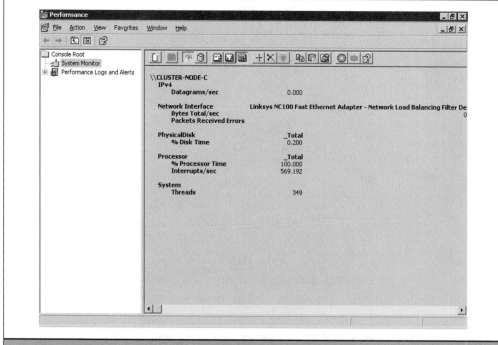

Figure 8-4. Viewing reports in the System Monitor

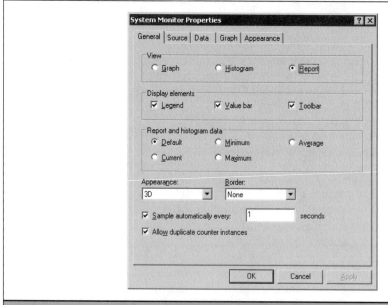

Figure 8-5. Configuring the General tab

In Figure 8-5, you're looking at the *General* tab, which enables you to configure the views just discussed (Graph, Histogram, and Report), and other display-oriented properties.

The next tab is the Data tab, as seen in the following illustration. In the *Data* tab, you can view the added counters or add more counters. You can add counters by clicking the big plus sign on the toolbar, as well as removing them with the big X. You can also adjust the colors and bar widths, if necessary.

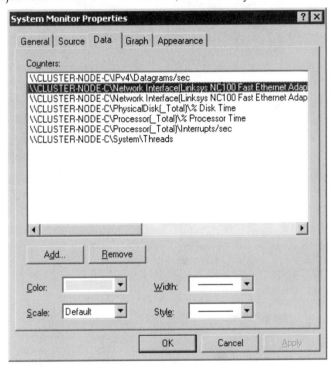

Now that you've looked at basic customization, let's add counters and monitor your server to obtain performance data for troubleshooting or to create a simple baseline.

1. Make sure you have an open Performance Console and have the System Monitor selected in the left-hand pane of the MMC, as shown in Figure 8-6.

2. Now select the plus sign and begin to add the counters to be monitored. I'm using the graph and have multiple counters configured.

3. To add counters, you can click the plus sign or utilize the System Monitor properties. I'll add counters on one of my cluster nodes to be monitored. Once you select Add Counters, you open the Add Counters dialog box, as seen in Figure 8-7. You need to understand what you see in this dialog box because this is basically all you need to know to configure monitoring of the server. This is difficult to read and it can be confusing without an explanation of what you're looking at.

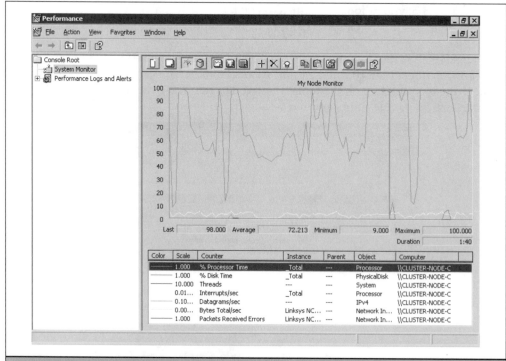

Figure 8-6. Viewing counters within the System Monitor

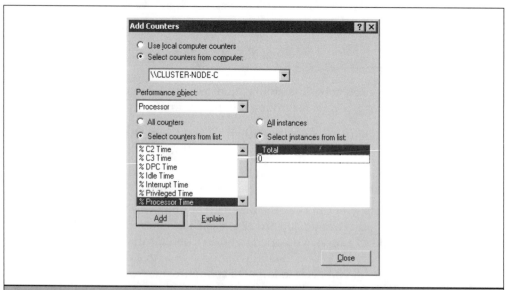

Figure 8-7. Adding counters

4. Windows Server 2003 platform enables you to click the Explain button to find more information about something you highlighted. I highlighted % Processor Time to read more details about it, as shown in the following illustration, before I add it as a counter on my graph.

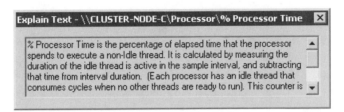

That's it for adding counters. Just go through and look at what you need to monitor, see the explanation if you aren't sure what they are, and then add them, as necessary, to get baseline information or to help you troubleshoot problems.

Now that you know how to manipulate the System Monitor, let's look at how to work with alerts.

Performance Alert Configuration

Now that you have your counters set up to monitor your systems, let's look at configuring a basic alert while monitoring the system. Again, this book isn't trying to teach you the inner workings of every configuration change you can make in Windows Server 2003 or Windows 2000, it's trying to teach you the concepts of high availability. Alerts warn you immediately when a problem occurs. Here, you look at configuring an alert based on a counter problem.

First, you will want to open the Performance Console again so you can look at the System Monitor. This time, you select the Performance Logs and Alerts icon, so you can configure an alert, as seen in Figure 8-8.

1. Once you open the Performance Console, select the Alerts icon in the left-hand pane of the console. Right-click it and select New Alert Settings. You open the New Alert Settings Dialog Box and you can give it a new name there. I named it as High CPU, as you can see in the next illustration. You can select whatever you want, but make sure you create a name that makes sense to you and is effective. In other words, if you select a name like System Issue and you monitor CPU processing issues, what happens after you have ten new alerts? Will you remember what this one was for? Try to keep this organized to make your life easier.

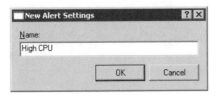

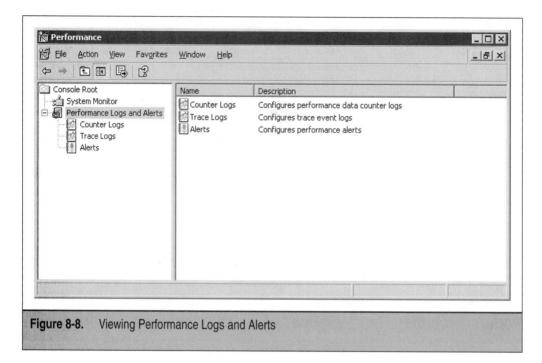

Figure 8-8. Viewing Performance Logs and Alerts

2. Once you select a name, click OK, and you'll open the New Alerts Properties sheet, in this case, High CPU, as seen in the following illustration.

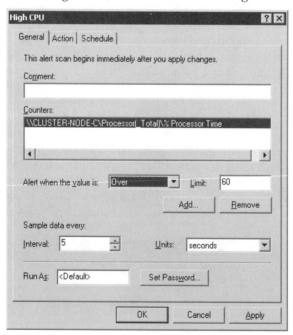

3. Once you open the new alert, you're on the General tab first. Here, you can add your counters to set alerts. In the Counters section of the dialog box, you can add counters by clicking the Add button right below it. Click Add and you'll be given a list of counters to select from that's identical to the one you saw in Figure 8-7 when we added counters to the System Monitor. This time, add them to the new alert you're creating.

4. You now want to set the actual alert parameters in the new alert you just created. Still in the General tab, you can see that below the counter you added, you have a setting that gives you an alert when the value is either over or under a specific number. Because we're talking about overall CPU usage, 60 will be the processor time and anything above it issues an automatic warning. Now, before you look at the actual warning, you need to set the data-sampling period. Each setting is different, depending on which counter you select.

5. Next, you need to go to the Action tab, as seen in the next illustration. In the *Action* tab, you have multiple options for what the system should do when the alert is tripped, but I'm sticking with the Application Event Viewer log for now. You can, however, select many other things, such as custom scripts and programs, as well as a network message sent if configured to do so.

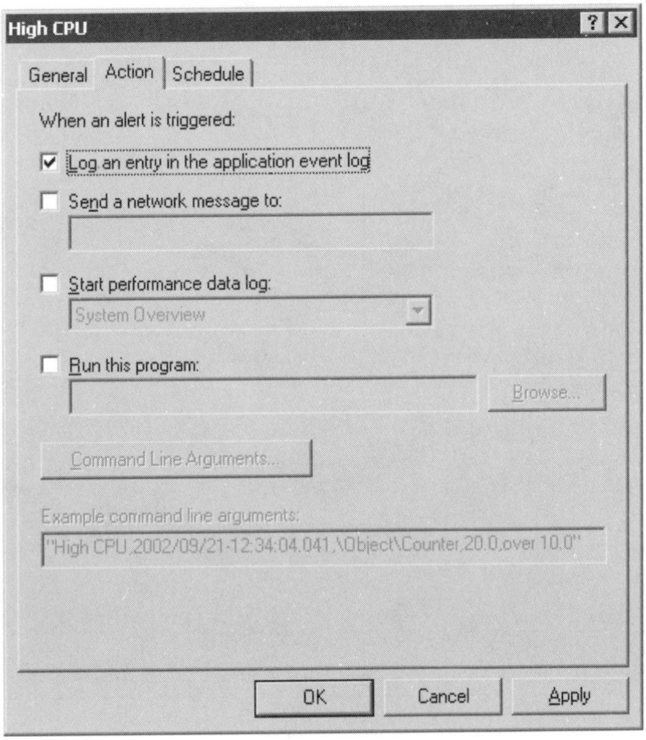

6. Once you finish setting the logging of the alert to the Application Log in the Event Viewer, click OK. You've now created your first alert. In Figure 8-9, you can see the alert was created, it's green in color, and operational.

7. Your next step is to see if the alert trips. I set this alert so low that on any normal system, it's going to trip a few times, no matter what happens to the system. I did this so you can set the alert and see it make an entry to the application log. You don't want to do this on a production system without monitoring the log itself because it will fill up quickly and could overwrite important entries from other subsystems.

8. In Figure 8-10, you can see I opened the Event Viewer on the Computer Management Console. Now you can see the logging and the SysmonLog source.

9. On opening one of the events, as seen in the following illustration, logging has occurred to the application log from the alert itself that the alert you set has tripped its threshold.

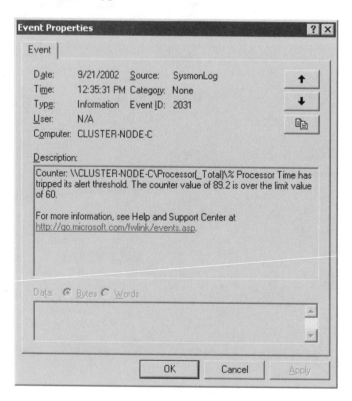

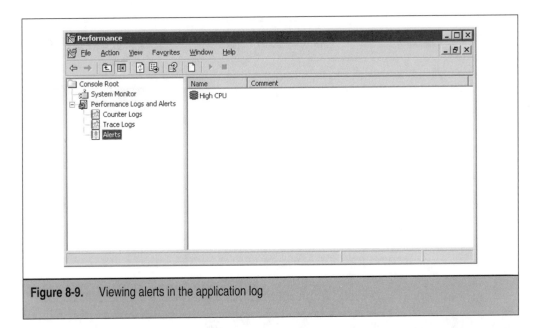

Figure 8-9.   Viewing alerts in the application log

10. The last thing you can see is the actual event in the Performance Console, which is now colored red, indicating it needs your attention because it's been tripped. You can see an example of this in Figure 8-11.

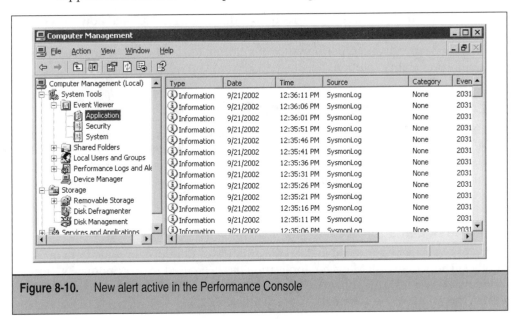

Figure 8-10.   New alert active in the Performance Console

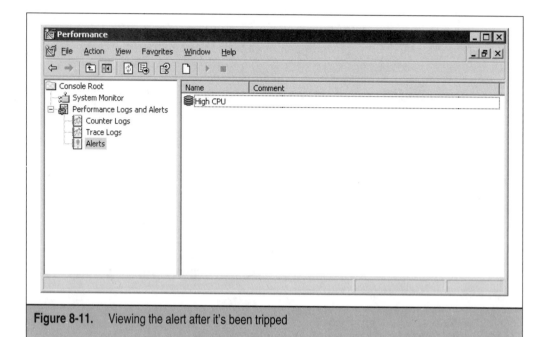

Figure 8-11. Viewing the alert after it's been tripped

Now you know how to set up alerts on Windows Servers 2003 and how to perform monitoring of your systems in case of disaster, so they're highly available. In the next section, you learn advanced performance monitoring techniques on your systems and your high-availability solution.

Advanced Performance Monitoring Techniques

Monitoring use, processes, services, and events is also critical in performance management, baselining, and disaster recovery of any solution, especially one that's highly available. Your responsibility is to make certain your systems are running. Using a tool like this is a quick way to monitor the performance of several things, which are discussed next. Let's look at the Task Manager in detail.

Using Task Manager

A Process Manager has existed in every incarnation of Windows in some form or another. The actual Task Manager application has been used from Windows NT to Windows Server 2003 and beyond. This is one of the handiest, most widely used tools within the Windows tool arsenal.

You can use any of the following methods to get to the Task Manager:

- Use the following key stroke: CTRL-SHIFT-ESC
- Type **taskmgr** into the Run dialog box or a command prompt
- Press CTRL-ALT-DEL, and then select the Task Manager button
- Right-click the taskbar and select Task Manager from the Properties menu

The Task Manager opens by default to the Processes tab. Click the Applications tab first, so we can go in order, from left to right.

The *Applications* tab contains your running applications, which is helpful to see if you have nonresponding applications here. The applications are listed under a task column but, for the most part, those listed denote entire applications like Word or Excel. In terms of high availability, you might want to check your systems and nodes to see if an application the system is running is hung up and needs to end. You can also start new tasks as easily as you can end currently running tasks.

The *Processes* tab, as shown in the following illustration, is the most-used tab in the tool. This is where you can see the running processes and what's using them, as well as the CPU and Memory usage, by default.

Image Name	User Name	CPU	Mem Usage
svchost.exe	SYSTEM	00	6,120 K
dfssvc.exe	SYSTEM	00	2,988 K
mmc.exe	Administrator	00	2,172 K
srvcsurg.exe	SYSTEM	00	3,816 K
svchost.exe	LOCAL SERVICE	00	1,112 K
llssrv.exe	NETWORK SERVICE	00	2,604 K
inetinfo.exe	SYSTEM	00	9,788 K
explorer.exe	Administrator	06	12,556 K
elementmgr.exe	SYSTEM	00	2,372 K
appmgr.exe	SYSTEM	00	3,952 K
FSHOT6.EXE	Administrator	56	19,104 K
msdtc.exe	NETWORK SERVICE	00	3,812 K
spoolsv.exe	SYSTEM	00	3,088 K
svchost.exe	SYSTEM	00	13,592 K
svchost.exe	LOCAL SERVICE	00	2,952 K
svchost.exe	NETWORK SERVICE	00	3,216 K
wpabaln.exe	Administrator	00	2,068 K
svchost.exe	SYSTEM	00	2,484 K
lsass.exe	SYSTEM	00	7,564 K
services.exe	SYSTEM	00	3,200 K
winlogon.exe	SYSTEM	00	4,532 K

Processes: 28   CPU Usage: 88%   Commit Charge: 126660K / 636968K

Use this tool to find the following:

- Runaway processes
- Memory leaks
- Trojan applications
- Nonresponding or hung process

That's not all you can find. You have the option to add more to it. If you go to the Task Managers View menu with the Processes tab selected, you can add more columns by going to the Select Columns option in the drop-down menu. Once you select it, you open the Select Columns dialog box, as seen in the next illustration.

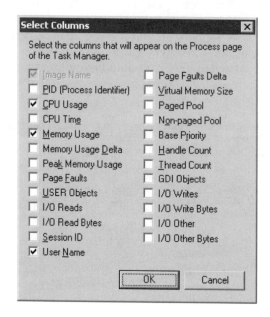

Viewing System Performance is also key for solving issues and monitoring performance within the Task Manager. In the *Performance* tab, you can monitor the following:

- Detailed CPU information
- Detailed Memory information

Use the Performance tab to see if Memory and CPU usage is at a normal level or if something could be wrong. For example, server performance degraded when I ran a CPU-intensive application on my cluster node. When I went to access resources on the server, it was a bit slow. I checked to see what the problem was and noticed (as seen in the following illustration) my CPU utilization was not only high, but also that it was consistently high.

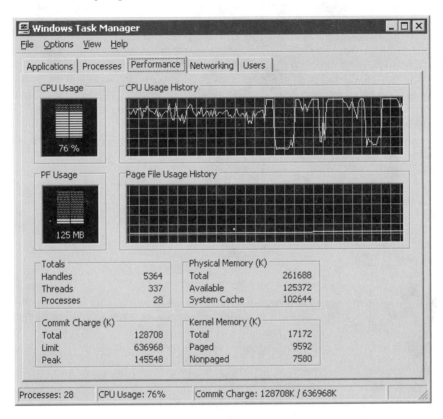

I returned to the Process tab to look for the process with the highest CPU usage within the list. I could then right-click the actual process and immediately stop it from running. The CPU utilization went down immediately.

If you're going to end something that's critical for the system to function, the Task Manager will let you know and stop you from doing it. Either way, you're using the tool to troubleshoot the performance on your system.

New to Windows Server 2003 is the Networking tab, which is an excellent tool for troubleshooting network interface performance issues quickly. As you can see, you get a graph to look at for each interface you configure. In the next illustration, you can see the Heartbeat and Local Area Connections that denote the interfaces on my cluster node. You can see, for the most part, utilization is low. You can watch this for traffic problems but, in my experience with the tool, it's hard to get a feel for your network traffic with this tool. I would still use the Network Monitor that comes with Windows Server 2003.

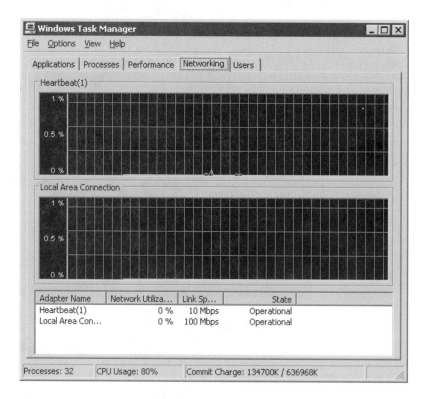

The last tab is the *Users* tab, which is used for viewing currently connected and logged-in users. From a performance standpoint, you might be interested in the information to see who's logged into the system and how many people are accessing resources on the system.

Next on the list of items to check for performance and baselining of your systems is to manage your system services.

Managing System Services

In this section, you learn how to manage your system's services, which can help you fix performance-related issues. We look at the benefits of being able to monitor services and how to do so. Services provide key functions to Windows systems and, up until now, might have been transparent to you. To manage system services, you use the Services icon located in the Computer Management console, as seen in Figure 8-12.

A Services Console is also located within the Administrative Tools folder. Either way, you can get to services installed on your systems.

With critical services, such as the Cluster Service in Figure 8-13, you need to make sure the service is running, started, in a state where it isn't running (indicating a possible problem), or even disabled. To get to Services properties, right-click the service you want, and then select Properties. In Figure 8-13, you can see I disabled the Cluster Service on my Windows Server 2003 because I'm running load balancing and

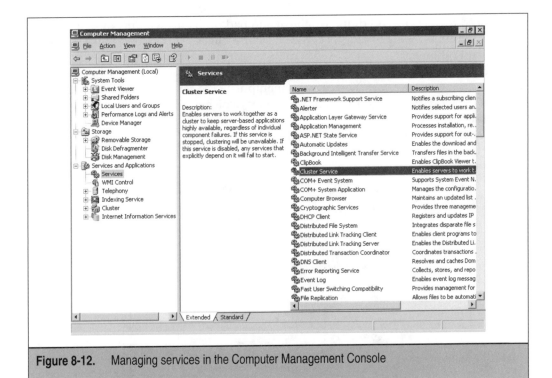

Figure 8-12.   Managing services in the Computer Management Console

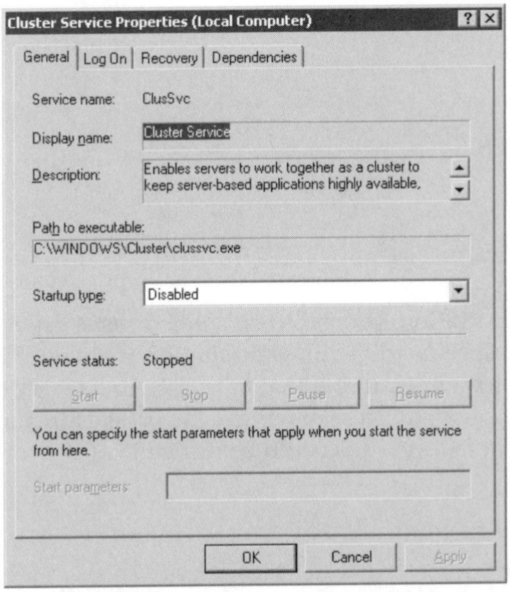

Figure 8-13.   Viewing a service

I don't need this service. If I didn't disable it and had problems with my system, such as getting load balancing to work, I could check the Cluster Service and make sure it isn't up and running.

In the Cluster Service Properties dialog box, you can do more than see how a service is configured to start. You can also manipulate the service within this dialog box. And, you can get a description of the service, which is always helpful when troubleshooting.

The *Log On* tab, as shown in the next illustration, enables you to designate an account that will operate with the service. You can leave this as the default.

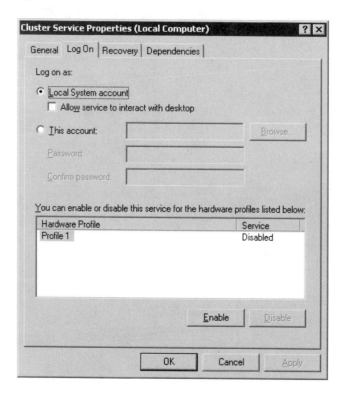

In the following illustration, you get to do some disaster recovery by using the Recovery tab. You can specify what you want the service to do if it does fail. I set it here to try to restart a few times and, if that fails, then to let it try to reboot the server. Be careful with this because services sometimes fail on startup and, if you configure it to restart on subsequent failures, this could be difficult.

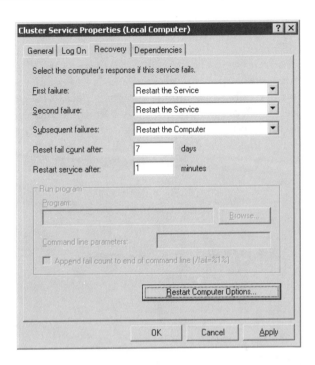

If you want to use the Restart options, you can select the Restart Computer Options button. Once selected, you can configure a message to be sent, as seen in the next illustration.

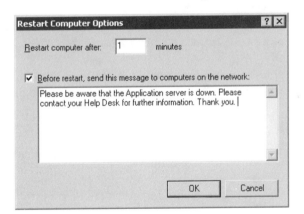

Again, use this option, but be careful with your settings and what you select to have the computer rebooted for.

In the following illustration, you see the *Dependencies* tab, where you can see what services depend on other services. In other words, you can see here that the Cluster Service depends on the remote procedure call (RPC) Service. If RPC isn't functional, then the Cluster Service won't operate correctly. This is important to know because, many times when you're troubleshooting the Cluster Service, you get RPC error problems. The services are dependent on each other for the Cluster Service to operate and this information can help you troubleshoot your problem more quickly and easily.

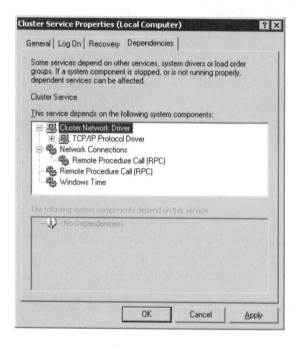

Now you can troubleshoot and use services to gauge your system's performance. And, know you know how to fix your system if it isn't performing properly.

Using Event Logs

One of the most important performance-monitoring tools you can use is the *Event Viewer*, which is located within the Computer Management Console, located in the Control Panel. Once you open the Computer Management Console, the Event Viewer is found close to the top of the console under an icon named System Tools, as seen in Figure 8-14.

For Windows Old Timers, this section will be old hat because the Event Viewer hasn't changed much from Windows 2000 to Windows Server 2003. The Event Viewer is a tool used to monitor and troubleshoot a Windows high-availability solution. This tool is the most critical troubleshooting aid you have because almost all system functions and processes are configured to report to the Event Viewer with informational, warning, or critical-level issues.

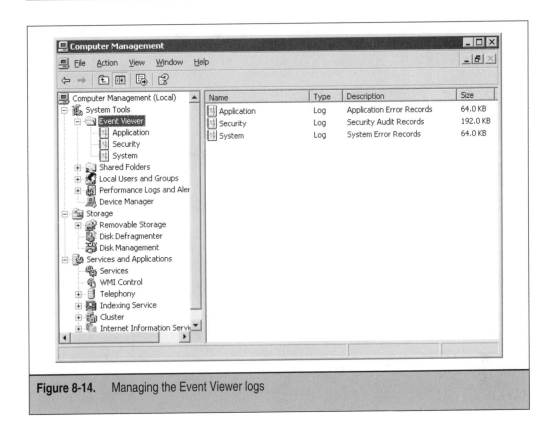

Figure 8-14.   Managing the Event Viewer logs

You can view the log contents simply by selecting one of the logs listed within the console. You see three logs by default:

- Application
- Security
- System

These logs monitor exactly what they say they do. Applications log to the Application log, Security violations, when configured correctly, log to the Security log, and system-level issues log to the System log. There are also options to have other logs in the Event Viewer, but such logs are also installed when new applications or services are installed on the system. In other words, when you install Active Directory on a server, it also adds a new log or two to the system under the Event Viewer. By default, you'll see the three, as shown in Figure 8-14.

To view a log, click it and it shows you the events it recorded within the right-hand side of the MMC console. You can view a log's detail and properties by double-clicking any event you want to investigate. In the next illustration, I wanted to look at an informational event the WLBS service issued. Here, you can see the cluster node started and, when it did, it assumed a Host ID of number 2.

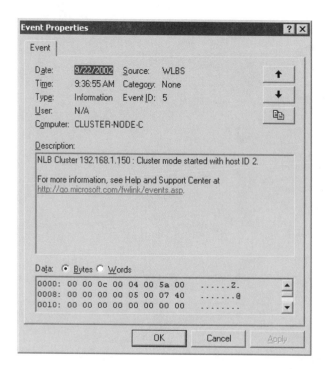

You can get more than simple informational events as well. You can get Warning and Critical. All events are important, but Critical means you have a problem that needs to be dealt with or investigated immediately.

You can also modify your logs, if needed. To modify a log, right-click the log you want to modify, and then select Properties. Once opened, you see a dialog box like the one in the following illustration. In this log, you can change many settings, such as the maximum log size. For a solution you implemented, you might find it sends out many informational events to the log. This is something to watch for because, if you set the log incorrectly, it continues to overwrite all the informational events. If you get a Critical event, it could be swallowed whole by the never-ending log that continues to delete old entries you consider as duplicates. Because of reasons like this, you should know how to configure the basic fundamentals of this log and what to look for. In high-availability solutions, you might need to rely on the information in a log file and, if you can get to it, you might have thrown out some evidence pointing to the problems your system could be having.

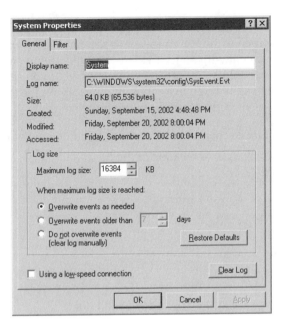

You can set the log size limit and have it overwrite old items, based on the size restrictions. Empty it manually, so you can see what your systems are logging by default when you first implement it.

You can also set Filter properties for the entire log, as seen in the next illustration. Here, you can adjust the type of events you want to view.

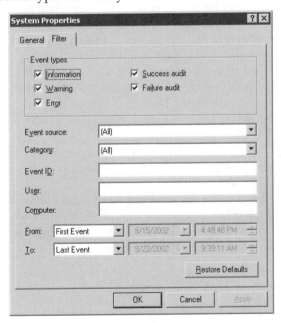

Save your log files over time for baselining purposes on events and for historical data. To save logs, right-click the log you want to save and select the option to save your log file. You can save it with an EVT extension. Only the Event Viewer can read the log files you created, unless you get a third-party tool. If you save log files all the time, you might want to store them in a separate directory on the system. Be sure to label the saved file logs correctly. I use the following system:

- Name the first three characters of your log file the name of the log.
- Name the next six figures the date of the file.

It would look like this:

- APP092002.evt
- APP092902.evt
- SEC092002.evt
- SYS092902.evt

As you can see, I made a system by log type and date.

CONCLUSION

In this chapter, you learned about advanced high-availability topics you can use to plan a solid high-availability solution. You need this information, so you can properly plan out the solution you want and have it work for you, rather than against you. This chapter was important because you might have lost a little focus from back in Chapter 1 where high-availability concepts were first discussed. In this chapter, you built on all the hands-on instruction you got from Chapters 2 through 7 learning how to design and build high-availability solutions. In this chapter, we finalized topics you need to understand in depth to get those hands-on exercises to production systems.

We also covered in great depth the DRP stage. This is, by far, the most important documentation you can do on any production system, especially for the high-availability solution.

Last, you learned some advanced monitoring you can do to monitor your high-availability solution and how to baseline it to avert future problems. Performance monitoring is the key to healthy systems.

Next, please look through the Appendixes, so you can learn some advanced troubleshooting and project management techniques for your high-availability solutions. I hope you enjoyed this book, found it full of helpful information, and had as much fun reading it as I had writing it.

APPENDIX A

Project Plan Sample

In this appendix, you look at creating a project plan for rolling out a high-availability solution. You see about 150 separate tasks set within a project that can be customized to your needs. The purpose of this appendix is to give you a tool to build your own project plan, if needed.

HIGH-AVAILABILITY PROJECT PLANNING

This appendix will be valuable to Project Managers, Team Leaders, Architecture Designers, and Supervisors. Anyone can use the appendix as an aid to help build a project plan for a high-availability solution.

Again, you can use this appendix as a guide and change it as you see fit. Many times, I use templates for projects.

Build the Project

In this section of the appendix, you see all the sections you need to plan before you begin the roll out.

First, get a vision of the project. Project Managers will call this a Scope Document, but I'll keep it simple enough for anyone to follow here. In Figure A-1, I started a project plan on a Gantt chart. You don't have to use Project 2000 to do this. The whole point is to organize everything, so you don't forget any steps and you have a way to track what's being done on the entire project.

	Task Name	Duration	Start	Finish
1	⊟ Envisioning	12 days	Mon 1/6/03	Tue 1/21/03
2	⊟ Create the vision/scope document	6 days	Mon 1/6/03	Mon 1/13/03
3	Define and write project vision statement	2 days	Mon 1/6/03	Tue 1/7/03
4	⊟ Define and write project scope	2 days	Wed 1/8/03	Thu 1/9/03
5	Identify business drivers and constraints	2 days	Wed 1/8/03	Thu 1/9/03
6	Identify critical dates	2 days	Wed 1/8/03	Thu 1/9/03
7	State assumptions	2 days	Wed 1/8/03	Thu 1/9/03
8	⊟ Gain vision/scope document approval	2 days	Fri 1/10/03	Mon 1/13/03
9	Plan the meeting	1 day	Fri 1/10/03	Fri 1/10/03
10	Obtain vision/scope document approval and signoff	2 days	Fri 1/10/03	Mon 1/13/03
11	⊟ Create the conceptual design	4 days	Tue 1/14/03	Fri 1/17/03
12	Develop the conceptual design	4 days	Tue 1/14/03	Fri 1/17/03
13	⊟ Write a high-level risk assessment	2 days	Mon 1/20/03	Tue 1/21/03
14	Assess risks and write risk assessment	2 days	Mon 1/20/03	Tue 1/21/03

Figure A-1. Viewing a Gantt chart

You must lay out the major tasks that need to be accomplished. In this appendix, we set up a project plan for a small company for a load-balanced solution with two nodes.

1. Group major tasks together. What are the major points at each transition of the plan? You need to start with a kick-off meeting. What about planning the design and getting a budget? Who will supervise the whole team? Who will work with all the teams within the group? You need to start thinking about people as resources. Where can you use them to get the project accomplished in a timely and accurate manner?

2. After you brainstorm the project, you need to commit it to paper (or electronically). You can group subtasks under major tasks. If you do this correctly, you'll have a list like this:

   - **Project Vision (Main Task)**

   - Create the vision/scope document: this is used to start the documentation of the NLB solution you want to roll out.

   - Define and write the project vision statement and scope: you need to assign someone to do this (as a resource). This will most likely be the Project Manager, if you have one.

   - Identify business drivers and constraints: what is driving this project? The customer needs a Highly Available solution and you need to provide it for them. However, they might be unable to afford what you propose.

   - Identify critical dates: does this have to be done before December when everyone will be shopping online?

   - Gain vision/scope document approval: you need stakeholders to sign off on the document, so you can get funding and approval to move forward.

   - Plan the meeting: this is your kickoff meeting where everyone meets and the project begins.

   - Obtain vision/scope document approval and signoff: you need signatures on the documentation you created. The kickoff meeting could be the place to do it when everyone is assembled.

   - Create the conceptual design: now that you're funded, you can begin the design. This can be done in many ways, but you can refer to the Visio diagrams provided within the book.

   - **Planning (Main Task)**

   - Define project structure: you can do this by explaining what you're presently creating—the structure of the project.

   - Assign project team roles and responsibilities: this is an important task because you need to know what people will be available, what they're going to do, and what their roles will be as the project progresses.

- Assess customer infrastructure: you can't deploy a project without having an idea on how your plan fits into it. This is critical to get the project solution to work.

- Acquire reference materials and software tools: of course, you need to make sure you have documents, books, tools, and anything else you need to get the job done.

- Assess and mitigate risks: what are the risks? Once you determine them, either make plans to back out of problems that occur (DRP) or get rid of risk altogether, if possible.

- Implement the testing resources: you need to make sure you have enough to pilot the solution or set up a test lab.

- Create a communications plan: communications are essential to success. If you're out of the loop, you might find it hard both to get tasks completed and to get them completed on time.

- Identify current network infrastructure: critical to the success of a load-balanced (or any other) solution. You must know the network layout and its data flows.

- Physical network topology: WAN and LAN charts are needed to help the planning of the high-availability solution.

- Protocol address management: you need to know the Layer 2 and Layer 3 (MAC and IP) addresses for the network if you're to populate it with a load-balanced solution.

- Remote access: will there be remote access to the NLB cluster? If so, then you need to plan it.

- Network operations/performance management: covered in detail in Chapter 8. You must know who will monitor and maintain the solution once it's in place.

- Training: are your people ready to implement and maintain this solution? If not, then you must train them.

- Identify current user environment: do you know who you have on the floor and how the new NLB cluster will affect them? What about web access or business partners?

- Assess infrastructure readiness: is your infrastructure ready to put this new NLB cluster in place? Will you have enough ports in the switch?

- Specify functionality to be delivered: you need to document what this solution will provide.

- Build the master project plan: a master project plan contains smaller grouped plans. In other words, you can make this one the master project plan, and then you can add the high-availability implementation into this one once you're ready to do it.

- Build the master project plan: now that you have the master plan, you need to build and document it.

- Update the master project plan: Now that it's ready to go or in the works, you need to keep it updated and manage it.

- **Developing (Main Task)**

- Create the logical design: now you need to develop the plan and the solution. This section is highly flexible and can be made to meet any needs your project has.

- Server installation and configuration: this can be broken down further but, for this example, let's keep it simple to the two nodes we'll implement.

- Install NLB node (select the first node): plan development.

- Install NLB node (select the second node): plan development.

- Install NLB drivers: plan development.

- Configure the NLB drivers to design specifications: plan development.

- Validate and approve logical design: now that you know what your install is going to be composed of, you need to make sure everyone else agrees with a peer review.

- Validate logical design: check, validate, and then sign off on the logical design.

- Implement the design into a pilot: this is where you can build the pilot based on the design you created.

- Conduct the pilot: make sure you build a good pilot and you demonstrate it properly.

- Complete the pilot and controlled introduction, and then document the results.

- Move from controlled introduction to enterprisewide deployment.

- **Deployment (Main Task)**

- Deploy the system: now you're ready to go! This is where you do the actual deployment. Again, this is something you can break down deeper, but for this plan, you can use the second half of Chapter 3 to fill in the various subtasks involved with NLB clustering.

- Monitor user satisfaction: test the solution and see if it works. Is it better? Simulate failures and see how long you take to get it back together.

3. Now, populate Microsoft Project with this, if you have it. If not, you can make a simple spreadsheet to keep track of what's listed.

4. Last, assign resources (this also includes people) to each task. This should complete a simple project plan for you.

Again, modify this as you see necessary. Understand, this is a template to help you build your own project plans as needed.

APPENDIX B

Advanced Troubleshooting: Event IDs

In this appendix, you look at Microsoft Cluster Server (MSCS) event messages. The intent of this appendix is to make it quick and easy for you to look up possible problems you might experience with your Windows-based high-availability solution. In this section, you look at Event IDs that appear in logs while working with high-availability solutions, such as clustering and load balancing. This appendix was created to consolidate the most-likely seen errors in one section of the book for easy reference. If you need to research some less-common events, you can search **http://www.microsoft .com/technet**.

Event ID 1000

- **Source**   ClusSvc
- **Description**   Microsoft Cluster Server suffered an unexpected fatal error at line ### of source module %path%. The error code was 1006.
- **Problem**   Messages similar to this might occur in a fatal error that could cause the Cluster Service to terminate on the node that experienced the error.
- **Solution**   Check the system event log and the cluster diagnostic log file for additional information. The Cluster Service might restart after the error. This event message could indicate serious problems that might be related to hardware or other causes.

Event ID 1002

- **Source**   ClusSvc
- **Description**   Microsoft Cluster Server handled an unexpected error at line 528 of source module X. The error code was 5007.
- **Problem**   Messages similar to this might occur after installation of Microsoft Cluster Server. If the Cluster Service starts and successfully forms or joins the cluster, they could be ignored. Otherwise, these errors could indicate a corrupt quorum logfile or other problem
- **Solution**   Ignore the error if the cluster appears to be working properly. Otherwise, you might want to try creating a new quorum log file using the -noquorumlogging or -fixquorum parameters, as documented in the *Microsoft Cluster Server Administrator's Guide*.

Event ID 1006

- **Source**   ClusSvc
- **Description**   Microsoft Cluster Server was halted because of a cluster membership or communications error. The error code was 4.
- **Problem**   An error could have occurred between communicating cluster nodes that affected cluster membership. This error might occur if nodes lose the capability to communicate with each other.

- **Solution** Check network adapters and connections between nodes. Check the system event log for errors. A network problem might be preventing reliable communication between cluster nodes.

Event ID 1007

- **Source** ClusSvc
- **Description** A new node, ComputerName, was added to the cluster.
- **Information** The Microsoft Cluster Server Setup program ran on an adjacent computer. The setup process completed and the node was admitted for cluster membership. No action required.

Event ID 1009

- **Source** ClusSvc
- **Description** Microsoft Cluster Server couldn't join an existing cluster and couldn't form a new cluster. Microsoft Cluster Server has terminated.
- **Problem** The Cluster Service started and attempted to join a cluster. The node might not be a member of an existing cluster because of eviction by an administrator. After a cluster node has been evicted from the cluster, the cluster software must be removed and reinstalled if you want it to rejoin the cluster. And, because a cluster already exists with the same cluster name, the node couldn't form a new cluster with the same name.
- **Solution** Remove MSCS from the affected node and reinstall MSCS on that system, if desired.

Event ID 1010

- **Source** ClusSvc
- **Description** Microsoft Cluster Server is shutting down because the current node isn't a member of any cluster. Microsoft Cluster Server must be reinstalled to make this node a member of a cluster.
- **Problem** The Cluster Service attempted to run, but found it isn't a member of an existing cluster. This could be because of eviction by an administrator or an incomplete attempt to join a cluster. This error indicates a need to remove and reinstall the cluster software.
- **Solution** Remove MSCS from the affected node and reinstall MSCS on that server, if desired.

Event ID 1011

- **Source** ClusSvc
- **Description** Cluster Node ComputerName has been evicted from the cluster.
- **Information** A cluster administrator evicted the specified node from the cluster.

Event ID 1015

- **Source**   ClusSvc

- **Description**   No checkpoint record was found in the logfile X:\Mscs\Quolog.log. The checkpoint file is invalid or was deleted.

- **Problem**   The Cluster Service experienced difficulty reading data from the quorum log file. The log file could be corrupted.

- **Solution**   If the Cluster Service fails to start because of this problem, try manually starting the Cluster Service with the -noquorumlogging parameter. If you need to adjust the quorum disk designation, use the -fixquorum startup parameter when starting the Cluster Service. Both of these parameters are covered in the *MSCS Administrator's Guide.*

Event ID 1016

- **Source**   ClusSvc

- **Description**   Microsoft Cluster Server failed to obtain a checkpoint from the cluster database for log file X:\Mscs\Quolog.log.

- **Problem**   The Cluster Service experienced difficulty establishing a checkpoint for the quorum log file. The log file could be corrupt or a disk problem could exist.

- **Solution**   You could need to use procedures to recover from a corrupt quorum log file. You might also need to run chkdsk on the volume to ensure against file system corruption.

Event ID 1019

- **Source**   ClusSvc

- **Description**   The log file X:\MSCS\Quolog.log was found to be corrupt. An attempt will be made to reset it or you should use the Cluster Administrator utility to adjust the maximum size.

- **Problem**   The quorum logfile for the cluster was found to be corrupt. The system will attempt to resolve the problem.

- **Solution**   The system will attempt to resolve this problem. This error could also be an indication that the cluster property for maximum size should be increased through the Quorum tab. You can manually resolve this problem by using the -noquorumlogging parameter.

Event ID 1021

- **Source**   ClusSvc

- **Description**   Insufficient disk space remains on the quorum device. Please free up some space on the quorum device. If no space exists on the disk for the quorum log files, then changes to the cluster registry will be prevented.

- **Problem** Available disk space is low on the quorum disk and must be resolved.
- **Solution** Remove data or unnecessary files from the quorum disk, so sufficient free space exists for the cluster to operate. If necessary, designate another disk with adequate free space as the quorum device.

Event ID 1022

- **Source** ClusSvc
- **Description** Insufficient space is left on the quorum device. The Microsoft Cluster Server can't start.
- **Problem** Available disk space is low on the quorum disk and is preventing the startup of the Cluster Service.
- **Solution** Remove data or unnecessary files from the quorum disk, so sufficient free space exists for the cluster to operate. If necessary, use the -fixquorum startup option to start one node. Bring the quorum resource online and adjust free space or designate another disk with adequate free space as the quorum device.

Event ID 1023

- **Source** ClusSvc
- **Description** The quorum resource wasn't found. The Microsoft Cluster Server has terminated.
- **Problem** The device designated as the quorum resource couldn't be found. This could be because the device failed at the hardware level, that the disk resource corresponding to the quorum drive letter doesn't match, or that it no longer exists.
- **Solution** Use the -fixquorum startup option for the Cluster Service. Investigate and resolve the problem with the quorum disk. If necessary, designate another disk as the quorum device and restart the Cluster Service before starting other nodes.

Event ID 1024

- **Source** ClusSvc
- **Description** The registry checkpoint for cluster resource resourcename couldn't be restored to registry key registrykeyname. The resource might not function correctly. Make sure no other processes have open handles to registry keys in this registry subkey.
- **Problem** The registry key checkpoint imposed by the Cluster Service failed because an application or process has an open handle to the registry key or subkey.
- **Solution** Close any applications that might have an open handle to the registry key, so it might be replicated as configured with the resource properties. If necessary, contact the application vendor about this problem.

Event ID 1034

- **Source**   ClusSvc
- **Description**   The disk associated with cluster disk resource name couldn't be found. The expected signature of the disk was signature. If the disk was removed from the cluster, the resource should be deleted. If the disk was replaced, the resource must be deleted and created again to bring the disk online. If the disk hasn't been removed or replaced, it might be inaccessible at this time because it's reserved by another cluster node.
- **Problem**   The Cluster Service attempted to mount a physical disk resource in the cluster. The cluster disk driver couldn't locate a disk with this signature. The disk could be offline or it might have failed. This error could also occur if the drive has been replaced or reformatted. This error might also occur if another system continues to hold a reservation for the disk.
- **Solution**   Determine why the disk is offline or nonoperational. Check cables, termination, and power for the device. If the drive has failed, replace the drive and restore the resource to the same group as the old drive. Remove the old resource. Restore data from a backup and adjust resource dependencies within the group to point to the new disk resource.

Event ID 1035

- **Source**   ClusSvc
- **Description**   Cluster disk resource %1 couldn't be mounted.
- **Problem**   The Cluster Service attempted to mount a disk resource in the cluster and couldn't complete the operation. This could be because of a file-system problem, a hardware issue, or a drive-letter conflict.
- **Solution**   Check for drive-letter conflicts, evidence of file-system issues in the system event log, and for hardware problems.

Event ID 1040

- **Source**   ClusSvc
- **Description**   Cluster generic service ServiceName couldn't be found.
- **Problem**   The Cluster Service attempted to bring the specified generic service resource online. The service couldn't be located and couldn't be managed by the Cluster Service.
- **Solution**   Remove the generic service resource if this service is no longer installed. The parameters for the resource might be invalid. Check the generic service resource properties and confirm correct configuration.

Event ID 1042

- **Source** ClusSvc
- **Description** Cluster generic service resourcename failed.
- **Problem** The service associated with the mentioned generic service resource failed.
- **Solution** Check the generic service properties and service configuration for errors. Check system and application event logs for errors.

Event ID 1043

- **Source** ClusSvc
- **Description** The NetBIOS interface for IP Address resource has failed.
- **Problem** The network adapter for the specified IP address resource has experienced a failure. As a result, the IP address is either offline or the group has moved to a surviving node in the cluster.
- **Solution** Check the network adapter and the network connection for problems. Resolve the network-related problem.

Event ID 1044

- **Source** ClusSvc
- **Description** Cluster IP Address resource %1 couldn't create the required NetBIOS interface.
- **Problem** The Cluster Service attempted to initialize an IP address resource and couldn't establish a context with NetBIOS.
- **Solution** This could be a network adapter or a network adapter driver-related issue. Make sure the adapter is using a current driver and the correct driver for the adapter. If this is an embedded adapter, check with the OEM to determine if a specific OEM version of the driver is a requirement. If you already have many IP address resources defined, make sure you haven't reached the NetBIOS limit of 64 addresses. If you have IP address resources defined that don't have a need for NetBIOS affiliation, use the IP Address private property to disable NetBIOS for the address. This option is available in SP4 and helps to conserve NetBIOS address slots.

Event ID 1045

- **Source** ClusSvc
- **Description** Cluster IP address IP address couldn't create the required TCP/IP Interface.

- **Problem**   The Cluster Service tried to bring an IP address online. The resource properties might specify an invalid network or malfunctioning adapter. This error could occur if you replace a network adapter with a different model and continue to use the old, or inappropriate, driver. As a result, the IP address resource can't be bound to the specified network.

- **Solution**   Resolve the network adapter problem or change the properties of the IP address resource to reflect the proper network for the resource.

Event ID 1056

- **Source**   ClusSvc

- **Description**   The cluster database on the local node is in an invalid state. Please start another node before starting this node.

- **Problem**   The cluster database on the local node might be in a default state from the installation process and the node hasn't properly joined with an existing node.

- **Solution**   Make sure another node of the same cluster is online first before starting this node. On joining with another cluster node, the node will receive an updated copy of the official cluster database and should alleviate this error.

Event ID 1061

- **Source**   ClusSvc

- **Description**   Microsoft Cluster Server successfully formed a cluster on this node.

- **Information**   This informational message indicates an existing cluster of the same name wasn't detected on the network and this node elected to form the cluster and own access to the quorum disk.

Event ID 1062

- **Source**   ClusSvc

- **Description**   Microsoft Cluster Server successfully joined the cluster.

- **Information**   When the Cluster Service started, it detected an existing cluster on the network and was able to join the cluster successfully. No action needed.

Event ID 1063

- **Source**   ClusSvc

- **Description**   Microsoft Cluster Server was successfully stopped.

- **Information**   The administrator stopped the Cluster Service manually.

Event ID 1068

- **Source** ClusSvc
- **Description** The cluster file share resource resourcename failed to start. Error 5.
- **Problem** The file share can't be brought online. The problem could be caused by permissions to the directory or the disk in which the directory resides. This might also be related to permission problems within the domain.
- **Solution** Check to make sure the Cluster Service account has rights to the directory to be shared. Make sure a domain controller is accessible on the network. Make sure dependencies for the share and for other resources in the group are set correctly. Error 5 translates to Access Denied.

Event ID 1069

- **Source** ClusSvc
- **Description** Cluster resource Disk X: failed.
- **Problem** The named resource failed and the Cluster Service logged the event. In this example, a disk resource failed.
- **Solution** For disk resources, check the device for proper operation. Check cables, termination, and log files on both cluster nodes. For other resources, check resource properties for proper configuration and check to make sure dependencies are configured correctly. Check the diagnostic log (if it's enabled) for status codes corresponding to the failure.

Event ID 1070

- **Source** ClusSvc
- **Description** Cluster node attempted to join the cluster, but failed with error 5052.
- **Problem** The cluster node attempted to join an existing cluster, but was unable to complete the process. This problem could occur if the node was previously evicted from the cluster.
- **Solution** If the node was previously evicted from the cluster, you must remove and reinstall MSCS on the affected server.

Event ID 1071

- **Source** ClusSvc
- **Description** Cluster node two attempted to join, but was refused. Error 5052.
- **Problem** Another node attempted to join the cluster and this node refused the request.

- **Solution** If the node was previously evicted from the cluster, you must remove and reinstall MSCS on the affected server. Look in Cluster Administrator to see if the other node is listed as a possible cluster member.

Event ID 1104

- **Source** ClusSvc
- **Description** Microsoft Cluster Server failed to update the configuration for one of the node's network interfaces. The error code was errorcode.
- **Problem** The Cluster Service attempted to update a cluster node and couldn't perform the operation.
- **Solution** Use the net helpmsg errorcode command to find an explanation of the underlying error. For example, error 1393 indicates a corrupted disk caused the operation to fail.

Event ID 1105

- **Source** ClusSvc
- **Description** Microsoft Cluster Server failed to initialize the RPC services. The error code was %1.
- **Problem** The Cluster Service attempted to use required RPC services and couldn't successfully perform the operation.
- **Solution** Use the net helpmsg errorcode command to find an explanation of the underlying error. Check the system event log for other RPC-related errors or performance problems.

Event ID 1107

- **Source** ClusSvc
- **Description** Cluster node node name failed to make a connection to the node. The error code was 1715.
- **Problem** The Cluster Service attempted to connect to another cluster node over a specific network and couldn't establish a connection. This error is a warning message.
- **Solution** Check to make sure the specified network is available and functioning correctly. If the node experiences this problem, it might try other available networks to establish the desired connection.

Event ID 5719

- **Source** Netlogon
- **Description** No Windows domain controller is available for the domain "domain." (This event is expected and can be ignored when booting with the

No Net hardware profile.) The following error occurred: No logon servers are currently available to service the logon request.

- **Problem**   A domain controller for the domain couldn't be contacted. As a result, proper authentication of accounts couldn't be completed. This could occur if the network is disconnected or disabled through system configuration.

- **Solution**   Resolve the connectivity problem with the domain controller and restart the system.

Event ID 7000

- **Source**   Service Control Manager
- **Description**   The Cluster Service failed to start because of the following error: The service did not start because of a logon failure.
- **Problem**   The service control manager attempted to start a service. It couldn't authenticate the service account. This error can be seen with Event 7013.
- **Solution**   The service account couldn't be authenticated. This could be because of a failure contacting a domain controller or because account credentials are invalid. Check the service account name and password, and then ensure the account is available and credentials are correct. You might also try running the Cluster Service from a command prompt (if you're currently logged on as an administrator) by changing to the %systemroot%\Cluster directory (or where you installed the software) and typing **ClusSvc -debug**. If the service starts and runs correctly, stop it by pressing CTRL-C and troubleshoot the service account problem. This error could also occur if network connectivity is disabled through the system configuration or hardware profile. Microsoft Cluster Server requires network connectivity.

Event ID 7013

- **Source**   Service Control Manager
- **Description**   Logon attempt with current password failed with the following error: There are currently no logon servers available to service the logon request.
- **More Info**   The description for this error message might vary somewhat based on the actual error. For example, another error that could be listed in the event detail might be: Logon Failure: unknown username or bad password.
- **Problem**   The service control manager attempted to start a service. It couldn't authenticate the service account with a domain controller.
- **Solution**   The service account could be in another domain, or this system isn't a domain controller. It's acceptable for the node to be a nondomain controller, but the node needs access to a domain controller within the domain, as well as

the domain the service account belongs to. Inability to contact the domain controller could be because of a problem with the server, the network, or other factors. This problem isn't related to the cluster software and must be resolved before you start the cluster software. This error could also occur if network connectivity is disabled through the system configuration or hardware profile. Microsoft Cluster Server requires network connectivity.

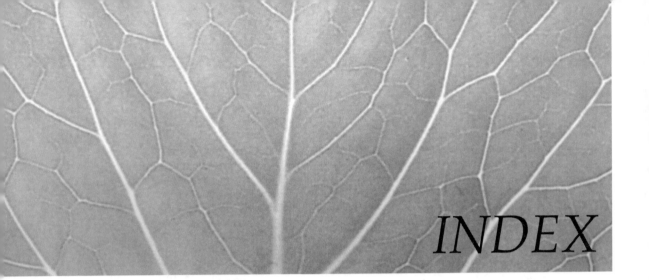

INDEX

E

 F

 G

 H

❖ **I**

❖ **L**

R

 S

INTERNATIONAL CONTACT INFORMATION

AUSTRALIA
McGraw-Hill Book Company Australia Pty. Ltd.
TEL +61-2-9900-1800
FAX +61-2-9878-8881
http://www.mcgraw-hill.com.au
books-it_sydney@mcgraw-hill.com

CANADA
McGraw-Hill Ryerson Ltd.
TEL +905-430-5000
FAX +905-430-5020
http://www.mcgraw-hill.ca

GREECE, MIDDLE EAST, & AFRICA
(Excluding South Africa)
McGraw-Hill Hellas
TEL +30-210-6560-990
TEL +30-210-6560-993
TEL +30-210-6560-994
FAX +30-210-6545-525

MEXICO (Also serving Latin America)
McGraw-Hill Interamericana Editores S.A. de C.V.
TEL +525-117-1583
FAX +525-117-1589
http://www.mcgraw-hill.com.mx
fernando_castellanos@mcgraw-hill.com

SINGAPORE (Serving Asia)
McGraw-Hill Book Company
TEL +65-6863-1580
FAX +65-6862-3354
http://www.mcgraw-hill.com.sg
mghasia@mcgraw-hill.com

SOUTH AFRICA
McGraw-Hill South Africa
TEL +27-11-622-7512
FAX +27-11-622-9045
robyn_swanepoel@mcgraw-hill.com

SPAIN
McGraw-Hill/Interamericana de España, S.A.U.
TEL +34-91-180-3000
FAX +34-91-372-8513
http://www.mcgraw-hill.es
professional@mcgraw-hill.es

UNITED KINGDOM, NORTHERN,
EASTERN, & CENTRAL EUROPE
McGraw-Hill Education Europe
TEL +44-1-628-502500
FAX +44-1-628-770224
http://www.mcgraw-hill.co.uk
computing_europe@mcgraw-hill.com

ALL OTHER INQUIRIES Contact:
McGraw-Hill/Osborne
TEL +1-510-596-6600
FAX +1-510-596-7600
http://www.osborne.com
omg_international@mcgraw-hill.com